P9-DWJ-595

My grandmother first introduced me to tabletop gaming at the ripe age of three, and my love for it grew exponentially over the years. As a teenager, it wasn't exactly the cool thing to do, but as I learned and grew not only did I realize I didn't mind doing uncool things but I found a flourishing community of welcoming people who would change my life forever. As a single mother at nineteen years old, I struggled with fitting in and finding friends who shared my interests. I had always been passionate about art, music, and storytelling; this passion quickly morphed into a love of narrative gaming and eventually all tabletop gaming. When I came back to tabletop gaming, I found myself at home for the first time, surrounded by people who valued spending quality time together. May anyone feeling lost share this world with our community and lose herself or himself in the wonder of the adventures, exploration, and endless universes to discover.

THE EVERYTHING®

TABLETOP GAMES BOOK

From Settlers of Catan to Pandemic, find out which games to choose, how to play, and the best ways to win!

Bebo of *Be Bold Games*

ADAMS MEDIA

New York   London   Toronto   Sydney   New Delhi

COPYRIGHT

Adams Media
An Imprint of Simon & Schuster, Inc.
57 Littlefield Street
Avon, Massachusetts 02322

An Everything® Series Book.
Everything® and everything.com® are registered trademarks of Simon & Schuster, Inc.

First Adams Media trade paperback edition July 2019

ADAMS MEDIA and colophon are trademarks of Simon & Schuster.

For information about special discounts for bulk purchases, please contact Simon & Schuster Special Sales at 1-866-506-1949 or business@simonandschuster.com.

The Simon & Schuster Speakers Bureau can bring authors to your live event. For more information or to book an event contact the Simon & Schuster Speakers Bureau at 1-866-248-3049 or visit our website at www.simonspeakers.com.

Photographs © Simon & Schuster, Inc.
Interior design by Colleen Cunningham
Interior images © Getty Images/yclam, Vectorios2016

Manufactured in the United States of America

10 9 8 7 6 5 4 3 2 1

Library of Congress Cataloging-in-Publication Data
Names: Bebo (Game expert), author. | Be Bold Games (Gaming website)
Title: The everything® tabletop games book / Bebo of Be Bold Games.
Description: Avon, Massachusetts: Adams Media, 2019.
Series: Everything®.
Includes index.
Identifiers: LCCN 2019006897 | ISBN 9781507210628 (pb) | ISBN 9781507210635 (ebook)
Subjects: LCSH: Board games.
Classification: LCC GV1312 .B39 2019 | DDC 794--dc23
LC record available at https://lccn.loc.gov/2019006897

ISBN 978-1-5072-1062-8
ISBN 978-1-5072-1063-5 (ebook)

DEDICATION

This book is for Hailey, Enver, Link, Eliza, Percy, James, Margot, Gabe, Lucy, and all of the other young and inspiring gamers who continue to make tabletop gaming flourish and grow with the passing of time.

Be bold, play games, be you.

Thank you to every single board game designer, publisher, playtester, artist, graphic designer, and gamer out there for helping create a board game industry that is thriving and bringing joy to tables one game at a time. Watching the industry grow the past six years has been inspiring and thrilling. I've made an incredible number of friends who are now some of the most important people in my life. Watching my friends' and colleagues' careers grow and flourish alongside my own has been a magical journey, and I couldn't be more grateful for their never-ending support and encouragement.

As our industry continues to grow I ask that we keep in mind the importance of sharing, learning, and growing together as a community. Education is critical, and sharing the information we have with new designers, publishers, and gamers keeps the tides rising as games and user experiences improve along the way. It's our duty to ensure that all gamers feel welcome and safe, and in order to provide that we must empower underrepresented groups and actively listen to and support them sharing their stories, talent, and passions.

CONTENTS

CONTENTS

CONTENTS

CONTENTS

INTRODUCTION

Ticket to Ride. Pandemic. Fireball Island. Exploding Kittens. Today there are hundreds of tabletop games on the market, and it's tough to know what to play. Here in *The Everything® Tabletop Games Book* you'll find dozens of games that are smart, challenging, and fun.

This book will introduce you to games ranging from widely available classics such as Carcassonne and Settlers of Catan to deck-building games like Dominion to cooperative games like Betrayal at House on the Hill and Pandemic. These and the other widely popular games featured in this book will introduce you to the types of tabletop games on the market and help you decide what kind of game suits you best, for every occasion. Each entry includes:

- Difficulty on a scale of one to five
- Recommended age range for players
- How many players are needed
- How long it'll take you to play it
- Some good times to play it
- When it was released
- The publisher's name
- Who the designer is

Then there's a short description of what it's like to play the game. Finally the entry lists the top game expansions that have been published. If the game has no expansions, we indicate that.

As tabletop gaming flourishes, it's drawing in more and more people who regularly gather together to enjoy these games—whether at home, at a local game store, or elsewhere. There are even conventions such as Origins and Gen Con at which thousands of tabletop games are played by people from around the world. So, whether you want to explore new worlds and futures, fight off threats to the earth, solve complex puzzles, or more, you'll find the game you're looking for.

Now let's start playing!

JOIN IN:

TABLETOP GAMING CULTURE

As you'll quickly discover when you start playing tabletop games, there's a whole culture that goes along with them. At local game stores, clubs, libraries, and elsewhere people who are either friends or perfect strangers bond over game boards. In this chapter, you'll learn a bit about this culture: where tabletop games are played, the main types of games, a bit about the history of tabletop gaming, and how to assemble a gaming group.

GETTING STARTED

One of the fantastic aspects of game design is that you can take any subject from the real world and transform it into a captivating project. Tabletop games take artwork, storytelling, and system design and weave them into a magical experience for a table of players to share, creating memories and friendships that can last a lifetime. Tabletop games give players an experience they won't soon forget and encourage table talk and shared joy in order to give everyone at the table not only a better understanding of each other, but also a better understanding of themselves.

Just as with any hobby, there are different types of tabletop games to choose from. Some you'll like and some you won't. The number one rule of tabletop gaming is: don't let anyone tell you if a game is good or bad. Ask yourself if it's the right game for the people you're playing with at the time. If it is, then go ahead and play it! Different games work better with different kinds of people. A game that's perfect to play with your mom and grandma may not be perfect to play with your friends from college.

One of the most important aspects of gaming is enjoying yourself and creating memories with people you care about. If a game isn't doing it for you, talk about that with the other players. Explain what you did or didn't like about a game so the next time you're picking, you can find one that better suits the group. After all, the whole point of playing games is to have fun, and if you're not, then it's time to move on to a different game.

As you're reading this book, make note of which games seem to suit you best. Remember, everyone has a different idea of fun, so games that work for some people won't for others. Each entry includes information on the number of players and the time it takes to play the game. That will help you winnow things down right from the start; after all, if a game is meant for four players and there are just two of you, it's best to choose a different game.

FACT

Something that's been very conducive to the rise of tabletop games in recent years is the development of crowdfunding websites. *Kickstarter* is among the best known of these. If you go on the *Kickstarter* site you will find hundreds of tabletop games that are competing for investor dollars.

Once you've got a list of games you're interested in, start thinking about people who might like to play them with you. And ask yourself, when's the best time to play these games.

WHEN SHOULD YOU PLAY TABLETOP GAMES?

One of the great things about tabletop games is that they fit on, well, a table. They come in a variety of sizes and take different amounts of time to play. For each of the games described in this book, we've listed some times and places that would be good to play. These times and places reflect the culture of tabletop gaming, which includes family gatherings, a group of friends getting together for an evening of game play, tabletop gaming at your local game store, and much more. What connects all these options is the idea of people coming together over games.

Here's the list. Keep in mind that it's not written in stone; if you want to play one of the games in this book somewhere other than what we suggest, go for it.

- **When you're at a dinner party.** Dinner parties are a great time to break out a game. After all, your guests are already sitting around a table, and games can supplement your sparkling conversation. Generally games that are good for dinner parties don't last too long (your guests can't stay up all night gaming) and aren't super-strategic, since after a good dinner no one wants to think too hard.
- **When you're just getting started with tabletop games.** If you've never played tabletop games before—or at least nothing more complicated than Monopoly—it's best to start with something comparatively simple, like these games. Have someone who knows the game teach you how to play.
- **When you have a spare ten minutes.** Some of the games in this book take a couple of hours to play. But others can be played

in five or ten minutes. If you've got a friend and just a little time, a short game is the way to go.

- **When you have a few spare hours.** Maybe it's a lazy Sunday afternoon. Maybe it's a rainy day and you don't feel like watching TV. Whatever the case, there are plenty of tabletop games that take a few hours to play and can keep you and your friends busy.
- **When you're having a game night.** One of the great things about an organized game night is that there can be several games going at once. The games with this designation take about the same amount of time to play, so everyone will finish at about the same time. They also require about the same number of players, so it's easy to split up your guests between several games.
- **When you're at your local game store.** As you'll see later in this chapter, local game stores are at the center of gaming culture. Most of these stores not only sell games; they also have space to play them. The games with this designation are a bit harder to find outside of game stores or are sufficiently advanced that some expert advice (such as you find at game stores) is welcome.
- **When you're ready to explain rules.** Come on! Admit it. Sometimes it's fun to be the one to explain rules. And when you teach a new person how to play a game, you're making a new gaming friend who can join your circle. These games aren't super hard, but they've got a lot of rules, and it's fun to explain them to newbies.
- **When you're in a large group.** Some of the games in this book are meant for parties—they're aimed at involving a large number of people. These can be crazy fun and can help break the ice if people at the party don't all know each other. Keep in mind that your gregarious friends probably won't love deck-building or heavier strategy games as much as your quiet or focused friends. Ask your friends what games they enjoy, and let their answers guide your choice.

- **When you love solving puzzles.** Lots of tabletop games depend on players' ability to figure out problems—some of them kind of complicated. If you like exercising your brain, there are lots of games in this book for you.
- **When you want to play on a team.** Most games in this book are competitive—but some are not. Those games depend on everyone playing cooperating with each other. In a sense, you're all playing against the game itself. Games with this designation depend on team play.
- **When it's time for a little competition.** Although some of the games described in this book depend on teamwork, others… not so much. If you're keen to beat out your opponents and show them who's king of the mountain, you'll find lots of ultra-competitive games here. Be ruthless, have no mercy on your foes, and rise to the top.
- **When the whole family is around.** Perhaps when you were little, your family played Monopoly or Chutes and Ladders. Now, when you get together, it's time to try something a bit more challenging—one of the games described in this book. These games aren't difficult, and they don't require a lot of strategy. They're just fun and pretty casual—just right for a family atmosphere.
- **When you want to learn more about your gaming friends.** No matter how well you think you know your friends, there's always a bit more to find out. Some of the games in this book will help you do that—often by asking challenging and sometimes very personal questions.
- **When you want to play something challenging.** Some of the games in this book are simple. Others, such as the ones with this designation, require careful strategizing, plotting out your next series of moves to take advantage of your opponents' weaknesses. If you like a challenge, you'll find what you're looking for here.
- **When you're in a tabletop game marathon.** There are few things more fun than getting your friends together for an

ARE TABLETOP GAMES THE SAME THING AS BOARD GAMES?

Not quite. A tabletop game is anything that's played, well, on top of a table. Board games are a subset of tabletop games and use a game board where pieces, cards, and sometimes miniatures are moved around. Not all the games in this book are board games (although most are). Some are card games, and several are role-playing games, which don't use a board.

entire day (and night, sometimes) of gaming. The games with this designation are flexible in how many people can play, can last for hours of gaming fun, and don't take themselves too seriously.

- **When you want a game you can carry with you.** Some of the games we'll discuss are pretty big. Others, like these games, you can put in your pocket. If you never know when you'll find the opportunity to game, stick a copy of a tabletop game in your pocket and you're good to go.

- **When you need to relax.** Whether you're competitive or cooperative, tabletop gaming is a great way to kick back and have fun. These games aren't especially difficult, aren't hyper-competitive, and aren't likely to get anyone mad. They're just relaxing, easygoing games.

- **When you want something fun and easy.** Although some of the games in this book are pretty complicated, others, such as the ones with this designation, you can learn in ten minutes. There are times you don't want to devote a lot of your mind to a game. Sometimes it's not so much about the game play but about the conversations over the game board you have with friends and family. You'll find that in these pages too.

- **When you feel like adventure.** Tabletop games can have very mundane settings; after all, what's more ordinary than building a railroad? But games can also take you right out of this world. Whether it's climbing a mountain with a mysterious temple clinging to its side or sidling cautiously through dank dungeon corridors, an ear cocked for goblins, tabletop games are a gateway to mystic and exotic destinations. These games are an entry to weird and enchanting worlds.

- **When you're at a gaming convention.** Gaming conventions are everywhere these days, and there's bound to be one happening soon near you. Surrounded by thousands of enthusiastic gamers, you'll find yourself playing new tabletop games and immersing yourself in gaming culture. The games with this designation are commonly found at conventions (along with hundreds, if not thousands, of others). This style of play lends itself to tournaments and other forms of organized play—something you may want to take part in as you gain experience with these games.

LOCAL GAME STORES

One of the best places to play games and find others to play them with you is your local game store. Finding a local game store is simple. A quick online search will reveal any in your area. However, a word to the wise: they tend to be located in urban areas.

It's important to find the right local game store for you. Some game stores are more kid-friendly. Others cater to a specific genre of games and players. They may have broad appeal or be more specialized in their offering. They are as diverse as their owners and community. If you have young children, it's a good idea to try to find a game store owned by people who also have children.

If you are new to the hobby and want to explore, look for a few things when you enter the store:

- Does the store provide an open gaming space?
- Are tables clean and organized?
- Is the staff friendly and inviting?
- Do they provide opened demo copies of games for you to "try before you buy"?
- Can you rent games?

If the answer is "yes" to most or all of these questions, you've found a friendly local game store (FLGS), and those are the best! Be sure to return. Also check for events. Most stores have a weekly open board game night (although there may be a fee). Some stores have specific game nights for gamers in their twenties and

> **FACT**
> If you're not one for kids, however, it's a better idea to avoid those stores that might have a more kid-focused environment. Don't be afraid to admit that a store might not be right for you, although it's probably best if you don't tell the store that.

thirties, the LGBTQIA+ community, gamers over sixty-five, and families. Check to see what is offered, and don't be afraid to ask. If they don't offer it, maybe it is because they haven't had the right person to organize it, and the right person could be you.

In smaller cities, game stores may not have a large selection available. It's important to consider asking your game store how to pre-order games that you may have heard are coming out. Game stores live and die by their regular client base, so if you find a space that you love, be sure to show your appreciation to them by making your purchases there. In larger cities there are even game stores with fees where you can pay to play games for a set number of hours using their game collection in case you don't have the money or space to invest in your own.

FINDING YOUR GAMING GROUP!

The most important thing about your gaming group is that you should have fun together. Even if there are things you don't have in common (and there almost certainly will be), you all like games, and that's a great unifier. It may take some time to find out who your core of gamers are, but that's okay. After a couple of regular game nights, some people may drop out, but others will probably want to join in the fun.

When planning a game night there are only a few rules:

- Avoid sticky or messy snacks
- Be ready for anything (group size, personality type)
- Have the right space to accommodate the games being played
- Have a designated teacher

You always have the option to plan your own game night or find one at a local game store, café, or public event space. For families with children, it's often easier to find other families to game with, especially if your children are around the same age. Family and party games are excellent choices if you want to include the children in the game. However, there are also plenty of dexterity games you can give the kids to play while you play a complex strategy game with the adults.

Board game cafés are becoming more common, and if you have a local café in the area that doesn't currently have them, consider talking to the owner about adding tabletop games to his or her café. There are plenty of abstract strategy games that can even be displayed as gorgeous works of art sitting on a shelf. These games are so striking that they garner the interest of folks who have never given tabletop games a second thought. They are fantastic tools to create new tabletop gamers and will help you to find your perfect game group.

Make New Friends

When looking to form a new tabletop gaming group it's critical to tap your other friend groups, whether they're from church, trivia night, or your local Pokémon Go group. You'll want to consider using websites like MeetUp.com or *Facebook* to garner interest in game nights. You can also put up flyers, but the most essential component in having a successful tabletop game night is matching up the right game with the group in front of you.

Player Count

A majority of tabletop games are designed for two to four players. If you plan on having more than four players at your game night, it's essential to have more than one game or games that accommodate more players. Titles like Citadels, Red Flags, Cash 'n Guns, Codenames, and Mysterium are prime examples of games that can accommodate large groups of people.

Accommodations

If you want everyone to have a good time, it's important to plan when setting up a game night. Consider creating a *Facebook* event and asking people to RSVP. While a large room with many

CAN I FIND GAME STORES ONLINE?

Yes, many game stores have an online presence. Not all game stores are listed online, though, which is why asking around for a local game group can be a great alternative to looking up a store. Also, many coffee shops have small game collections. Every day more libraries add tabletop games to their collections, and it's never too late to convince them to start one.

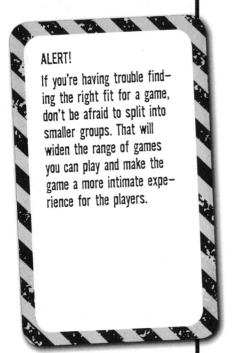

tables can be ideal for more rules-heavy games that tend to be on the quieter side, if you plan on playing party games, you might consider accommodations that have multiple rooms.

Party games tend to require a lot more communication and table talk, and can get loud. If you're playing party games, make sure you do it in a place where noise isn't an issue, especially if there are other tabletop games going on nearby. There's nothing worse than trying to play an attention-heavy board game and having your concentration broken by shouting. Consider this when planning your game nights.

HOW TO DECIDE ON A GAME

For everyone to have the best time, it's important to pick the right game. Some people are rowdy and outspoken—they probably won't do well with a game that requires a lot of concentration and strategic thought. Other people are quieter and more interested in the complex process of planning and executing complicated game strategies. They'll enjoy different kinds of games than the first group.

Above all, *have fun*! When everything's said and done, that's really what this book is all about.

Don't be rigid about following the advice given here. Be willing to try new games. It's possible you and your friends might enjoy some of these games even if they're recommended for different kinds of people. Don't be afraid to ask the players throughout the game play if they are having a good time. It's okay to have a miss at game night and set it aside for a better game that ends up being a win for everyone!

BEGIN HERE:

CONTEMPORARY CLASSICS

Evergreen games are the widely known popular games that keep game stores in business. These are the titles that have become or are expected to become household names. They are almost always easy to teach, easy to learn, and widely available in game stores, local libraries, and cafés. Without these games, tabletop gaming as it is today would not exist. As tabletop gaming continues to grow, the most accessible games will always be the best-selling ones. However, as the quality of art and pieces improves with the influx of money in the tabletop industry, we have to ask ourselves if these games will change. The larger publishers have put a lot of work into updating the look and feel of many classic games in an effort to stay relevant. It will be interesting to see if the tides will change, or if these modern classics are here to stay because of the ways they resonate with players through a distinct combination of gorgeous artwork, relatable or fun mechanics, and fast or engaging game play.

Munchkin

Difficulty: ✷ ✷ ✷ ✷ ✷

Age Recommendation: 8+

Number of Players: 3–6

Play Time: 1–2 hours depending on how vicious your friends are

Release Date: 2001
Publisher: Steve Jackson Games
Designer: Steve Jackson

 ## THE GOAL

Be the first player to reach level ten by defeating a monster!

 ## LET'S PLAY!

There are some board games that are so classic in the board game industry that experienced gamers stop taking them seriously. Munchkin is one of those games, but you should play it anyway because it's also one of the few games that consistently excites new players and brings new enthusiasts to the hobby. That's thanks to how easy it is to learn and play, and also because of the way it strikes just the right balance between luck and skill in its game play.

In Munchkin, your only task is to make it to level ten. This sounds simple until you realize that your friends are working together to stop you every step of the way. In the game, there are many kinds of cards but only two stacks on the table: treasures and doors. Each player starts the game with four treasure cards and door cards. If the players have been dealt any equipment, race, or class cards in their hand, they put them into play immediately. Players may only ever have one race and one class card in play at any given time. Equipment is limited to one body armor, two hands to carry weapons, one foot gear, and one head gear. These help

IS IT EASY TO FIND COPIES OF MUNCHKIN FOR SALE?

Yes. It's available through online retailers and almost every game store stocks it. You might not be able to find it at bigger retail stores like Target and Walmart, but with a little searching you can easily lay your hands on a copy.

ALERT!

Munchkin is entirely capable of ruining relationships. Arguments are built into it. Please play this game with caution!

players defeat the wide variety of monsters they face! Players may choose to replace these with better cards, and there are even some cards that allow players to ignore these limits.

Each heroic player kicks off her or his turn by kicking open a door. This is done by flipping the top card of the door deck over. If the player encounters a monster, a level is listed at the top center of the card. Defeating a monster is simple: the active player, using all of her class, race, and equipment cards, must have more strength than the monster's level. Some of these monsters have special text that makes them stronger or weaker against certain races, classes, or equipment. Almost all monsters have "bad stuff" listed on their cards. This is what happens to players if they fail to defeat the monster. If they succeed, they'll acquire the amount of treasure listed on the card.

Players do not choose if they would like to fight the monster; instead, they *must* fight the monster. That said, no hero has to go into battle alone. The active player may ask the other players for help on her turn by negotiating for their treasures, or even offering the other players her equipment in play in return for their one-time help. Then the players who have decided to fight the monster add their overall scores together. Negotiations need to be enticing if you want them to be effective, so don't be afraid to part with some of your favorite armor.

To make matters a bit more complicated, the players who aren't helping a munchkin in combat can work against her by playing curses to hinder her and her allies, cards that stop the combat, or even wandering monsters whose strength can be added to the active monster's strength.

If the active player cannot defeat the monster or obtain help, she may choose to run away. The player rolls a die and if she rolls a five or higher, she can run away from the combat. If she fails, the bad stuff on the card becomes her unfortunate fate.

Not all doors have monsters behind them. Some have a simple curse behind them, which impacts the player immediately. Fortunately, sometimes what's behind the door is neither a curse nor a monster, in which case the player may take the card and simply put it into her hand to use on a rainy day—or she may play it immediately.

If you didn't find a monster when you kicked open the door you can either:

- Play a monster from your hand and enter combat with it.
- Loot the room by taking the top card of the door deck.

None of the other players are allowed to see what you drew this time.

At the end of each round, players must have five or fewer cards in their hand, and since players don't have a limit on the number of cards they can play, they can manage their hand size fairly easily. However, if a player winds up with more than five cards, she must donate her extra cards to the player with the lowest level. If she is the character with the lowest level, she may discard her extra cards.

FACT

Munchkin was never intended to be a very serious game. Instead, it was initially designed as a parody of role-playing games like Dungeons & Dragons. It's a simplified, silly parody of the genre, and it's perfect for introducing new players to tabletop games. Its designer, Steve Jackson, also designed the Generic Universal Role Playing System (GURPS), which was intended as an alternative to D&D.

EXPANSIONS

Deluxe Base Sets:

- Munchkin Shakespeare Deluxe
- Munchkin Legends Deluxe
- Munchkin Zombies Deluxe

Settlers of Catan

Difficulty: ✶ ✶ ✶ ✶ ✶

Age Recommendation: 12+

Number of Players: 3–4

Play Time: 1–2 hours

 **THE GOAL**

Be the first player with 12 points. You gain these points through having the longest road, building settlements, upgrading those settlements to cities, and buying development cards.

👥 LET'S PLAY!

Chess. Monopoly. Dungeons & Dragons. Magic: the Gathering. Settlers of Catan. These are some of the most well-known and revolutionary tabletop games in history. In an industry where most board games make less than 5,000 copies, breaking one million copies sold is pretty powerful stuff. Catan has sold more than 18 million copies worldwide, which is a huge accomplishment for a modern tabletop game.

The theme of Catan is a classic one: settlers venture into a new, unexplored land, which must be tamed and civilized. Its mechanics first appear to be dice rolling and network building. However, at the heart of Catan lies a fierce negotiation and trading game that will permanently ruin your relationships with your family members in the same ways you fondly remember playing Monopoly with your grandmother.

WHEN TO PLAY:

- When you want to play something challenging

- When you're at a gaming convention

- When you're ready to explain rules

Release Date: 1995
Publisher: Mayfair, Catan Studios
Designer: Klaus Tueber

CONTEMPORARY CLASSICS

In Settlers of Catan, you build roads to build more settlements, but you need wood and clay to build those roads. In the game, there are five resources that you trade:

1. Wheat
2. Wood
3. Stone
4. Sheep
5. Clay

The board is made up of fourteen hexagonal shapes. Each hexagon represents one of the five resources and is assigned a number between two and twelve, excluding the number seven. The closer the numbers are to seven, the more common that number appears to be on the board. The intersections of these tiles are where players place their settlements and build roads between them. All settlements must be at least two roads away from each other in order to be placed. This can, of course, lead to some cutthroat competition!

Development cards can be purchased. These consist of five different abilities, which can't be used until the player's next turn:

1. The **knight** allows you to move the robber and steal a resource from the owner of an adjacent settlement or city (and if you have the most of them, award yourself the "largest army" bonus).
2. The **year of plenty** card allows you to select two resources of your choice from the bank.
3. The **road building** card lets you build two roads for free.
4. The **monopoly** card allows you to announce one kind of resource and then take everyone's entire supply of that resource.
5. **Victory point** cards award you an extra victory point.

ARE THERE VERSIONS OF SETTLERS OF CATAN THAT AREN'T BOARD GAMES?

Yes. There is a card game and a dice game based on Settlers. It should be noted that Settlers was the game that established hobby board games in the United States and Europe.

To start the game each player is given two settlements to place on the board. The starting player places his first settlement, and then players continue clockwise placing settlements until the last player places her first settlement and then also places her second settlement.

The placement of settlements then slingshots back around counterclockwise until the first player has placed his second settlement, then the game is ready to begin!

Each player begins his turn by rolling two six-sided dice. Each settlement is placed at the intersection of one to three six-sided tiles and each player may only place one settlement per turn. Each tile represents a resource and has a number on it.

Any time that number is rolled by those two six-sided dice, the players with a settlement on the intersection of the tiles receive one of its resources. When they've upgraded their settlement to a city by paying the necessary resources, they collect two resources each time that number is rolled.

EXPANSIONS

- Settlers of Catan:
  5–6 Player Extensions
  1996, 1999, 2000, 2001

- Settlers of Catan:
  Seafarers
  1997

- Settlers of Catan:
  Cities & Knights
  1998

- Settlers of Catan:
  Traders & Barbarians
  2007

- Settlers of Catan:
  Explorers & Pirates
  2013

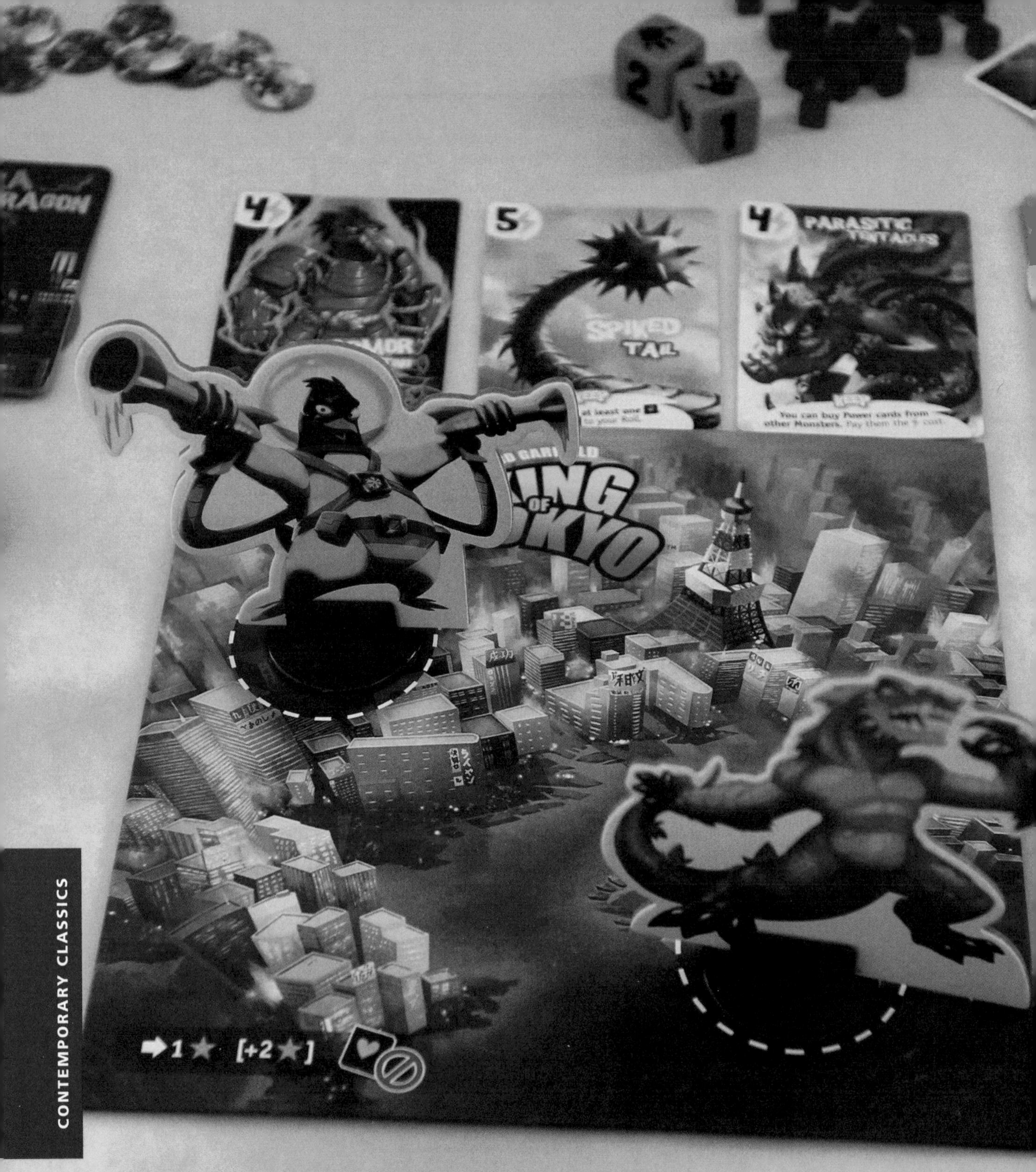

SPIKED TAIL
You can buy Power cards from other Monsters.

King of Tokyo

Difficulty: ★ ★ ★ ★ ★

Age Recommendation: 6+

Number of Players: 2–6

Play Time: 30–60 minutes

 THE GOAL

Be the last Kaiju standing by defeating the other players or the first player to score 20 points!

 LET'S PLAY!

Yahtzee. Everyone's heard of it, if not played it. It's estimated that Yahtzee sells more than 50 million copies per year. King of Tokyo took Yahtzee's popular game mechanic (roll the dice three times) and turned it into the perfect Kaiju-smashing party game. In King of Tokyo, each player selects an epic Kaiju monster to play; the monster is represented by a gorgeous colorful character standee.

Players choose from cybernetic kitties, intimidating Kaiju, mechanical dragons, aliens, krakens from the seas, and even penguins from outer space! These monsters vie for control of Tokyo where they face off, dealing damage to one another and gaining power so that they may be crowned the King of Tokyo.

In the center of the table is Tokyo, the battleground of the game. Players may only enter Tokyo if they roll at least one paw or, if there is already a player in Tokyo, they deal damage to the active player in the city. If the game has more than four players, two players may be in Tokyo at any given time.

WHEN TO PLAY:

- When you're having a game night
- When you're at a dinner party
- When you're at your local game store

Release Date: 2011
Publisher: Iello Games
Designer: Richard Garfield

FACT

Kaiju refers to a film genre in Japan in which giant monsters—often the result of radioactive mutation—attack cities like Tokyo. The word translates to "strange beasts" and originally referred to monsters and creatures from ancient Japanese legends.

CONTEMPORARY CLASSICS

Placed next to the Tokyo board is a number of cards that can be purchased by any player if he has enough energy cubes to pay the cards' cost.

At the beginning of each player's turn he takes hold of six vibrant, chunky dice, each one of which has hearts, lightning bolts, and monster paws on it as well as numbers from one to three. Similar to Yahtzee, players roll the six dice, and if they don't like the results, they may roll them again. They may reroll up to two times.

Each of the symbols on the dice has a different purpose, and keeping a few of them from round to round will prove useful for the players. If a heart is rolled and the player is not located in Tokyo, he may heal one health for each heart he rolled. If the monster paw is rolled while the player is in Tokyo, the player may deal one damage to each player outside of Tokyo. If the player is outside of Tokyo, he deals one damage for each monster paw rolled to each player in Tokyo. If the lightning bolt is rolled, the player collects one energy cube for each lightning bolt rolled on his turn. If a number is rolled, the player gains power if he rolls at least three of the same number on his turn.

There are two ways to be crowned the King of Tokyo. Players can either eliminate all of their opponents by dealing the final blow to them and taking their initial ten health all the way down to zero, or they can gain a total of twenty power and be forever crowned the King of Tokyo. Well, at least until next game night.

EXPANSIONS

- Power Up! Expansion
- Monster Expansions

Ticket to Ride

Difficulty: ✱ ✱ ✱ ✱ ✱

Age Recommendation: 8+

Number of Players: 2–5

Play Time: 60 minutes

WHEN TO PLAY:

- When you're having a game night

- When it's time for a little competition

- When you're just getting started with tabletop games

Release Date: 2004
Publisher: Days of Wonder
Designer: Alan R. Moon

🎯 THE GOAL

Be the player at the end of the game who's built the longest or the most railroads and thus has the most points!

🧍🧍 LET'S PLAY!

Ticket to Ride is an award-winning tabletop game that continues to win hearts and minds for its creativity and simplicity, as well as for its many expansions. In a world where there's a cult of the new, Ticket to Ride has earned its place among the classics, offering an edge-of-your-seat engaging play experience by beautifully blending just the right amount of player interaction with a race to the finish line.

To start the game, each player is dealt out three destination cards. Between the players sits a map with colorful train cars connecting various US cities to each other. On each of the cards players have been dealt are two locations on the map and a point value. Players obtain points at the end of the game if they've managed to connect the two cities using their train car playing pieces. These cards are kept a secret from the other players.

Players are each dealt three destination cards, but they only have to keep two of the three they are dealt. They may keep all three if they so choose. They also gain bonus points at the end by connecting cities and by having the longest continuous train at the

- Ticket to Ride: USA 1910

- Ticket to Ride: Europa 1912

- Ticket to Ride: Alvin & Dexter **2011**

FACT

Alan Moon's first game ever was published in 1981. It's called Black Spy and is a variation on the classic game Hearts!

end of the game. Players lose points at the end of the game if they have incomplete train cards.

Each player starts the game with four train cards randomly dealt to them. Players use these train cards to connect locations on the map. For example, if a player is trying to get from El Paso to Houston, she needs a total of six green train cards to connect the two cities. In order to complete a destination card and acquire those victory points, the players need to connect multiple cities.

On their turns, players can take a variety of actions. They may draw two cards from the faceup available train cars, they may draw two cards from the facedown stack of cards, or they may take one of each. If there is a rainbow locomotive available from the five faceup cards, that card can be used as any color train car when placing trains onto the map; however, it costs both of the player's draw cards on her turn. If there are ever three rainbow locomotive cards in the faceup cards, all five cards are discarded and replaced with five new ones.

Instead of drawing cards, players may also choose to play a set of colored train cards to complete a route between two cities. They play the number of train cards needed to connect one city to the next, of the appropriate matching color. Players each start the game with forty-five train cards, and they must use them wisely throughout the game. Players may also choose to draw three additional destination cards and keep one to three of them instead of drawing cards or completing routes.

When any one of the players has two or fewer train cars on his or her turn, players get an equal number of turns and then the players add up their points. As in many modern strategy games, you need to add points together from multiple sources to determine the final outcome. Each player adds together the points from his or her completed destination cards and subtracts the points from his or her incomplete destination cards. The player with the longest continuous route receives a bonus.

Thanks to its ease of play and interesting strategy, Ticket to Ride is a staple in game collections. It's one of the easier games to introduce new players to, and it's great for most ages.

Carcassonne

Difficulty: ★ ★ ★ ★ ★

Age Recommendation: 8+

Number of Players: 2–5

Play Time: 45 minutes

 THE GOAL

Place walls, roads, buildings, and meeples in such a way that you're the player at the end of the game with the most points!

 LET'S PLAY!

A flourishing fortified city awaits you in the breathtaking landscape of southern France. Carcassonne is the largest walled city in Europe, and its mighty appearance is a sight to see for any traveler who stumbles upon it. In the game, players place tiles and score points a number of ways in an effort to be the most successful city builder around.

Each player draws and places a tile with a portion of a southern French landscape on it. The tile might feature part of a city, a road, a cloister, or some combination of these features. Any time a player places a tile, he may also choose to play a meeple onto that tile. Each player has just seven meeples so it's important that he place them strategically. When a meeple is placed onto a tile, it cannot be moved, and it is only returned to the player after it has scored points.

A road scores points when it has both a beginning and an end. When that happens, the player scores 1 point for each tile that makes up the completed road. A castle scores points when it

WHEN TO PLAY:

- When you're having a game night

- When you're at a dinner party

- When you're ready to explain rules

Release Date: 2000
Publisher: Z-Man Games
Designer: Klaus-Jürgen Wrede

CONTEMPORARY CLASSICS

is completely surrounded by castle walls to form a city. However, if more than one meeple is on the same city when it's completed, then the points must be divided, unless one player has more meeples on the city than the other player, in which case winner takes all. Some castle pieces are worth double because of the little checkered icon placed in the corner of the tile. These are each worth 4 points instead of just 2. Cloisters score when they are entirely enclosed by other tiles, which can be challenging if you can't find just the right tile to fit, so be careful with your placement. They are each worth 1 point for every tile touching them plus 1 point for the cloister itself for a total of up to 9 points.

Some meeples don't score points until the end of the game. While most meeples stand up on tiles, meeples placed in the fields are placed lying down. These meeples score points for the castles connected to the fields in which they are lying. They score 3 points for every castle touching the field that they are scoring. If there is another player in that field, the first player must split the points with her unless he outnumbers her, in which case winner takes all.

The game ends when the last tile in the game is placed. If some of your roads, castles, and cloisters are incomplete, don't worry! Roads are still worth 1 point for every tile of the road. Castles are worth half the points, and cloisters are worth the full points. After all of the points have been added up, the winner is determined. She may ask the other players to pay for their trip to Carcassonne. It's likely that the other players will decline, but it's always nice to try.

EXPANSIONS

- The River
  2001

- Hills & Sheep
  2014

- Under the Big Top
  2017

Splendor

Difficulty: ✱ ✱ ✱ ✱ ✱   **Number of Players:** 2–4

Age Recommendation: 10+   **Play Time:** 30 minutes

 ## THE GOAL

Be the first player to have 15 prestige points.

LET'S PLAY!

In Splendor, players are merchants of the Renaissance and are tasked with buying gems and then transporting them to shops all in the name of acquiring prestige points. This is a game of chip collecting and card development. There are three tiers of beautifully illustrated cards, and on each card is a cost of tokens in the lower left-hand corner. The bottom row is the least expensive, and cards become increasingly costly with each row moving upward. There are a set number of poker gem tokens depending on the number of players in each game. The value of the cards increases with the cost increase, meaning that the game can ramp up quickly.

Each player may take one of three actions on his turn. He may take three tokens of different colors, take two tokens of the same color if there are four or more left of that color, or purchase a card from the table using his tokens.

Additionally, each player has the option to influence one of the nobles before his turn ends. Each noble

WHEN TO PLAY:

- When it's time for a little competition

- When you're having a game night

- When you're in a table-top game marathon

Release Date: 2014
Publisher: Space Cowboys
Designer: Marc André

FACT

Splendor took the world by storm in 2014, selling out almost instantaneously. As the game took a while to reprint, the demand for it only grew, and it skyrocketed its way up the *BoardGameGeek* hot list and eventually settled into its home in the top 200. The challenging economics of the game, the weighted poker chips, and the breathtaking artwork make the game look as good as it feels to play.

CONTEMPORARY CLASSICS

tile on the table is worth 3 points. On each noble tile is a card requirement. In order to claim a noble the player must have acquired the appropriate number of cards in the specified gemstone color, typically between three and four of each card and somewhere between two and three different gemstone card colors.

As players take their gem tokens they race the other players to claim the various trade deals. Pay close attention to what other players are doing because what they're up to is as important as what you're doing. The push and pull of this game keeps the tensions high and the energy at the table even higher.

The first player to reach 15 points activates the end of the game; however, he or she isn't guaranteed the win. If any one of the other players manages to gain more points than the player who triggered the end of the game, that person could snag the win right out of his or her hands!

EXPANSIONS

- Cities of Splendor
  2017

BUILD YOUR DECK:

DECK-BUILDING GAMES

3

In a deck-building game the construction of a card deck is the primary focus. While most people think of Magic: The Gathering when they think of deck builders, when you move into the board game space there are many deck-building games. A major distinction between these and collectable card games such as Magic: The Gathering is that these board games are self-contained; that is, they don't require the purchase of any expansions or other cards to play the game. Unlike Magic: The Gathering and other collectable card games, where decks are built before game play, something that often requires the purchasing of many packs of cards, a deck-building game is one where the deck is built during the game. It's easy to start off with a simple deck builder and work your way into increasingly complex deck builders. This is a great place to start in tabletop gaming if you're seeking many hours of fun without too much rule book reading. In this chapter, we'll start some simpler deck builders and work our way up in complexity.

ommon Cards

Letters

Letters

Letters

Letters

ne End

The Toughest Lesson Of All
Ø
PAIGE TURNER
5¢ ★4

A LAND OUT OF TIME
Ø
PAIGE TURNER
8¢ ★7

VICIOUS TRIANGLE
Ø
PAIGE TURNER
11¢ ★10

LADY of the WEST
Ø
PAIGE TURNER
17¢

L
3¢
rd uses all
cards, +2¢

U
2
4¢
Attack:
-1 card next hand
4¢

Y
3
5¢
Attack:
Cannot draw more
than 5 cards
5¢

G
3
6¢
Attack:
Cannot use letters
that cost 8¢ or more
6¢

V
4
7¢
Attack:
Words cannot be mor
than five letters
7¢

Ø
2¢ 1

T
1
1¢

Editor

At the end of the game,
the player with the fewest
wilds in their deck gains
this card.

Award 5

Paperback

Difficulty: ✱ ✱ ✱ ✱ ✱   **Number of Players:** 2–5

Age Recommendation: 8+   **Play Time:** 45 minutes

WHEN TO PLAY:

- When you want to play something challenging
- When you're at your local game store
- When you love solving puzzles

Release Date: 2014
Publisher: Fowers Games
Designer: Tim Fowers

THE GOAL

Be the player at the end of the game with the most fame points as you write a book!

LET'S PLAY!

Paperback is a deck-building game about writing a paperback novel. It requires players to write a book, one word at a time. Paige, the main character of the game, happens to be an aspiring novelist who is willing and ready to work hard to make her way onto the bestsellers list. As the players write novel after novel they see Paige on the cover of each story, imagining herself as the heroine of every tale she tells.

Each card has four bits of important information on it:

1. Letter   3. Ability
2. Score   4. Cost

On her turn, each player must spell a word using the cards in her hand, in order to play the cards from her hand. All cards are discarded at the end of the player's turn whether she used them to make the word or not. This would seem like a very daunting task were every player not given a number of wild letters to use as they see fit.

- **Letter:** The player uses this to spell her word.
- **Score:** This is the number of points that the letter is worth when used in a word.
- **Ability:** This is what action the player takes when the card is used.
- **Cost:** This is how many cents the player must pay to acquire the card into her deck.

Each player starts the game with five common letters, T, R, S, L, and N and five wild cards. Four "fame cards" are put out onto the table; these are fame point value wild cards that players compete to acquire. The higher the cost of these fame cards, the higher the fame point value. They score 0 points when used in a word, much like the other wild letter cards in the game.

Between all players is a market of cards called "the Offer." There are seven general costs in each row: the two-cent pile, the three-cent pile, the four-cent pile, the five-cent pile, the six-cent pile, the seven-cent pile, and then the final pile, which includes a mixture of the eight-, nine-, or ten-cent cards. Each of these piles, excluding the two-cent pile, then takes its top card and places it faceup below the stack. This is an alternate card, allowing the players to have more options when selecting a card to purchase.

On her turn, each player draws her first hand of five cards. Each player in turn must then create a word, check its length to see if she earns the common vowel, which is a vowel card she can then take into her hand and use in the next round. Resolve any abilities, score the word, buy cards, discard her remaining

ESSENTIAL

To check a word's length, count the number of letters in the player's word, including wildcards. If the word is equal or longer than the highest number shown on the length track, you gain the common card. This reveals the next common card for everyone to use and expands the length required to gain the next card. When the last common card is gained, the game is over, but that's not all that the cards do!

T
1

T

1¢

Editor

...he end of the game, ...player with the fewest ...ds in their deck gains this card.

5

Award

hand, and draw a new hand. Then, on her next turn, she may create a word using the cards in her hand. She doesn't need to use all of the letters in her hand, and of course, like most word games, no proper nouns are allowed.

After checking the length, the players resolve any abilities. The abilities on your cards are all activated if they are used in the word you've chosen to play. Make note of any abilities that give you additional cards on your next turn. Then, using the score of your word, you may purchase from the visible cards in the offer, including the four fame cards that are faceup on the table. Any unused cards are then discarded, and you draw five cards to form your next hand plus draw any additional cards granted by abilities. If you run out of cards to draw, you shuffle your discard pile and create a new one.

There is also a range of card abilities available in the game and important keywords that trigger different abilities. When players are tasked with trashing a card, it does not mean to discard it but instead to remove it entirely from the game. Depending on the ability, players may also add cards to their discard pile or hand.

Paperback is a simple deck-building game that's great for families or casual game nights. While it doesn't have the same competitive spirit of many other deck-building games, it's the perfect game for a low-key game night, and it plays fairly quickly. If you're hesitating spending the money on the full version of the game, you can find the mobile version of the game on iOS and give it a try before purchasing the physical version of the game. Paperback has a sequel as well! You might have guessed—it's called Hardback.

FACT

There is also a cooperative version of the game in which players work together to win the game by accomplishing the goal of buying all of the fame cards before any card gets five tokens on it. They form a pyramid of cards with one at the top and four at the bottom.

ALERT!

Most deck-building games don't have requirements to play cards such as spelling a word out. Keep this in mind as you add more cards to your deck, as it becomes more difficult to acquire your best cards into your hand.

EXPANSIONS

- Paperback: Unabridged **2017**

DC Comics Deck-Building Game

WHEN TO PLAY:

- When you're just getting started with tabletop games

- When you want something fun and easy

- When you need to relax

Release Date: 2012

Publisher: Cryptozoic Entertainment

Designers: Matt Hyra and Ben Stoll

Difficulty: ★ ★ ★ ★ ★

Age Recommendation: 10+

Number of Players: 2–5

Play Time: 45–60 minutes

 THE GOAL

Defeat supervillains to be the player with the most victory points at the end of the game.

 LET'S PLAY!

Growing up everyone wanted to play their favorite superheroes. In the DC Comics Deck-Building Game you have the opportunity to act as your favorite hero and call upon your superfriends to aid you in your quest to defeat the villains posing a threat to the city! Using standard deck-building mechanics, the players buy cards to defeat supervillains in an effort to gain victory points. The player with the most at the end of the game wins and is crowned the hero who saves the day!

Between all of the players sits a board with a city deck, and from that deck, players turn five cards faceup. This is the lineup of cards they are permitted to purchase. Above this pool of cards sits a supervillain deck; only the top card is turned faceup for all of the players to see. The game ends when the last villain in this deck has been defeated. Before the game begins, a player shuffles seven random supervillains with Ra's al Ghul on top of the deck and returns the other four supervillains to the box.

Next to this deck sit weakness cards, facedown. Turn one of those faceup next to that deck so players know that if they gain a weakness, that's the one they take. Beside that sits the kick deck, the top card of which is always available to all players, allowing them to improve their deck even if they cannot afford one of the cards from the city lineup.

Before the game begins, each player is given a hero, and on that hero is a special ability. The players each start the game with seven punch cards that give the player +1 power, as well as three vulnerability cards that give no power and simply take up space in the player's hand and deck.

Players shuffle these ten cards together and then draw five at the start of their turn. Then they play all of the cards from their hand and gain the power on each card. Then the player may buy any number of kick cards in the lineup with the power that she's generated. The card's cost is listed in its bottom right-hand corner. However, what you need to pay special attention to is in the left-hand corner, where inside a bright yellow star is the number of victory points each card is worth. At the end of the game, players add up these points, and the person with the most wins the game.

The DC Comics Deck-Building Game plays quickly, is easy to learn and teach, and while players technically compete against each other, because you all work together to defeat the villains, you have a sense of comradery with the other players. While there are cards that you can play to make the other players suffer, the impact isn't immediately felt in the same way as with most games, so your resentment is delayed long enough that you won't immediately despise the people helping you fight the big bads.

EXPANSIONS

There are currently no expansions for this game.

Dominion

Difficulty: ★ ★ ★ ★ ★

Age Recommendation: 13+

Number of Players: 2–4

Play Time: 45–60 minutes

Release Date: 2008
Publisher: Rio Grande Games
Designer: Donald X. Vaccarino

 THE GOAL

Be the player at the end of the game with the most victory cards in your deck.

LET'S PLAY!

Dominion was one of the very first deck-building games that was simple and elegant enough to make deck-building truly accessible to people who hadn't played dozens of games before. In this game, you are a monarch and a ruler of a small peasant kingdom of rivers and evergreens. You have hopes and dreams to create a more pleasant kingdom with more rivers and a wide variety of trees in hopes of uniting the people under one banner, your banner. Unfortunately for you, several other monarchs have the same plan, and you race them to gain as much unclaimed land as possible.

In Dominion, the players build a deck of cards by using action and treasure cards from the available card piles in the supply. Each player starts the game with seven copper cards and three estate cards. They shuffle these together and draw a hand of five cards.

In Dominion, there are sets of kingdom cards. Take the stacks of each of these cards and put them between each player. There are a number of different kinds of actions a player can take on her turn; however, she must choose just one to take.

WHEN TO PLAY:

- When you're in a table-top game marathon

- When you're at your local game store

- When you're at a gaming convention

HOW SIMILAR IS DOMINION TO MAGIC: THE GATHERING?

Somewhat similar. Designer Donald Vaccarino was an enthusiastic player of Magic: The Gathering and corresponded with M:TG creator Richard Garfield about ideas for M:TG. So it would be surprising if some elements of M:TG didn't creep over into Dominion. But ultimately, Dominion is its own game.

DECK-BUILDING GAMES

EXPANSIONS

Partial List

- Seaside
  2009

- Alchemy
  2010

- Cornucopia
  2011

- Empires
  2016

- Renaissance
  2018

Attack cards allow players to make other players discard cards or put cards on the top of their deck to hinder their next turn. If the player decides to buy instead he can choose to cash in his treasure and purchase additional cards. This gives the player coins, which he can use to buy cards but only if the card played has a buy action listed on it. If the card has a curse on it, the player loses 1 victory point at the end of the game, and if the card has victory points on it, the player gets points at the end of the game. Finally, a player may choose to take an action. These cards allow players to draw cards, discard cards, trash cards (remove them from the game), or even shuffle their deck into their discard pile.

There are placeholder cards facedown at the bottom of each pile to better help the players keep track of the piles running out, indicating the end of the game. On her turn each player takes the following three phases in order and then passes play:

Action Phase: Play one action card and take as many actions on it as possible. You can still play a card even if you cannot take all of the actions listed on it. If the card states that you can take additional actions, take those too.

Buy Phase: Gain one card from the supply by paying its cost. Put it into your discard pile.

Clean-Up Phase: Place all of the cards in your play area and any left in your hand faceup onto your discard pile. Draw five new cards for the next round.

After the end game condition has been met (when three stacks of cards have been entirely purchased or the stack of provinces has been depleted), all players add up their points and the person with the most victory points wins the game.

Whether you enjoy this game or not, there is no denying its monumental influence in tabletop gaming, and we're happy to see it continue to hold its place in the top 100 board games of all time on *BoardGameGeek*.

Harry Potter Deck-Building Games

Difficulty: ★ ★ ★ ★ ★

Age Recommendation: 10+

Number of Players: 2–4

Play Time: 45–90 minutes

 ## THE GOAL

Work together to defeat the villain for the scenario!

 ## LET'S PLAY!

In Harry Potter Deck-Building Games players face off against a villain such as Draco Malfoy, Crabbe, Goyle, or Quirinus Quirrell. In this game, players work together to defeat the villain before that villain and his henchmen take over all of the locations in the game. Part of what makes this game unique is that it takes place over seven scenarios and each game played progresses the game from one scenario to the next, evolving the game play with each scenario. As the scenarios progress your heroes, Harry, Ron, Hermione, and Neville, gain special abilities; however, the villains also progress in difficulty, and new mechanics are introduced throughout the game.

Each hero starts the game with a unique deck that contains a special item particular to her and a special ally that only she has. The rest of the deck is comprised of minor spells that grant the player one influence, which is used as purchasing power throughout the game. While each player starts the game with ten cards, at the start of the game each player draws only five cards.

Release Date: 2016

Publisher: USAopoly

Designers: Forrest-Pruzan Creative, Andrew Wolf, and Kami Mandell

FACT

Finding art was challenging for the publishers due to the fact that there were limited art assets of certain characters from the first movie. For example, the filmmakers hadn't anticipated how important Neville Longbottom would be as the movie series progressed. Once they realized this they took better photos of Neville in later films, and you see this reflected in the artwork of the game as the story progresses.

DECK-BUILDING GAMES

FACT

The Harry Potter novels are among the most success-ful novels of all time. As of February 2018, more than 500 million copies of the books have been sold worldwide.

EXPANSIONS

- Harry Potter: Hogwarts Battle—The Monster Box of Monsters **2017**

When learning new spells with their influence points, the upgraded cards grant one of several abilities. The player may be allowed a card draw, allowing him to draw an additional card to play on his turn. He could also be granted attack tokens, which allow him to place damage tokens on the villain to work toward defeating him or her. Players may also gain influence for purchasing additional cards and health, which allows them to heal either themselves or other players.

Between all players sits a board with a market of six faceup cards that players spend their influence to acquire. All the while, one of the three villains is faceup and the players are tasked with defeating him or her. Players have a limited number of health points, however. At the start of each player's turn, a dark arts card is flipped, and as you can guess, nothing good can come of that. In the starting game one of four events can occur, but keep in mind that as the scenarios progress, these events grow increasingly difficult.

A dark arts card is revealed at the start of each player's turn. Four things can happen when a dark arts card is flipped over. If a petrification card is flipped, all players lose a card and cannot draw extra cards this turn. If the players fall subject to expulsion, they lose 2 health points, and if they experience a Flipendo, they lose a health point and discard a card. If they encounter "He Who Must Not Be Named," they're forced to add a skull token to the location, bringing their impending doom ever closer. After this card is revealed, the player plays her cards faceup onto the table one at a time and gains the appropriate tokens with each card she plays.

If a player ever loses all ten of her starting health points, she must discard all tokens and half of the cards in her hand rounded down. She also adds one skull to the location and resets her health to 10 points. She comes back into the game on her next turn. However, should the villains manage to take over all of the available locations by adding enough control tokens to each one, then all players collectively lose the game, and if they want to move forward to the next scenario, they're going to have to try again.

Ascension

Difficulty: ★ ★ ★ ★ ★

Number of Players: 1–4

Age Recommendation: 13+

Play Time: 30–60 minutes

 THE GOAL

Be the player to gain the most honor points through building your deck and acquiring cards and gems throughout the game.

LET'S PLAY!

A majority of people fall in love for the first time between the ages of fifteen and eighteen. Gamers might fall in love every day with Ascension: Chronicles of the Godslayer. In this game, the goal is simple. Have more honor points at the end of the game than your opponent. Each player starts the game with a starting deck that's not very powerful, and every turn they play all the cards in their hand in order to acquire new cards in the center row by paying the cost listed on the card.

In this game there are monsters you can defeat. Once defeated, they are then discarded.

There are several different factions of cards you can purchase: void, mechana, lifebound, and enlightened. Typically, a player focuses on one specific faction to collect, as they work well together. Some even have abilities that activate with the presence of another card of the same faction.

Void cards allow you to thin your deck by removing them from the game. That might not sound like much, but in a majority

Release Date: 2010

Publisher: Stone Blade Entertainment

Designers: Justin Gary and John Fiorillo

WHEN TO PLAY:

- When it's time for a little competition

- When you're at a gaming convention

- When you're ready to explain rules

DECK-BUILDING GAMES

EXPANSIONS

Partial List,
Standalone Expansions:

- Ascension:
  Storm of Souls
  2011

- Ascension:
  Dreamscape
  2015

- Ascension:
  Gift of the Elements
  2017

- Ascension:
  Delirium
  2018

of deck-building games this is a powerful action that allows you to thin your deck, creating a more cohesive engine. The fewer cards you have and the more powerful they are, the better your engine is going to function. Some of these cards may even give you additional purchasing power or fighting strength when activated.

Mechana cards are designed to play off one another. For example, many of them state that if you have another mechana card in your hand or in play, you can gain purchasing power or a special ability that in some way would typically break the rules of the game otherwise, such as putting a card directly into your hand or even directly into play! Due to their high purchasing price, they tend to be worth quite a few points as well.

Lifebound cards can combo off of one another. They tend to be hero heavy and allow players to acquire heroes at a much faster rate. Heroes are a subset of cards within the game that tend to provide a high number of end game victory points for a low amount of purchasing power within the game.

Enlightened cards are all about making your engine more efficient by allowing players to draw cards at a more rapid pace. They also help you acquire cards at a much faster rate. These cards are ideal for defeating monsters and acquiring more cards, rapidly.

What sets Ascension apart from other deck-building games is that the game is broken (that is to say, there's an advantage built into it if you can find it). If one player can get an engine up and running before the other players, she's sure to take the win. While the game plays very well with two players, it scales fairly well provided that all players are actively paying attention to the kind of decks the other players are building. This is a no-cell-phone-at-the-table kind of game if you're really looking to experience how immersive and engaging this game can be.

Ascension now has what might be considered a sequel game called Shards of Infinity. It implements many similar mechanics but takes place in a science fiction setting.

Clank! A Deck-Building Adventure

Difficulty: ★ ★ ★ ★ ★

Age Recommendation: 12+

Number of Players: 2–4

Play Time: 30 minutes per player

 THE GOAL

Be the player at the end of the game with the most points and make it out alive without losing all of your health! Secondary goal: be the first player to escape the dungeon with at least one artifact.

 LET'S PLAY!

Clank! A Deck-Building Game, oftentimes simply referred to as Clank!, truly revolutionized the genre. While it may not have been the first deck-building game to add a board to a deck builder, it was the first wildly popular one to do so.

Each player starts the game with a set of ten cards, and between all of the players sits a dungeon in the form of a board. Players need to rush their way through this to collect secrets, treasures, and artifacts, all while avoiding waking an angry, fire-breathing dragon. Along the way each player makes noise, also known as "clank," and as a result, suffers the dragon's unending wrath.

Below the dungeon sits a dungeon row of cards to be purchased by the players to improve their deck throughout the game. Below the dungeon row is a reserve of cards that may

WHEN TO PLAY:

- When it's time for a little competition

- When you want to play something challenging

- When you're at your local game store

Release Date: 2016
Publisher: Renegade Game Studios
Designer: Paul Dennen

DECK-BUILDING GAMES

always be purchased or defeated using skills or swords. This ensures that a player's turn never feels useless and that no matter how hopeless the dungeon row might look, the player can always work toward improving her deck.

What made Clank! unique at the time of its release was its ability to seamlessly merge a deck-building game with the action adventure of a dungeon-delving game. Within the game there are five resources: boots, gold, fight, points, and skill. You use boots to move your adventuring meeple around the board. To move one space, you must have one movement, unless there are footsteps between you and your next room, in which case you need two movements (movement is shown by boots on the cards).

There are four resources in the game, which are granted by the cards played each turn. Gold is the first resource, often given to players through playing cards and discovering secrets in the dungeon. It can be used to purchase items from the marketplace. Swords help the players fight monsters in the tunnels when moving from one room to the next and monsters from the dungeon row. Players need to do their best to not ignore the goblin, who is always around to beat up on if they need extra gold. Skill is another resource of great importance because skill points allow the players to purchase new cards from the dungeon row. They must be spent on the turn they are played or else they vanish into the abyss. Movement, the final resource, allows the players to travel from room to room in the dungeon. Finally, each card has a number of victory points on it, which indicate the number of points given to the player at the end of the game. Points are the only resource that truly matters in the end, since this secures victory when all is said and done!

Each player starts the game with the same set of cards: stumble, sidestep, burgle, and scramble, as well as thirty clank cubes. Each player is given two stumble cards, one sidestep, six burgles, and one scramble. Stumble forces the player to put one clank onto the board; they stumble around the dungeon and make too much noise, enraging the dragon. Sidesteps allows the player to move without making noise. Burgle allows the player to gain skill; players use this to purchase increasingly good cards from the dungeon row. Scramble provides the player with both skill and movement, helping the player escape the dungeon before the dragon attacks.

When the dragon attacks, all clank cubes on the board are poured into a bag that holds twenty-four black dragon cubes. There are a set number of cubes randomly drawn from the bag. If a black cube is drawn, nothing happens. If a player's color cube is drawn, it's placed upon the board where it damages his health. (Each player starts the game with 10 health points.)

Players gain points in one of two ways: either by purchasing cards from the dungeon row using her skill or by exploring the dungeon. Any time a player makes her way into a room there are a number of special things she may run into, treasures that she can steal from the dungeon. Minor secrets can contain skill, gold, healing, strength, card removal, or a magical dragon egg containing victory points. These come at a price of enraging the dragon. Major secrets contain healing, skill, treasure, card draw, or a chalice, which contains victory points but does not enrage the dragon. Artifacts are victory points ranging from 5 to 30 points but be wary—these are coveted by the dragon, and when he realizes they are gone, he grows increasingly angry. Monkey idols are each worth 5 points and may interact with special cards within the game.

When a player moves into a room with any one of these items, she may choose to pick it up. While it's almost always advantageous to pick up secrets and idols, players may choose to be pickier when choosing to pick up an artifact due to the fact that they can only carry one of these unless they obtain a backpack, in which case, they may carry two. How does one obtain a backpack? Purchase it from the marketplace. Any time a player enters into the marketplace, she may spend seven coins to purchase one of the marketplace items.

> **FACT**
> Deck-building games are a staple of tabletop gaming, and when Dominion first gained popularity in 2008, it seemed as if the entire genre took off. The market saw new games like Tanto Cuore imitate the game play of Dominion. In 2010 Thunderstone and Ascension hit the market, followed by Rune Age and Penny Arcade: The Deck-Building Game, which kicked off a line of licensed, accessible deck-building games.

The master key is used to unlock locked rooms anywhere on the game board. Once a player has obtained one, she can unlock any lock on the board. The backpack allows the player to hold one additional artifact that can be worth up to 30 points! If you see a player with a backpack and an artifact, it might be in your best interest to do something to thwart him. Finally, the crown is worth the number of victory points shown. The highest-value crown is worth 10 points, and they decrease with each one purchased from the marketplace.

Any time a player takes an artifact from the dungeon, the dragon's rage track increases. Where the dragon starts on the track depends on the number of players. Any time a small secret egg is revealed and taken from the board or an artifact is taken, the dragon moves up on the track. There are also cards that can be faceup in the dungeon row that make the dragon draw an additional cube from the bag when he attacks. For every space the dragon moves up on the rage track, there are additional cubes that must be pulled from the back when he attacks.

The first player to escape the dungeon stops playing the game normally. On his turn, he becomes the dragon, drawing cubes from the bag as the dragon himself. The game escalates quickly from here as all players attempt to scramble their way out of the dungeon! If a player does die before escaping the game board, all hope is not lost. If the player dies aboveground, then he still scores all of his points as normal. However, he misses out on the 20-point bonus one would receive for escaping the castle entirely. If the player dies belowground, he does not receive any points and he cannot win the game.

Clank! takes the classic take on a deck-building game and turns it into an adventure no player soon forgets. It's fiercely addicting, and each game feels truly unique. If you can convince your game group to play any of the simpler deck-building games, Clank! should be an easy sell.

EXPANSIONS

- Clank! Expeditions: Gold & Silk
  2018

- Clank! The Mummy's Curse
  2018

LAYING IT ALL DOWN:
TILE–LAYING GAMES

Tile-placement games have been popular since the invention of dominoes, which has inspired countless games. These are games that feature placing pieces onto a board to score victory points, often based on the other tiles directly adjacent to them. There can also be set collection in this, which gives the player points based on the same types of tiles connected to or directly adjacent to them.

Carcassonne is the most notable and popular tile-laying game thanks to how accessible it is, but tile-laying games are not always simple. Some of the most notorious "heavy" games such as Twilight Imperium and Eclipse are tile-laying games as well. These games come in all different kinds of shapes and sizes and for all kinds of age ranges. Some take two minutes to learn and fifteen minutes to play; others take sixteen hours just to play them.

Due to the nature of tile-laying games, they tend to have gorgeous table presentation, making them easier to convince people to play. They also tend to be on the more family-friendly side of games thanks to their lighter rule sets, which means you shouldn't have much trouble teaching anyone the games in this chapter.

Kingdomino

Difficulty: ★ ★ ★ ★ ★

Age Recommendation: 6+

Number of Players: 2–4

Play Time: 15–25 minutes

 ## THE GOAL

Be the player at the end of the game with the most prestige points by acquiring the best land tiles.

LET'S PLAY!

You are a lord or lady seeking new lands to expand your kingdom! You must explore all of the lands, wheat, fields, lakes, and mountains to spot the very best plots. You compete with other players to acquire the best land tiles to form a 5-by-5 tile grid, preferably in a way that allows the players to score the most prestige points! The grid of tiles may never be expanded beyond five tiles high and five tiles wide.

The game comes with forty-eight dominoes, and depending on the player count you use twenty-four, thirty-six, or all forty-eight of them. If you are playing a three- or four-player game, you use one meeple. If you are playing in a two-player game, you need two meeples each.

Between all of the players sits the domino row. Dominoes are always placed facedown, number-side up to start. Before players make the selections, the four numerical tiles are placed in order and then turned faceup. The higher the number, the more valuable the tile. However, the player who selects

WHEN TO PLAY:

- When the whole family is around

- When you need to relax

- When you want something fun and easy

Release Date: 2016
Publisher: Blue Orange Games
Designer: Bruno Cathala

FACT

Bruno Cathala, the designer of this game, has said he only works on games he would want to play himself.

FACT

Kingdomino was initially a game designed for a ski resort and was called K'dominoz!

ESSENTIAL

Meeples are game pieces that look more or less like people. They feature in a lot of tabletop games. They are *not* miniatures; those are realistic–looking plastic or metal people or creatures used in tabletop gaming.

EXPANSIONS

- Age of Giants

the higher-value tile is the last player to select a tile on the next round. Players take their meeple and the domino under it in order from left to right and then flip them over to their landscape side. When they take their domino, they must place it into their kingdom. When placed into their kingdom, it must either touch their castle or another domino that matches at least one matching landscape square on it.

If you can't play the domino, you have to discard it, which costs you points in the end. While your castle does not have to be in the center of the 5-by-5 tile grid, you receive bonus points at the end if it is.

Players earn points only at the end of the game for connecting squares of the same landscape, and the points they earn are dependent on how many crowns they have in those sections. Players go one by one, scoring points for each different landscape region in their city. They simply take the number of squares of that same landscape type and multiply it by the number of crowns in that region. If a region has no crowns in it, the player scores no points for that region. The crowns come up on various tiles in limited numbers, so they're likely to be highly sought after. If you see one, it might be worth fighting for.

The game ends when all of the tiles in the game have been used. Kingdomino is an easy-to-play, easy-to-learn accessible game that doesn't have a huge amount of physical demand. It's a great introduction to European-style worker placement games, and while the box says ages eight and up, most six-year-olds could play this game without much trouble.

Seikatsu

Difficulty: ★ ★ ★ ★ ★

Age Recommendation: 8+

Number of Players: 1–4

Play Time: 15–30 minutes

 **THE GOAL**

Your objective is to find the best place to put the tile on the board in order to have the best view.

LET'S PLAY!

Seikatsu is a gorgeous game set in a Japanese garden flourishing with flowers and birds. *Seikatsu* means "life" in Japanese, and in this game you compete with the other players to have the most breathtaking view of the finished garden between you. You take turns drawing garden tiles from a cloth bag, each featuring a bird and a flower.

Between all of the players sits a gorgeously illustrated colorful garden board. At the start of the game, each player takes a flower-scoring pawn in either pink, blue, or green.

Each player starts the game by drawing two poker-like tiles from the bag. Players take turns placing one of those two tiles on the board. There are two types of scoring in Seikatsu: immediate scoring for birds and end-of-game scoring for flowers.

The way scoring works for birds is different than the way scoring works for flowers. Not only do birds score immediately; they score a number of points based on the number of similar

WHEN TO PLAY:

- When you want something fun and easy

- When you need to relax

- When you're just getting started with tabletop games

Release Date: 2017

Publisher: IDW Games

Designers: Matt Loomis and Isaac Shalev

HOW ELSE COULD *SEIKATSU* BE TRANSLASTED?

Another possible translation of *seikatsu* is "chores."

birds directly adjacent to them. You score 1 point for the bird you placed and 1 additional point for each adjacent bird that matches that bird's type. It's important to note that it's only tiles directly adjacent to that bird.

The way flowers score is all based on perspective. Each player scores rows of flowers based on the view from their pagoda. The matching flowers do not need to be touching or in order. They simply need to be in the same row in order to count for points. Each row is tallied up by the flower with the *most* of the same kind in that row. One flower is worth 1 point, two are worth 3 points, three are 6 points, four are 10 points, five are 15 points, and finally, six flowers are worth an astounding 21 points!

Also in the game are beautifully illustrated koi tokens that count as wild tiles upon their initial placement as birds, as well as wild tiles when it comes to scoring points for flowers. They do not count as wilds when you are placing other birds adjacent to them. Koi fish only score once upon placement and do not count as additional points for any other player, yourself included, after their initial placement.

The game ends when all tiles on the board have been filled. Then players add up their flower points and add them to the bird points they have been tracking throughout the game.

EXPANSIONS

There are currently no expansions for this game.

Cottage Garden

Difficulty: ✴ ✴ ✴ ✴ ✴

Age Recommendation: 8+

Number of Players: 1–4

Play Time: 45–60 minutes

WHEN TO PLAY:

- When the whole family is around

- When you're in a table-top game marathon

- When you want something fun and easy

Release Date: 2016
Publisher: Stronghold Games & Edition Spielwiese
Designer: Uwe Rosenberg

THE GOAL

Plant the most attractive garden.

LET'S PLAY!

A colorful sea of flowers framed by walls, paths, and hedges. As ambitious gardeners, you face the challenge of filling the beds in every corner of your garden with plants!

The objective of the game is to be the player at the end of the game with the most points. The game takes place over four phases: the refilling phase, the planting phase, the scoring phase, and the gardener phase.

The refilling phase is only activated if the gardener row from which the player is about to pick has fewer than two flower tiles in it. During this phase, you take the flower tile that is in the queue directly in front of the wheelbarrow. Place it into the empty space of the gardener row. Then push the wheelbarrow to the next empty space of the gardener row and repeat this process until all spaces in the gardener row are filled.

During the planting phase the active player takes one of the available flower tiles from the gardener spaces. The die at the start of the game starts in this space. Players may only take from the spaces in that row or column, the exception being the diagonal spaces from

EXPANSIONS

There are currently no expansions for this game.

which a player may take in a diagonal line (note that these spaces are only used in a four-player game). The most important rule to note is that tiles may *not* ever overlap. After selecting the flower tile they'd like to place, players then tetris that tile into one of their two available garden plots. Then they move on to the scoring phase.

The scoring phase in this game is tricky because players choose which of their score trackers to move up the track and they receive points at the end of the game based on where those trackers are located. Every time a cube crosses this red line, the player gains an extra cat, which can be placed in her garden to take up a single space. They're not worth points but they make your garden purrrfect.

When a player completes a garden plot by filling every available space on the plot, the player then scores her blue and orange flower pots for points. She can move one blue cube up for every blue pot on that garden plot and one orange cube up for every orange pot. Blue cubes are worth 2 points each and each orange cube is worth 1 point for most of the track; however, there is a value increase in the final track space where orange points jump from 15 to 20 and blue from 14 to 20. The orange track gains 5 additional points for its last movement, and the blue gains 6 points for its last movement. When a player scores a garden plot, she *may not* split the points between two point trackers; she must pick one blue cube and one orange cube to move and only move those two up. Then the player moves on to the gardener phase.

In the gardener phase the active player must move the gardener die, located on the edge of the board, one space, moving clockwise. Whenever the sixth round is reached, you need to pay for every additional action you take, and to start, you must immediately discard any flowerbeds that have two or fewer flower tiles in them. Then you must pay either one blue space moving back or two orange spaces moving back to continue taking each additional turn for the rest of the game. Players can stop whenever they choose and not pay to take additional actions.

At the end of the game players add up all of their points and the player with the most points wins!

Takenoko

Difficulty: ★★★★★

Age Recommendation: 8+

Number of Players: 2–4

Play Time: 45–60 minutes

 THE GOAL

Grow a beautiful garden so you're the player at the end of the game with the most points.

LET'S PLAY!

In Takenoko you're tasked with growing a beautiful bamboo garden. You're also tasked with destroying a beautiful bamboo garden! Why? Because while you move around a gardener who grows bamboo shoots in the imperial garden, he also has a bit of a rival: a rascally little panda, given to the Emperor of China as a symbol of peace, who also needs all of that yummy bamboo in his robust tummy.

The hungry panda eats any bamboo he comes into contact with. However, bamboo can't grow without proper irrigation. Players need to irrigate the lands as they go, as well as plant the plots of land where the bamboo grows. Each player is given two actions per turn; these include placing a tile, irrigating, moving the gardener or panda, and acquiring an objective card.

When placing a tile, draw three plots from the stack of plot tiles and choose one to place onto the board. It must be touching at least two other tiles on the map, including the irrigation plot. When a player chooses to take and/or place

WHEN TO PLAY:

- When you want to play something challenging

- When it's time for a little competition

- When you're having a game night

Release Date: 2011

Publisher: Asmodee North America

Designer: Antoine Bauza

WHERE DOES THE WORD TAKENOKO COME FROM?

Takenoko translates from the Japanese into "bamboo shoot!"

TILE-LAYING GAMES

an irrigation they take a water irrigation token. These only irrigate tiles parallel to their long sides. Once a tile is irrigated, it automatically spouts one bamboo piece. If the player decides to move the panda or the gardener, he may move it in a straight line to one tile. The gardener adds one bamboo piece to that tile and any adjacent tiles of the same color. The panda chomps down on bamboo and then the player may put it on his player board. Then, he may choose to turn those bamboo in for points on his objective cards. If a player is out of objective cards, he may choose to draw one as an action on his turn from the panda, plot, or gardener objectives.

For scoring purposes, players each start the game with one of each of the secret objectives. The panda objectives represent two or three bamboo shoots. You can play these objective cards by trading in bamboo you've eaten as the panda. The plot objectives have three to four adjacent plots represented on them, and in order to score them the player must irrigate plots in the formation indicated on the card. The gardener objectives represent one of three potential situations, which are either a single bamboo shoot with four bamboo and one specific improvement on it, a single bamboo shoot with three bamboo and no improvements on it, or a group of several bamboo shoots of three sections without any improvement constraints.

Before his turn, the player always rolls a die, which allows him to take one of five actions based on the number rolled, and there is one wild action that allows the player to pick which of the five actions he would like to take. When a sun is rolled, the player gains an additional action. When rain is rolled the player may place a bamboo section on the irrigated plot of his choice. When the wind is rolled the player may take two identical actions this round instead of two different actions. When a storm rolls in the player can put the panda on the plot of his choice. The panda eats a piece of bamboo when it arrives. If a player rolls clouds he may take an improvement chip into his reserve, which can be placed immediately on a play or stored on his player board for use on a later turn.

There are three improvement chips that can be placed on bamboo tiles. They improve the bamboo plot by enclosing it, fertilizing it, or turning it into a watershed. The enclosure protects the bamboo in its plot from that pesky panda that might try to eat it. The fertilizer increases the growth of bamboo on its plot. Each time a bamboo piece would grow here, instead, two bamboo pieces grow. The watershed provides the bamboo in its plot with all the water it needs, so it doesn't need to be conventionally irrigated.

Takenoko is an unbearably cute, beautifully approachable, serious strategy game that's great for serious gamers and families alike. Its one flaw is that it is common for one of the players to run away with the win. Once a player has figured out how to accomplish his objective cards, it can be difficult to stop him unless the other players are anticipating his actions. This is a game that you want to always settle over a rematch once you know your opponent just a little better.

ALERT!

Takenoko is a great family game with younger players in mind, but advanced players should always play with the advanced rules. These specify that if they draw an objective card that has already been completed in the bamboo garden, they must draw a new one in the category of their choosing.

EXPANSIONS

• Chibis

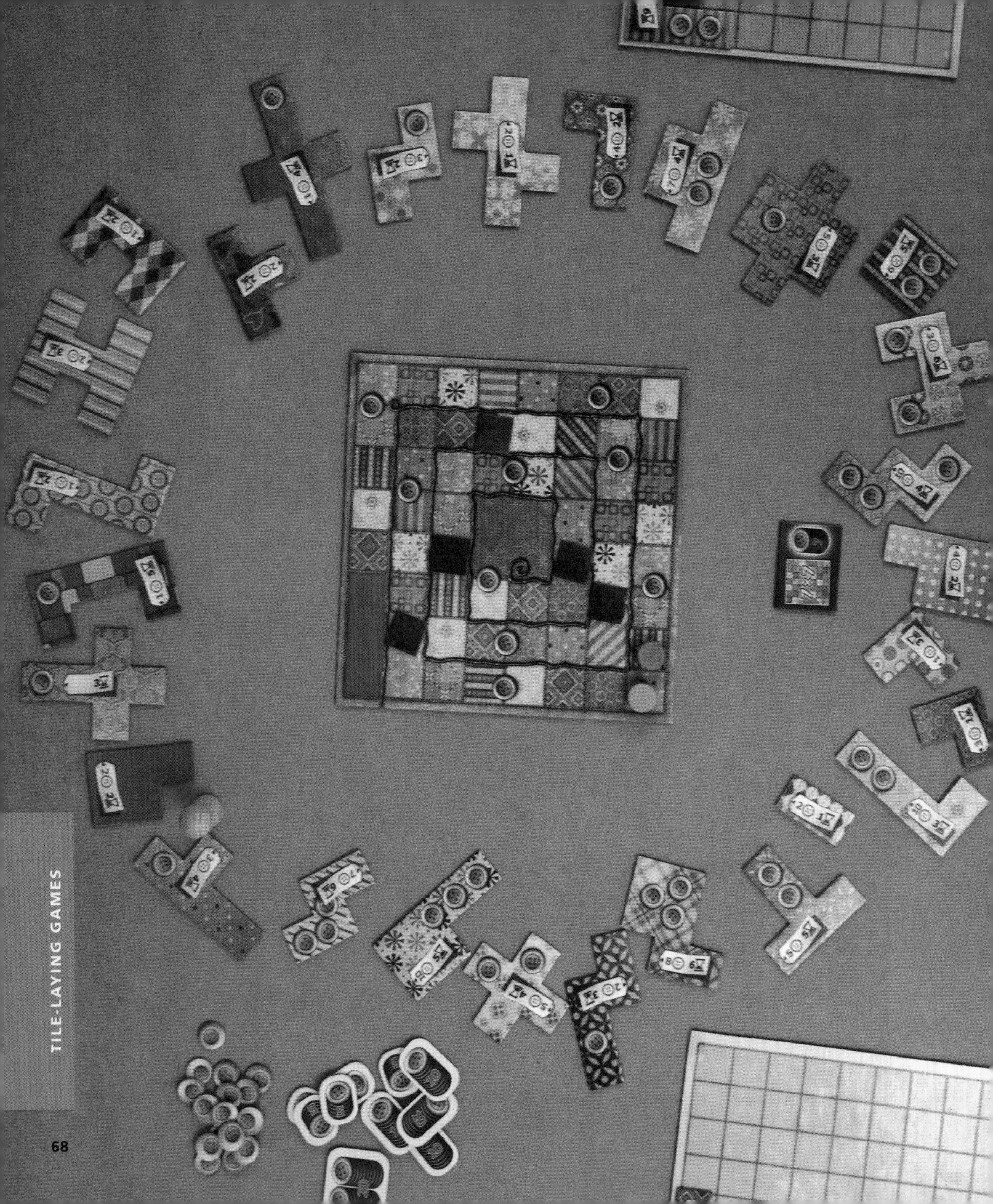

Patchwork

Difficulty: ★ ★ ★ ★ ★

Age Recommendation: 8+

Number of Players: 2

Play Time: 20–30 minutes

 **THE GOAL**

Be the player at the end of the game with the most buttons.

LET'S PLAY!

Patchwork is a two-person game that brought back the appeal of Tetris-like blocks to tabletop gaming. Each player sews a gorgeous quilt by selecting a tile in front of him and placing it on his board. If the player is the first to completely fill a 7-by-7 patchwork tile quilt on his board, he receives a bonus of seven buttons toward his end game score.

At the start of the game each player takes a quilt board and a time token with five buttons, which act as a currency to purchase quilt pieces. Between the players sits a board with a limited number of spaces on it and around them in a large circle sit all of the randomly sorted tiles. At the start of the game the pawn is placed in front of the smallest patch and the one in front of it.

In front of the pawn sit many patches. On his turn each player may select one of the three in front of the pawn, but he may only take a patch if he can afford to pay its cost in buttons. Each patch has a number of buttons listed on it as well as a timer with a number next to it. When a player selects a patch,

WHEN TO PLAY:

- When you love solving puzzles

- When you want to play something challenging

- When you're at your local game store

Release Date: 2014
Publisher: Lookout Games
Designer: Uwe Rosenberg

he pays its cost in buttons and then moves the number of spaces forward on the board as indicated next to the timer.

One unique mechanic in Patchwork is the player turn order. Whichever player is the farthest back on the board is the next player, so at times, taking low sand-timer tiles can be very advantageous, as it means acquiring even more turns before your opponent gets one.

Scattered around the board are various patches made up of squares that are used as units of measurement, and if a player is the first person to reach that patch and cross in front of it, he gets to add it to his board. These prove to be incredibly useful when attempting to complete that 7-by-7 patch grid, keeping in mind that each player's board is a 9-by-9 patch grid.

Also scattered around the main board are buttons. Any time a player passes one of these buttons he gains a button income for every button currently visible on his quilt. The fabric placed around the board has buttons randomly placed on it. He then uses these buttons to purchase even more quilt pieces on his future turns. When each player has reached the end of the track, the winner is determined by adding together the number of buttons he has left with the special +7 tile if someone earned it. Then each player subtracts 2 points for each empty space on his or her quilt board.

The player with the highest score wins the game, and in the case of a tie, the first player who got to the end of the board wins.

The elegance and ease of play of Patchwork makes it a delightful game for any two people who have a half hour to spend together. It's also a game, due to the nature of its mechanics, that you can pick up and put down as you go, so if you're meeting up with a friend to catch up, this game is easy enough to teach that you can have a normal conversation over a play of it.

Uwe Rosenberg has created many other games with similar tile play such as Cottage Garden, Spring Meadow, and Indian Summer, which are all beautifully unique games inspired by their sister, Patchwork.

HOW DO I KNOW WHOSE TURN IT IS?

The player who is farthest back on the tracks has the next turn, and she can sometimes take multiple turns in a row.

EXPANSIONS

- Patchwork Automa **2018**

Blokus

Difficulty: ★ ★ ★ ★ ★

Age Recommendation: 5+

Number of Players: 2–4

Play Time: 20 minutes

 THE GOAL

Finish the game with the most points by playing as many of your pieces as you can and preventing your opponents from playing all their pieces.

 LET'S PLAY!

Each player starts the game with twenty-one tile pieces that are made up of between one and five blocks each. At the end of the game, each tile not played loses the player the same number of points as there are blocks on the tile.

The blue player goes first, then the yellow, red, and green. When placing a piece, it diagonally touches a piece of the same color, but only diagonally. The pieces cannot come into contact with an edge. That said, there are no rules against coming into contact with the edge of another player's color tile.

When each player places her starting piece, it must fill her starting corner. If she manages to play all of her pieces, she gains 15 points, and if the last piece she plays is the one tile square she gets a bonus 5 points.

WHEN TO PLAY:

- When the whole family is around
- When you love solving puzzles
- When you're having a game night

Release Date: 2000
Publisher: Mattel
Designer: Bernard Tavitian

ALERT!
Blokus is known for its fast game play but also has a reputation for being positively addictive!

This game requires some quick strategy tips before you play!

- Unlike the real world, you can take up as much space as possible, so spread out and leave as many options open as possible from placing some of the pieces. Exploit the empty space left and do what you can to prevent the other players from placing their final pieces.
- Pay attention to your opponents' pieces. You might be able to block them from placing some of the pieces. Exploit the empty space left and do what you can to prevent the other players from placing their final pieces.
- When given the opportunity, always block another player's corners. They'd do the same to you, so it's up to you to stop them before they stop you!
- Learn to use your pieces offensively and defensively. Every piece in the game is unique and has different advantages and disadvantages.

Blokus is one of the easiest games to teach, but it's also one of the most challenging to master. Knowing your opponents and anticipating their strategy is key. If you're a part of a couple, this is a great game to get competitive over. The more you play together, the more challenging the game becomes.

EXPANSIONS

There are currently no expansions for this game.

Cacao

Difficulty: ★ ★ ★ ★ ★

Age Recommendation: 8+

Number of Players: 2–4

Play Time: 30–60 minutes

WHEN TO PLAY:

- When you're having a game night

- When you're just getting started with tabletop games

- When you're at a dinner party

Release Date: 2015
Publisher: Z-man Games
Designer: Phil Walker-Harding

 THE GOAL

Be the player at the end of the game with the most gold!

 LET'S PLAY!

Cacao takes the players into the exotic worlds of the fruit of the gods! In this game players place tiles in a jungle; along the way they gain wealth by growing and trading cocoa for gold coins.

Each player is given a player board. On it are three sun-worshipping places and a water field with numbers from -10 all the way up to 16. These are the number of victory points the player scores at the end of the game if she manages to bring her meeple to that place on the board. Each player starts the game at -10 points. There are also five storage spaces to hold cocoa fruit.

At the start of the game each player picks a color and takes the corresponding meeple along with her player tiles. Depending on the player count, certain tiles are removed from each player's stack of tiles.

Shuffle these tiles and put them facedown into a draw pile next to your village board. Between all of the players sit two tiles, a plantation, and a marketplace, as the starting tiles.

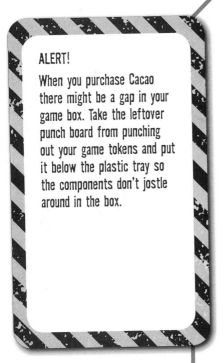

The jungle draw pile is a mixture of tiles composed of marketplaces, plantations, water, sun-worshipping sites, and gold mines. When a player's tile is placed next to a marketplace he may sell one cocoa for each meeple placed next to a marketplace for the price indicated on that tile. When a player's tile is placed next to a plantation he may gain one cocoa to his storage space for each meeple next to the tile multiplied by the number of cocoa plantations on that tile, which is either one or two. If a player places a tile next to a water tile he moves his meeple up on his water field track the number of spaces equal to the meeples on the board. He does not gain any points until the end of the game. If a player places a tile next to a sun-worshipping site he may take one sun token for each meeple placed directly next to a sun-worshipping site. These can be used later in the game to place one of his worker tiles over a tile he's already placed in order to regain the resources from the surrounding jungle tiles. If a player places a tile next to a gold mine he gains the number of gold tokens equal to the number of meeples on the tile directly adjacent to the gold mine multiplied by the value of the gold mine, which is either one or two.

When a player places one of his worker tiles, it automatically reveals the surrounding jungle tiles if they are not already revealed. While the jungle draw pile is shuffled there are always two jungle display tiles faceup on the table; with his worker tile placed on the board, he then takes the jungle display tiles and places them next to the empty edges of his worker tile and gains the resources or sells the cocoa as specified.

Cacao is one of the simpler tile-laying games, so it's good for first-time players. It's a great game to step into after you've given Carcassonne at try. If one player can learn the rules, it's fairly easy to explain how the game is played as you go. Just make sure you cover the sun-worshipping place and storage spaces before you start the game so the other players don't feel like you have an unfair advantage.

EXPANSIONS

- Cacao: Chocolatl
  2016

- Cacao: Diamante
  2017

Quadropolis

Difficulty: ★ ★ ★ ★ ★

Age Recommendation: 10+

Number of Players: 2–4

Play Time: 45–90 minutes

 THE GOAL

Be the player with the best city at the end of the game by having the most victory points!

 LET'S PLAY!

You have been tasked with building a metropolis! However, the town next door is also competing to have the best shops, parks, public services, and other structures within its city limits. You bid on the contractors to build those structures within your city. There are two modes of this game, classic and expert. This section deals with the classic mode; however, if you want to try the expert mode after playing classic, it's highly recommended in order to get the full effect of the game.

Between the players sits a 5-by-5 tile grid with randomly placed buildings, and on them is an architect. When a player places an architect she may place it on the edge of the 5-by-5 grid on any line or column from the north, south, east, or west sides. When you've decided where to place your architect, count the number of spaces on the tile away from it and take that building. Once an architect is placed in a space on the board, another architect cannot be placed there this round. The architect also cannot be pointed at the urbanist pawn, which is

WHEN TO PLAY:

- When you're having a game night

- When it's time for a little competition

- When you're ready to explain rules

Release Date: 2016
Publisher: Days of Wonder
Designer: François Gandon

FACT

The designer of Quadropolis had the idea for the game while lying in bed. The next morning he designed the prototype for the game!

TILE-LAYING GAMES

placed wherever the last building has been taken and moves every turn. Place the chosen building onto your player board.

When you take the building to place it onto your player board, you must place it onto your 5-by-5 tile grid. However, you must place it into a row or column that matches the number on that architect. If you take a tile with a four on it, for example, you must place it into the fourth row or column on your player board, each of which is marked with these numbers to indicate this information.

In the upper left-hand corner of each building sits the number of resources the players gain from placing the building; they gain these upon placement. In the bottom right-hand corner of each building sits the required resources to power the building in order to score points for it. If you don't acquire enough resources to power that building by the end of the game, you won't be able to score it at the end of the game.

If you can't place your building, or don't want to, you may discard it with no penalty. However, you may not collect any resources for a building unless it's placed onto your player board. The building types each have their own unique scoring mechanism. Residential buildings score points based on how tall they are. You can stack them on top of each other, increasing their value as they increase in height. Shops score points based on how many customers they have in them, which you gain as a resource in the form of bright transparent blue meeples. Public services score based on the number of districts in your city that have them. Parks score based on the number of residential buildings next to them. Harbors score based on the longest row or column of activated harbors in your city. Factories score based on the number of adjacent shops and harbors.

There are also some buildings that are simply worth victory points that are listed on them. Once the end of four rounds has been reached, players add up all of their buildings on their handy score sheet, and the player with the most points wins the game.

EXPANSIONS

- Quadropolis: Public Services

GET BACK TO WORK!:

WORKER PLACEMENT GAMES

Worker placement is like being taught to take your turn in preschool before selecting candy from the candy box. Players are given a set number of workers. They can use these workers to gather resources or perform actions in order to use them to accomplish other goals. The genre grew in popularity in the mid to late 2000s with the creation of games like Carcassonne, Stone Age, and Agricola.

As the genre grew, so did the number of games being produced. The real board game renaissance hit around 2014–2015, when these games exploded in popularity.

In 2009 the crowdfunding site *Kickstarter* was launched, and from there worker placement games gained even more popularity since publishers and designers could now find financial backing for their games.

Then in March 2012, the board game web series called Tabletop hosted by actor Wil Wheaton launched, making the community even more mainstream.

Thanks to the newly engaged audience, the hobby was able to grow and game stores boomed with popularity. The industry saw hundreds of new stores open up across the country, and while some failed to survive the volatile market, many stores have flourishing communities that come back to their stores regularly to play in tournaments, meet up with friends, and even just hang out and grab a snack and have some drinks.

Lords of Waterdeep

Difficulty: ★ ★ ★ ★ ☆

Age Recommendation: 12+

Number of Players: 2–5

Play Time: 1–2 hours

WHEN TO PLAY:

- When you're ready to explain rules

- When you're having a game night

- When you have a few spare hours

Release Date: 2012
Publisher: Wizards of the Coast
Designers: Peter Lee and Rodney Thompson

 THE GOAL

Complete enough quests to earn more victory points than any other player.

 LET'S PLAY!

City of Splendors. The Crown of the North. The city of Waterdeep is known just as much for its wondrous sights as a bustling trade hub nestled on the shores of the Sword Coast as it is for its back-alley swashbuckling skullduggery. As one of the secret lords or ladies of a clandestine council that controls the city, you will send your agents to various buildings across the city to hire adventurers to further your schemes and plots.

Lords of Waterdeep is a prime example of worker placement. Your goal is to complete quest cards to earn victory points before the end of eight rounds. To accomplish this you have a number of agents (workers) to use on your turn. You place a worker on one of the available building spaces and take the action that corresponds to that building. One of the core mechanisms in worker placement is employed in Waterdeep: blocking. Agents already placed by other workers block you from using those spaces. If you have no more workers to place, play skips to the next person until no one has workers to place.

FACT

Lords of Waterdeep was an unofficial side project between its two designers while working at Wizards of the Coast. It took months of testing before they finally felt comfortable pitching it to their bosses.

WHO ORIGINALLY CAME UP WITH THE IDEA OF THE CITY OF WATERDEEP?

Waterdeep was the creation of Ed Greenwood, a Canadian gamer. It was part of his campaign setting for his D&D game called the Forgotten Realms. TSR, the original publishers of D&D, bought the Forgotten Realms setting from Greenwood in 1986.

EXPANSIONS

• Scoundrels of Skullport
2013

Building spaces gives you different-colored cubes that represent different adventurers based on the classic D&D classes:

- Fighter
- Rogue
- Wizard
- Cleric

Once you acquire the right combination shown on the quest card into your tavern, you send workers off to complete the quest and collect the points, gold, or bonuses you receive by completing the quest.

You also get to purchase building plans with gold to build all new buildings where you and other players can place their agents. You receive a bonus when other players place their agents there since you're the one who built it.

Now obviously you can't let the other lords take too much of the city without interfering with their plots while furthering your own. To this end you gain and play intrigue cards to throw a wrench in their schemes and make them use their precious resources in ways they didn't plan for.

The fun comes from the slow buildup of your actions to complete your quests. Scouring over the board and trying to plan your perfect turn while trying to predict where your opponents are going to place is an exhilarating brain exercise. Lords of Waterdeep is one of the hobby's classic examples of a game that's fairly easy to understand how to play. What keeps even experienced players coming back are the fun strategies and unpredictable elements of game play.

Kingsburg

Difficulty: ★ ★ ★ ★ ★

Age Recommendation: 12+

Number of Players: 2–5

Play Time: 60–90 minutes

WHEN TO PLAY:

- When it's time for a little competition

- When you have a few spare hours

- When you want to play something challenging

Release Date: 2007

Publisher: Fantasy Flight Games

Designers: Andrea Chiarvesio and Luca Lennaco

 THE GOAL

Be the player most successful in defending the kingdom.

 LET'S PLAY!

In Kingsburg players are lords sent by the king to protect the kingdom in its frontier territories. In each year there are three production seasons for collecting resources, building structures, and training troops. Then winter comes, and players must fight the invading armies. If they succeed, they are rewarded by the king; however, if they fail, the invading armies cost them structures within their frontier territories.

At the start of the game each player is given a province board that matches his color along with three dice, three counters, and all of his building tokens. Players put their player boards in front of them. Players compete to earn victory points by building structures with the resources they gain from their dice, which are placed on advisors to acquire those resources. The rounds take place over eight phases, and during the first phase of the first year, each player receives a single good of his choice: wood, stone, or gold.

During the first phase, the player with the fewest buildings is awarded a white die to be used during the spring season, which

ESSENTIAL

The first edition of Kingsburg had an expansion but it was so well loved that it was made a part of the core game in the second edition.

EXPANSIONS

There are currently no expansions for this game.

is the season the game begins in. This won't take effect until the second year. Between all of the players sits a king's advisor board, and on it are advisors ranging from one to eighteen, the queen and king being seventeen and eighteen. On each of these advisors are goods that you take when removing your dice after influencing them.

During the production season, players roll the dice and adjust the turn order track. The lowest-rolling player places his dice first. The players take turns placing their dice on advisors one at a time. They may put one or more dice on any advisor as long as their total is exactly equal to the number on that advisor. The players collect their goods from each of the advisors from lowest to highest, and they may construct one building. If a player has the king's envoy marker, he may build two buildings.

As players upgrade their buildings, they have ways to manipulate the dice and resources they have each round as well as gain soldiers for combat later in the game.

The production season repeats for summer and fall, but between them, the player with the fewest buildings is given a king's envoy marker that allows her to influence an advisor who has already been influenced.

The players carry on into winter, but before then they may buy any number of soldiers at the cost of two goods each. Hopefully all players have built up buildings within their player boards to help gain strength and soldiers to fight off the monsters.

Then, the monsters attack. The top card of the enemies deck is turned over. Each player determines if she has defeated the monsters or been slain by them. If your attack is higher than the monsters, you win and receive the rewards listed on the enemy card! If it's equal, you get nothing but suffer no consequences. If you are lower than the monster's attack, you are defeated and suffer the losses listed on the enemy card. This typically involves losing one of your hard-earned buildings or some of your goods. Then players move the marker down one year on the track, and at the end of the fifth year, the game is over. The player with the most points at the end wins the game!

The only thing Kingsburg is missing is dragons and sorcery. Due to Kingsburg's dice-rolling worker placement method of play, the game feels infinitely replayable. There are also alternative building rows that players can put onto their province board to change up the game.

WHERE DID THE EXPRESSION TABLETOP COME FROM?

Tabletop was a popular web series starring Wil Wheaton, known for his roles in Star Trek: The Next Generation and The Big Bang Theory.

FACT

The first widely recognized worker placement game was published in 1998 under the name Keydom.

Release Date: 2016
Publisher: Stronghold Games
Designer: Friedmann Friese

ALERT!

End Game Condition: in a four- to five-player game three fabled juices are made, in a three-player game it's four fabled juices, and in a two-player game it's five fabled juices.

Fabled Fruit

Difficulty: ★ ★ ★ ★ ★

Age Recommendation: 8+

Number of Players: 2–5

Play Time: 20–30 minutes

 THE GOAL

Be the player at the end of the game with the most points.

 LET'S PLAY!

In Fabled Fruit players are animals living in a marvelous forest competing against each other for the very best fruits to devour! You are each tasked with acquiring fruit and trying to make the most juice. As you unlock abilities they change not just the game you're playing but future fable games.

The game starts in a relatively simple state. As you explore it, though, the game system, mechanisms, and your experience evolves.

The game starts with two hundred and forty location cards; there are four cards each for numbers one to fifty-eight, and eight cards are numbered fifty-nine. On each of these cards there is a price for the fabled juice and a text box of the location. There are also six wooden animals and six animal tokens along with sixty fruit cards of one fruit each and ten fruit-mix cards.

Players shuffle the sixty fruit cards and make a facedown stack next to the locations. This is where cards that are later added to the game come from. Do not shuffle these cards; they have been meticulously placed in order. The numbered location cards are not shuffled and the first six animal cards are placed onto the table. Whatever you do, do not shuffle the locations at any point. Deal two fruit cards to each player, and the rest go in a facedown stack next to the location stack.

The other tokens are placed around the board, and each player takes an animal meeple as well as its corresponding token. Players take turns in clockwise order. Each turn you must either move an animal to a new location and use its action in its textbox to collect fruits or, if you have enough fruits in your hand instead of using the location, you can buy it as a fabled juice. You must discard all of the fruit cards necessary to make your fabled juice as the fruits are being ground up and turned into that perfect juice!

In addition to normal fruits, some players may acquire a smoothie, which is a wild fruit that can be used in place of any fruit in the game. It's important to note that any time a fabled juice is purchased, the player draws the topmost single location card from the huge stack of locations. If it's the first card of a new location, you place a new small location stack for this location number and put all cards with that number onto the board. Every four cards of the new huge location stacks are incrementally grouped as sets of the same location. Any time a new location card with a new forest-dweller enters the game, all players can now use the new action or buy the new juice.

If you buy the juice of a location stack and it's the last one, that action is no longer available, and you take your animal back and move it to a new location during your next turn. After a player buys his final juice, activating the end of the game, the game is played as normal until the end of the current round so that all players have had an equal number of turns. The players add up their fabled juices and the player with the most points wins.

Fabled Fruit is a great way to introduce new players to games that evolve over time. As the game progresses new cards are added to the game from the location deck and they add additional cards, animals, and fruits to the game.

ESSENTIAL

Fable games are a genre of games (also called legacy games) that evolve with every play, permanently altering future games.

FACT

Stronghold Games, the publisher of this game, is well known in the board game industry for its European-style games.

EXPANSIONS

• The Lime Expansion

Release Date: 2017

Publisher: Brotherwise Games

Designers: Jason Harner and Matthew Ransom

ESSENTIAL

Designers Matthew Ransom and Jason Harner originally pitched Unearth as a game called Petals, in which players competed as hives of bees attempting to gather the most flowers and pollen. Unearth's iconic art is called isometric vector art. Artist Jesse Riggle is one of the pioneers in this style.

Unearth

Difficulty: ★ ★ ★ ★ ★

Age Recommendation: 8+

Number of Players: 2–4

Play Time: 45–60 minutes

 ## THE GOAL

Build new cities on the ruins of older ones to gain points.

 ## LET'S PLAY!

Long ago, your ancestors built great cities across the world and now your tribe must explore the surrounding areas of these lost cities. You are tasked with claiming them, building places of power, and restoring the glory of a bygone age.

Between all players sit five faceup earthly ruins, which players try to claim in order to collect sets of the ruins, which they score for points. Each ruin has a number in its top left-hand corner. This is the number that must be met between all dice placed on that card before it can be claimed by a player. It's always claimed by the player with the single highest dice placed on it. Any players who had dice on the ruin but did not get to take it receive power-up cards from the delver deck, which give them powerful abilities they may use throughout the game.

Upon reaching this number the ruin is reclaimed and goes into the claimed ruins pile. The player who did not claim the ruin gains one delver deck card for every die she had placed on the claimed ruin card. These cards are used to assist players throughout the game and contain varying powerful abilities.

Players score points two ways: through building monuments by acquiring stones and placing them in a formation to enclose the monument; and by acquiring ruins, which score points at the end of the game. Each turn players roll one of their five dice, but they must first select which ruin they would like to place their dice on. There are no bad rolls in the game, which gives the players perks when they roll poorly. If the player rolls between a one and a three she takes one of the stones available on that ruin. If there are no stones available on that ruin she simply places her die on that ruin. Either way, the die remains on that location. Should the player roll a four or greater, she leaves her die on the ruin in hopes she may claim it when the top left-hand number is broken. She does not gain any stones.

Collecting stones by rolling low is what players do to build wonders. When they have six total stones enclosing a space, they may select a monument to place inside of it. Some monuments have stone conditions that must be met in order to place them inside, so placing your dice strategically is critical to securing your win in Unearth.

Players choose from one of four of the faceup available wonders. They may select a greater wonder if they have a fully enclosed space of all of the same-colored stone, or a lesser wonder if they have varying types of stone enclosing their wonder.

Scoring of the ruins cards is unique: you get 5 points for every set of five different types of wonder cards you have, but you also receive points for having more of the same type of card as well. Players receive 2 points for any one color, 6 points for two, 12 points for three, 20 points for four, and 30 points for having five of the same-colored ruin. Small wonders are worth between 2 and 4 points while large wonders are worth 7 to 9 points. Unique wonders score points based on the text listed on each of their cards. The winner is the player with the most points!

FACT

Publisher Brotherwise Games had only one title out before Unearth: the best-selling game Boss Monster.

WHAT'S CONSIDERED A BAD ROLL IN UNEARTH?

There are no bad rolls in Unearth, but victory depends on employing a dynamic strategy that pays attention to your opponent's board as much as your own.

EXPANSIONS

There are currently no expansions for this game.

WHEN TO PLAY:

- When you feel like adventure

- When you're at your local game store

- When you're having a game night

Release Date: 2017
Publisher: Red Raven Games
Designer: Ryan Laukat

EXPANSIONS

- Near and Far: Amber Mines

Near and Far

Difficulty: ✶ ✶ ✶ ✶ ✶   **Number of Players:** 2–4

Age Recommendation: 13+   **Play Time:** 1–2 hours

 **THE GOAL**

Join an adventure and be the player at the end of the game with the most points.

 **LET'S PLAY!**

Have you ever wanted to go on an epic adventure but found yourself not really feeling like putting in all of that actual legwork? What if someone told you that you didn't have to leave the couch to have an epic adventure all of your own? In Near and Far players play through a book. No, really. There is a book that is page after page of maps, and in addition to that, as you go on your adventure you're directed to another book that's filled with stories and tough decisions that you need to make along the way. In this box there are several game modes that encourage your gaming group to get this gem to the table!

To start off there is a first adventure that assists players in learning how the game play works so they can get a grasp of what they are hoping to accomplish and how to make it happen. Each turn you are given two options: to either visit a space in the town or to leave town and begin your adventure!

In town there are many locations! You can visit the town hall, which will allow you to trade in goods for other goods and discard cards from your hand. You also have the option to increase or decrease your reputation in exchange for money and gems. You might also visit the saloon, where you meet with other adventurers who might want to join your party. You can head to the stables where you can recruit pets that help you in your journey. You can head to the general store to earn some extra money in exchange for some good old labor.

When you decide that you have enough goods to leave town you pick up the storybook and hand it to another player. Then you are given a short story read aloud to you by the other player, and you are faced with a decision, one you must face partially based on your skill and combat capabilities. Then you choose which of the two options provided to you that you would like to proceed with. Roll a die and check to see if you've accomplished your mission. The other player with that book then reads those results to you, allowing you to reap the benefits or suffer the punishments prescribed in the book.

The game ends when any one player has expended all of her tents on either the map or in the mine through combating various bandits. Each player scores points for coins, gems, tokens, trade routes, pets, treasure, and tents they've spent during the game! The player at the end, is, of course, the winner!

Near and Far is one of those games that takes a story from your childhood and turns it into something you can experience and interact with meaningfully. Everyone wants to choose her own adventure, but Near and Far gives players more than just two choices: it puts an entire universe in front of you and asks what you'd like to explore next. If you like telling stories, reading aloud, or simply meeting simple townspeople to piece together the puzzle pieces of a greater picture, Near and Far might be the game for you.

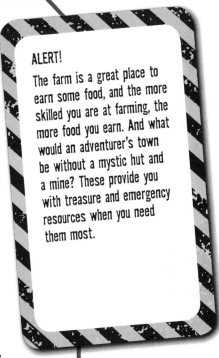

ALERT!
The farm is a great place to earn some food, and the more skilled you are at farming, the more food you earn. And what would an adventurer's town be without a mystic hut and a mine? These provide you with treasure and emergency resources when you need them most.

WORKER PLACEMENT GAMES

Stone Age

WHEN TO PLAY:

- When you're at a gaming convention
- When you're ready to explain rules
- When you're in a table-top game marathon

Release Date: 2008
Publisher: Z-Man Games
Designer: Bernd Brunnhofer

Difficulty: ★ ★ ★ ★ ★

Age Recommendation: 10+

Number of Players: 2–4

Play Time: 90 minutes

 THE GOAL

Gather resources and use them to improve circumstances for your workers.

LET'S PLAY!

Have you ever wondered what it might be like to be a caveman? Wonder no more! Stone Age is exactly the caveman simulator you've been searching for. In Stone Age, like most worker placement and Euro games, the objective is to be the player at the end of the game with the most points. You do so by deciding if you'd like to use your workers to either mine for resources, collect cards, build huts by spending your resources, or take one of three major actions. These include gaining additional workers, increasing your tool supply to better gather resources, or planting crops to better feed your workers each round.

In this game, there are four different resources: wood, clay, stone, and gold. Each one is needed to build the different huts that are out on the board. The eventual depletion of these huts also triggers the end of the game and provides valuable victory points to anyone who completes them. Each hut may only be completed by one player, and when it's obtained by her, she must place one of her workers on it to signify that she is going to build it. If she has the appropriate resources to build it, she may do so at the end of her turn. If she does not, then the worker returns to her to be used again in the next round.

Resource gathering, however, is no easy task. When you send your workers out to gather food, you roll one die for each worker placed at the resource-gathering location. Each die is six-sided; divide their total sum by the number associated with that location. Food is divided by two, wood by three, brick by four, stone by five, and gold by six. If you fall short, however, you can use those tools you gathered earlier in the game to bump your way up. You can add one to your total sum for each tool expended.

Your little caveman helpers can do more than just gather goods though. Workers who are sent to obtain the boat cards on the table need to pay the appropriate resources at the end of each round as well to acquire them. Then they are rewarded with that boat card, which has a bonus on it. These bonuses range from additional resources; sets that add to their end game victory points; and even end game bonus points that depend on how many workers, wheat, or houses they've built. These multipliers play a critical role in determining the winner of the game!

Stone Age is a fantastic way to introduce someone who has played a game like Carcassonne to the next stage of worker placement and European board games.

WHAT IF STONE AGE IS TOO COMPLICATED FOR MY CHILDREN?

There's a stepped-down version of the game called My First Stone Age that shares some mechanics but also serves as a supremely delightful children's memory game that's as fun and engaging for adults as it is for children.

EXPANSIONS

• Stone Age:
  The Expansion

MONASTERY

OUTPOST

MONASTERY

HARBOUR

HARBOUR

OUTPOST

GATE HOUSE

TOWN HALL

BARRACKS

HARBOUR

LONG HOUSE

OR

TREASURY

OR

ARMOURY

MILL

SILVERSMITH

OR

OR

Raiders of the North Sea

Difficulty: ★★★★☆

Age Recommendation: 12+

Number of Players: 2–4

Play Time: 1–2 hours

 ## THE GOAL

Impress the chieftain by carrying out daring raids and collecting valuables.

LET'S PLAY!

Raiders of the North Sea is a heavier European-style board game set in the central years of the Viking age. As Viking warriors you seek to impress the chieftain by raiding unsuspecting settlements. Players need to assemble a crew and collect provisions. They are also tasked with collecting gold, iron, and livestock as they raid the surrounding regions.

Between all of the players sits a beautifully illustrated, brightly colored player board, and on it sit resources for the taking. But first, players must build up their raiding team to make it over the treacherous waters in an effort to bring home their bounty.

At the start of the game, the starting player chooses to work or raid; all players take these same actions on their turns. Players continue taking turns until one of the three end game conditions has been met: if five of the six fortresses are raided, if all valkyries are off the board, or if the offering stack is empty. Each turn follows the same pattern: place a worker and resolve its action.

WHEN TO PLAY:

- When you feel like adventure
- When you have a few spare hours
- When you want to play something challenging

Release Date: 2015

Publisher: Renegade Game Studios

Designer: Shem Phillips

WORKER PLACEMENT GAMES

Hopefully players have acquired a solid crew because they need one in order to succeed in their raids. Players need to gather resources and prepare their crew, which is all done in the village at the bottom of the board. There are eight buildings there with various actions, and players place their one and only worker in an empty building before picking up a different worker from a different building where one is present.

Each of these buildings rewards resources such as gold, iron, livestock, and provisions or the ability to recruit additional warriors for future raids. On each warrior is a cost and on each of those cards next to his name and above that is the number of victory points each card is worth at the end of the game. When recruiting a warrior the players must pay their cost. Each warrior also has two abilities on his card. The one below the black card on it is the hired crew action. The one below the blue card is the town hall action.

The hired crew action allows the crew to offer additional military strength when raising specific settlements during raiding. The town hall actions are actions that the players take with their characters when they visit the town hall.

Once players have enough crew and provisions, they may choose to raid. To raid a settlement the player needs to meet three requirements: he must have a sufficient crew, enough provisions, and the required worker color. Raiding offers various ways of scoring. As the game proceeds, other colored workers (gray and white) enter the game, allowing players to raise increasingly challenging raids as they go.

Raiders of the North Sea is a gorgeous worker placement game with stunning board presentation that's sure to get anyone who hasn't played interested. However, it can look a bit intimidating with all those different resources on the table. It's important to have one of your players closely examine the rule book and guide the other players through their first game because, while the mechanics are simple, there is still a ton going on with this game that needs explaining.

EXPANSIONS

- The North Sea Runesaga
  2016
- Raiders of the North Sea: Fields of Fame
  2018
- Raiders of the North Sea: Hall of Heroes
  2018

GROUPTHINK:

COOPERATIVE GAMES

Working together is no simple task. However, with the right team assembled humans can accomplish anything! The games here range from two-player-only games to games where many players must work together to accomplish a shared goal. In themes, they touch on everything from simulating a romantic comedy to card-playing games where no one can talk to each other. Cooperative games require the players to work together not just a little, but entirely. There is also a sub-genre of games called semi-cooperative.

The most popular cooperative games include Pandemic and Gloomhaven, which are rules heavy but deeply satisfying. Cooperative games are great fun if you can get together just the right group but beware of quarterbacking. Nobody wants one person telling everyone else what to do! Communication is key in cooperative games, so get yourself some Ricolas and a glass of water because you're going to be talking—a lot.

Pandemic

Difficulty: ★ ★ ★ ★ ★

Number of Players: 2–4

Age Recommendation: 10+

Play Time: 45 minutes

 THE GOAL

Objective: Survive and cure the specified disease threatening humanity!

 LET'S PLAY!

Pandemic is a game that requires all players to work together to save humanity as a member of a disease-fighting team. Many consider Pandemic to be a modern classic and evergreen game as it quickly became one of the few games in local game stores that consistently sold for many years. Board gaming really started to take off around 2013, so having a hit prior to that time really gave some games an edge in the marketplace and allowed them to eventually hit the shelves of big-box retail.

Between all of the players sits a map on which players travel from city to city. Many of these cities contain a deadly disease, one of four, that threatens the human race. Players must work together to research cures and prevent additional outbreaks. Each player is given a unique role within the team and special abilities that can give their team an edge, but only if used properly.

WHEN TO PLAY:

- When you want to play on a team
- When you want to play something challenging
- When you're at your local game store

Release Date: 2008
Publisher: Z-Man Games
Designer: Matt Leacock

FACT

Matt Leacock was inspired by Reiner Knizia's Lord of the Rings: The Board Game (2000) and previously thought cooperative games were more aimed toward children. Before game design, Matt was a user interface designer and worked for Yahoo, AOL, and Apple.

Before starting the game, set all of your player pawns at the home base in Atlanta (home to the Centers for Disease Control and Prevention). Deal each player a random role card, two to four cards depending on the player count, and set the infection rate and outbreak tokens in their starting spots. Then begin the game by shuffling the infection cards and drawing nine cards. Place three infection cubes on each of the first three cities drawn, two on the next three, and one on the next three. Disease cubes are sorted by type; there are twenty-four of each in addition to five additional research tokens.

Before the game begins, one player prepares the player draw pile by shuffling all of the player cards together and then inserting epidemic cards every four to six cards depending on the difficulty level chosen by the players. When an epidemic card is revealed, three things happen: the infection rate goes up by one on the infection rate track, an infection takes place, and three cubes are placed in the city on the card (if that means a city would have more than three cubes, an outbreak occurs, and all the cities adjacent to the city that's at the center of the outbreak receive three cubes). Also, the players must increase the intensity of the infection by taking the infection discard pile, shuffling it, and putting it on top of the draw pile without shuffling it into the deck.

On his turn, each player takes a total of four actions; these can be basic actions or special actions. Basic actions are available to all players and special actions are character-specific. Basic actions include:

1. Driving or taking a boat to adjacent cities.
2. Flying to a city pictured on a card in a player's hand.
3. Flying to a research station.
4. Treating a disease by removing cubes from the city the player's pawn occupies.

The player also has the option to pass and skip one of his actions.

The special actions are unique to each player but allow the players to manipulate the board by taking what are essentially beefed-up basic actions that allow them to "break" the rules of the game. This can make it easier for them to move around the board, cure diseases, or research cures more effectively.

After taking his action, the player draws two cards to his hand, and if he has more than seven cards he must discard down to seven immediately. If another player is at his location, he can share knowledge with that player by giving her cards. There are special event cards and location cards. Special event cards may be played at any time and do not require an action to play. Players can use location cards to eradicate disease and travel around theworld.

The players are allowed to discuss strategies but do not immediately know everything the other players do. If you are playing in normal or heroic mode, you cannot show other players the content of your hand; however, you may freely talk about your hand. Since the game is a test of cooperation and not memory, the players can freely examine the contents of the infection and player discard piles.

At the end of their turn, players draw cards from the infection draw pile equal to the current infection rate and add one cube to the cities on the cards, using a cube of the same color as each card. Resolve the cards in the order drawn unless that disease has already been eradicated. If the infection causes the city to have more than three cubes then an outbreak occurs, and if the total outbreaks ever exceed eight, the players collectively lose the game.

The player may also lose the game if they need to add disease cubes to the board and there aren't any in the supply, as well as if there are not enough cards in the player draw pile when a player must draw cards.

The game is won when players find cures for all four diseases. Pandemic is a game that is fun provided that your group has a great sense of humor. Communicate well, and remember that it's okay to laugh at your failures.

ALERT!

Keep an eye on the long-term goals of the game. In Pandemic, it's important to focus on curing the diseases and not get too caught up in preventing outbreaks.

EXPANSIONS

- Pandemic: On the Brink **2009**
- Pandemic: In the Lab **2013**
- Pandemic: State of Emergency **2015**
- Pandemic: Legacy **2015**

COOPERATIVE GAMES

The Mind

Release Date: 2018
Publisher: Pandasaurus Games
Designer: Wolfgang Warsch

EXPANSIONS

There are currently no expansions for this game.

Difficulty: ★ ★ ★ ★ ★

Age Recommendation: 6+

Number of Players: 2–4

Play Time: 10–20 minutes

 THE GOAL

Avoid losing lives in order to become the only surviving player.

 LET'S PLAY!

Since its release in 2018, many have debated if The Mind is a game. Due to its simple rule set, many have claimed it's simply a puzzle or an activity and not an actual game. Experiences while playing this game vary quite a bit. While some are confounded by The Mind, others are elated by the game's simple elegance. The key to enjoying The Mind is to remember to have fun by celebrating your successes and laughing at your failures.

The Mind is an experiment and a team experience despite the fact that in this game no players are permitted to exchange information. No talking during this game is permitted at all. The deck contains one hundred cards numbered one through one hundred. Collectively, you must play these cards into the center of the table on a single discard pile in ascending order, keeping in mind, you are not allowed to communicate with each other about the cards in your hand.

Stare into your opponent's eyes and when the time is right, play your lowest card, because the goal is to play these cards from lowest to highest and it's critical that you don't mess this up. When you play your card, if no other player has a card in their hand that is lower, the game continues. If someone does, all players discard all cards lower than the card played, faceup, and then your team loses one life. You start the game with the number of lives equal to the number of players, but you have the opportunity to gain more throughout the game. If you happen to lose all of these lives, however, you lose the entire game.

Your team also starts the game with one shuriken. These are used to discard cards by allowing each player in the game to discard their lowest card faceup, giving everyone else information about what could potentially be in their hand. Players must silently communicate when they wish to use these, and it must be a unanimous decision when to use a shuriken.

For each level of the game, players are dealt that many cards. If you are playing level one, you are given one card, for level two, two cards, and so on. With each round, playing cards becomes increasingly difficult because between each round of the game, all cards from one to one hundred are shuffled together and dealt back out. No cards are ever permanently removed from the game. Players lose lives every time a card is played out of order.

The Mind is engaging, high stress, and high fun, and if you're not afraid to lose a bunch of times before you win, this might be just the game/puzzle/activity for you.

ESSENTIAL

It has been long debated between gamers whether The Mind is a game or an activity. It's important to choose the group you play this game with carefully because it's been one of the fiercest and talked about tabletop controversies in a while!

ALERT!

Players who are particularly good at reading each other might consider playing the game in extreme mode, where all players place their cards facedown into the stack and they aren't looked at until the end of a level.

WHEN TO PLAY:

- When you feel like adventure

- When you have a spare ten minutes

- When you want to play on a team

Release Date: 2010

Publisher: Z-Man Games

Designer: Shadi Torbey

Difficulty: ★ ★ ★ ★ ★

Age Recommendation: 8+

Number of Players: 1–2

Play Time: 15 minutes

 ## THE GOAL

Win the game by unlocking all of the oneiric doors before your dream time runs out!

 ## LET'S PLAY!

You are a Dreamwalker, lost in a mysterious labyrinth. Your goal is to find the eight oneiric doors and make your escape before the clock runs out.

Onirim is a game that can either be played cooperatively or as a solo game. The mechanics are elegant, simple, and easy to learn. You obtain doors either by playing three cards of the same color in a row or by discarding your powerful key cards. In both cases, you have to decide the best use of each card in your hand to carefully play around the nightmares that surprise you along the way. They are hidden within the deck and cause you horrible pain when revealed.

Within the deck of cards are eight door cards: two each of red, blue, green, and brown. There are also ten nightmare cards and fifty-eight labyrinth cards made up of chambers, keys, moons, and suns. At the start of the game, you draw five cards into your hand, and every time you play or discard cards, your hand should be immediately refilled to five.

There are three kinds of cards in the game: locations, doors, and nightmares. Location cards have a location on them as well as a color. If you play three in a row of the same color, you unlock a door. However, players can never play two cards of the same symbol in a row. The three symbols are the sun, the moon, and the key. If you draw a door from the deck and you have the corresponding key in your hand at the time you draw, you can choose to unlock the oneiric door of that color. If you draw a door and you do not have a key in your hand, it's placed into limbo, a temporary space for cards that are reshuffled into the deck at the end of the next turn.

When a player draws a nightmare card she must take one of several actions to resolve it: she can discard all of the cards in her hand, discard the top five cards of her deck, discard a key in her hand, or send a door she's already unlocked to limbo.

While the game sounds simple on paper, it grows increasingly difficult as the deck thins because the nightmares grow closer and closer together. If you have an easy start to the game, you better be prepared for disaster before long because eventually, your nightmares are going to catch up with you.

The base game also comes with three mini-expansions, which add cards that allow deck manipulation, additional victory conditions, time bombs that impede progress, and even one that makes it so you must find the doors in a specified order, which can prove to be incredibly daunting.

ESSENTIAL

Onirim is a great game to play with your partner; however, it's also a great solo game. You can also find the game on iOS and the Android marketplace available as a mobile app.

EXPANSIONS

- The three mini-expansions mentioned earlier, none of which have names.

NAVIGATOR

COPPER GATE

CORAL PALACE

CRIMSON FOREST

DUNES OF DECEPTION

FOOLS' LANDING

GOLD GATE

PHANTOM ROCK

HOWLING GARDEN

IRON GATE

LOST LAGOON

MISTY MARSH

OBSERVATORY

SILVER GATE

TEMPLE OF THE MOON

TEMPLE OF THE SUN

TIDAL PALACE

TWILIGHT HOLLOW

WATCHTOWER

CAVE OF EMBERS

WHISPERING GARDEN

BREAKERS BRIDGE

BRONZE GATE

CAVE OF SHADOWS

CLIFFS OF ABANDON

EXPLO...

Forbidden Island

Difficulty: ✶ ✶ ✶ ✶ ✶   **Number of Players:** 2–4

Age Recommendation: 8+   **Play Time:** 30 minutes

 THE GOAL

Capture all four treasures, get all players to Fools Landing, and have a helicopter lift cards upon arriving there.

👥 LET'S PLAY!

Forbidden Island is one of those games that people stare at because it's a gorgeous game that has stunning table presentation. In this game players take turns moving their pawns around the island, which is built with a number of location tiles. Unfortunately for the players, as the game progresses, more of the island tiles sink and become unavailable. As that happens the game speeds up because the water levels begin to rise even faster, which means sacrifices must be made.

In the game, you join a team of fearless adventurers on a do-or-die mission to capture four sacred treasures from the ruins of a paradise island. You work together against the clock to make your triumphant escape before you are swallowed into the watery abyss! Before starting the game one player sets up all twenty-four island tiles randomly placed color-side up. The first row is two tiles, the second four, the third and fourth are six tiles, the fifth is four again, and the final row is just two again, making for a beautiful island map. Next to the map sit the four treasures. To the left of

Release Date: 2010
Publisher: Gamewright
Designer: Matt Leacock

WHEN TO PLAY:

- When it's time for a little competition

- When you're having a game night

- When you're at your local game store

COOPERATIVE GAMES

the board are the shuffled treasure cards and to the right of the board are the shuffled flood cards along with the flood meter. The adventurer cards are also shuffled. One player draws six flood cards and flips over the corresponding tiles to identify that they are "flooded." Those six cards are put into the discard pile. The players pick a difficulty setting and set the water level marker on the water meter.

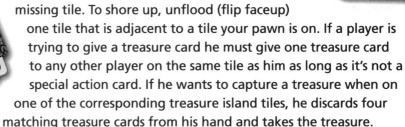

Each player starts the game with one adventurer card, which is read aloud to the other players. After all, you are working together. You also start with a pawn token, which is placed on the related island tile. Each player is dealt two treasure cards, which are kept faceup in front of each player.

Each player is given three total actions on his turn, but he does not have to take them all. He can move, shore up, give a treasure card, or capture a treasure card. When moving, the player moves one adjacent space. Players can't move onto or over a missing tile. To shore up, unflood (flip faceup) one tile that is adjacent to a tile your pawn is on. If a player is trying to give a treasure card he must give one treasure card to any other player on the same tile as him as long as it's not a special action card. If he wants to capture a treasure when on one of the corresponding treasure island tiles, he discards four matching treasure cards from his hand and takes the treasure.

There are also special movement rules laid out for each role.

- The **explorer** can move diagonally and can shore up tiles diagonally as well as swim diagonally.
- The **pilot** can jump to any time for one action but only one time per turn.
- The **navigator** can move other pawns up to two tiles for one action and can use the special movement power of the pawn when moving it for anyone but the pilot.

- The **diver** can move through as many flooded or missing tiles as desired for one action but must end his turn on a real tile.
- The **engineer** can shore up two tiles for one action.
- The **messenger** can give cards to a player not on the same tile as her.

After the player has taken his action on his turn he draws two treasure deck cards, which aid him in his journey, keeping in mind that he has a hand limit of five cards total. He can always use his special action card ability before discarding cards. Special action cards use no actions and can be used on other players' turns.

Unfortunately, after their turn players must draw flood cards equal to the water level, which could bring rising waters and danger. When a player draws a card for a tile that is not currently flooded, it flips facedown and is now flooded. When a player draws a card for a tile that *is* flooded, the tile is then "sunk" and discarded. Nothing can now save this tile, and any players on those tiles move to an adjacent tile of their choice.

The players only win the game if they capture all of the necessary treasure, have the helicopter lift card, and if every single player is safely located at Fools Landing.

ESSENTIAL

Forbidden Island is incredibly simple and fairly easy to teach. Kids as young as second graders can play the game with ease, although remembering some of the abilities of the various roles can at times be challenging for young children. It's a good idea to have an adult around to help remind them of these rules.

EXPANSIONS

There are currently no expansions for this game.

Betrayal at House on the Hill

WHEN TO PLAY:

- When you want to play on a team
- When you love solving puzzles
- When you have a few spare hours

Release Date: 2004

Publisher: Avalon Hill

Designers: Rob Daviau, Mike Selinker, Bruce Glassco, Bill McQuillan, and Teeuwynn Woodruff

Difficulty: ★ ★ ★ ★

Age Recommendation: 14+

Number of Players: 3–6

Play Time: 1–2 hours

THE GOAL

Survive and destroy the traitor.

👥 LET'S PLAY!

In this game players are tasked with navigating a haunted house and along the way they discover objects, weapons, and omens, which eventually leads to activating the haunt in the game. At that point, one of the players turns on the others and becomes the monster of the house. She is given an objective or a mission and is tasked with carrying it out to defeat the other players.

As the players who are not the monster make their way through the haunted house they uncover rooms, adding them to the ever-growing house. Why is there a pool on the second floor? Nobody knows or cares! They're too busy running from a massive werewolf!

At the start of the game each player is given a miniature of her character and a stat tracker that she uses to track her might, speed, sanity, and knowledge. These are unique traits that each character needs to use in the various challenges she faces either against the other players, the monster, or the room she is in. As players travel around the board and uncover rooms, some have omens. When they are revealed, players often must overcome an event that immediately happens.

After an omen is resolved, the player rolls a number of dice and if he exceeds the haunt number, then the haunt begins. A random player is selected to then become the player haunting the other players. The players stay in the room where the game is played, and the person selected to haunt goes into another room and reads his card. Then he must accomplish his mission, whatever that may be. Each game has endless possibilities, and the haunt is selected from a large book based on the events that occur during the game.

When Betrayal came out, it was unlike anything else the market had ever seen. The game play is a blast, if you're down with being scared.

FACT

Avalon Hill, the publisher of Betrayal at House on the Hill, was once an independent game company, dating back to 1952. It was sold to Hasbro in 1998, which placed it under the umbrella of Wizards of the Coast, a subsidiary of Hasbro.

EXPANSIONS

- Betrayal at the House on the Hill: Widow's Walk **2016**

The Grizzled

 THE GOAL

Survive the Great War together.

 LET'S PLAY!

In The Grizzled a small team of Frenchmen must struggle against the traumas of war long enough to see peace return to their homeland. Playing cooperatively, each player must survive the war or fall together defending Marianne.

The Grizzled is a cooperative card game about World War I, the Great War. As a cooperative war game, the game truly promotes a message of peace, fitting on the centennial of the war's armistice, November 11, 1918. The deck is built of the threats of war, traumatic events like a mortar strike or gas attack, cold snow or frigid rain, and culminating in shell shocks that can impact game play. Players cannot ever have more than three of the same threats on the table or they lose the round and suffer the consequences. In addition to these, the players will experience traumas within the game they need to overcome.

The traumas are important because not only can they add more threats of war to the table but they can only be removed by the love and support of their allies. Mute can make a player unable to communicate or use a speech to inspire the troops to prevail.

Release Date: 2015
Publisher: CMON
Designer: Tignous

Frenzied forces a player to be more reckless and draw two extra threats after a mission has been defined. If ever a player has four of these at the end of a round and cannot discard them, she falls victim to her ailments and the players collectively lose the game. Ailments are healed only at the end of the round when each player chooses which direction to lend support. Only the player with the most support may remove two of these or refresh her hero's power.

Leadership is a revolving post, and each player assumes command. The choice is hers to risk how much exposure to the war the team can handle. Each round the players are given a number of threat cards based on the mission they face, and as a result they must place as many of them as they can in an effort to make it through the tumultuous war at hand. For every card they cannot get rid of, they draw more cards onto the threat deck the next round.

Players place threats down, but if the same threat traumatizes the tired team three times, they fail the mission and their cause. Each character has a lucky charm, which they can use to neutralize a specific threat. But every successful mission brings your team closer to the white dove of peace.

While the mechanics of this game are relatively simple, it's not recommended for children under the age of thirteen due to its mature content.

FACT

The game was illustrated and designed by French artist Tignous, who delivered his contributions to this game just days before being killed at the *Charlie Hebdo* attack in Paris.

EXPANSIONS

- The Grizzled: At Your Orders **2016**

WHEN TO PLAY:

- When you want to play something challenging

- When it's time for a little competition

- When you're at a gaming convention

Release Date: 2017

Publisher: Asmadi Games

Designer: Chris Cielisk

One Deck Dungeon

Difficulty: ★ ★ ★ ★ ★

Age Recommendation: 14+

Number of Players: 1–2

Play Time: 30–45 minutes

 THE GOAL

Survive and escape with boatloads of treasure!

 LET'S PLAY!

Have you ever been described as roguelike? Now might be your opportunity to prove it! In this game, players are tasked with a dungeon delve that's different every time. It's difficult to survive, and you have a new character to build from scratch. The deck consists of various foes to battle and other perils, which may get the best of you along the way in the dungeon. However, if you manage to defeat the monsters, you are rewarded with experience, items, or skill. If you survive fighting the dungeon boss, you become a legend.

In One Deck Dungeon the players explore a dungeon represented by facedown door cards. When flipped over, there are monsters and rewards depicted on them. In order to defeat them, the players must match the dice rolled from their character's stats with the dice requirements as listed on the monster's card. Any spaces without a die on that card must deal damage or discard cards from the dungeon deck. Any hearts left open deal damage to your hero, and the hourglasses force the players to spend time by discarding cards from the deck, which speeds up the game. After the battle is fought, the player gains the loot listed on the card, which can add dice to her character's overall stats in the form of items; gains skill to help manipulate her dice; gains experience, which adds to the level of her character or maximum carrying capacity; or discovers a new potion to use later in the game.

As the players travel through the dungeon learning new skills and buffing up their character stats and dice, they grow increasingly strong and thus become capable of taking on even more dangerous creatures. Each time the players get through the encounter deck they find a staircase and may go even deeper into the dungeon. They shuffle all of the cards and go into the dungeon again, but this time things are even more challenging. Once they've completed all three levels, the players encounter a boss fight, which involves multiple rounds of combat. If the heroes manage to survive, they win the game. If any of the players ever have more damage on their character than they have health, they lose the game immediately and the game is over.

This can be played solo or with two players. With the expansion players can even play it as a four-player game. One Deck Dungeon has a simple rules set and loads of fun in a small box. The game does have a fair amount of setup, so be prepared to do some reading.

EXPANSIONS

- One Deck Dungeon:
  Forests of Shadows
  2017

Gloomhaven

Difficulty: ★ ★ ★ ★ ★

Age Recommendation: 14+

Number of Players: 1–4

Play Time: 1–2 hours

 **THE GOAL**

Be the player at the end of the game with the most points.

 **LET'S PLAY!**

Released in 2017, Gloomhaven is notable for the way that it shot up the *BoardGameGeek* rankings while redefining the dungeon crawl board game genre. Spun off from traditional pen-and-paper role-playing games (RPG), dungeon crawls focus on the tactical fighting, as opposed to role playing. While dungeon crawls are typically considered to be lighter games, Gloomhaven showed that a dungeon crawl board game can excel when it requires deep tactics, expansive character development options, and choices with harsh consequences.

At its core, Gloomhaven is a cooperative dungeon crawler for one to four players. It's designed to be played as a campaign across multiple gaming sessions with a consistent group. Unlike other games of its type, Gloomhaven also features a persistent world that can handle multiple groups playing concurrently in the same gaming world.

WHEN TO PLAY:

- When you feel like adventure

- When you want to play on a team

- When you want to play something challenging

Release Date: 2017
Publisher: Cephalofair Games
Designer: Isaac Childres

COOPERATIVE GAMES

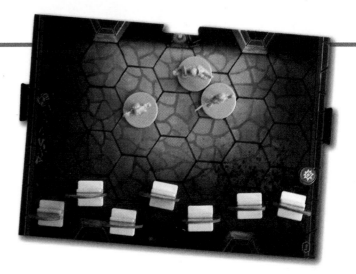

The enemies are controlled by a variable behavior deck and focusing rules rather than by one of the players. The story for Gloomhaven is branching, similar to computer RPGs like Mass Effect or Final Fantasy, but it plays a relatively more minimal role in the overall play experience. This story serves to connect the multiple tactical set pieces that make up the vast majority of the game play.

Each player chooses a pair of action cards from her hand:

- Each card has a different top action and bottom action that must be performed on the character's turn.
- Each card also has a number to show the initiative of the action, from one to one hundred.

Each player must, in secret, choose one of the two actions and then use its initiative numbers for the turn. Then the players reveal their number and flip over the cards that control each monster, which has its own initiative number. Then, from the lowest to the highest, each enemy or player activates and completes her turn.

This continues until the scenario is finished or the players'v characters are exhausted. Exhaustion occurs when the players can no longer play two cards. Cards are lost through resting, avoiding damage, or special abilities during the scenario, which also creates an effective turn limit for the players in the scenario.

Gloomhaven is an inspired design that is the current epitome of cooperative dungeon crawl games. It is highly recommended if you are interested in a game that centers on tactical depth and collaborative game play.

EXPANSIONS

- Gloomhaven:
  Forgotten Circles
  2019

Release Date: 2017
Publisher: Hush Hush Projects
Designer: Jacob Jaskov

Fog of Love

Difficulty: ★ ★ ★ ★ ★

Number of Players: 2

Age Recommendation: 16+

Play Time: 60–100 minutes

THE GOAL

Work together to achieve your personal secret objective, which can range from staying together as a couple and both achieving a certain level of happiness to intentionally breaking the other player's heart.

LET'S PLAY!

Love is no easy task. In this game players take on the roles of two characters who meet and fall in love. They are faced with challenges, and much like a romantic comedy there are awkward situations, lots of laughs, and so much compromise. Your goals as players might be at odds, or they might be fairly aligned; either way, you need to look deep inside your heart and decide if you're ready to change or if you're going to break your lover's heart. Happily ever after is never guaranteed, but life is full of surprises and you never know what's going to happen.

At the start of the game the players need to select the love story they are hoping to play through. The game starts with a tutorial, so don't worry if you don't know the game. It teaches you how to play as you go. Each player is given specific destinies that go in their hand as well as their starting hand, which is made up of sweet, serious, and drama cards from the deck. There is also a chapter outline that specifies the length of the chapters the players play out as well as the length of each chapter and which deck to draw these cards from.

Players sit across the board from one another. They build their characters by selecting three of the five trait cards that are dealt to them. Each player has varying trait goals, which they attempt to accomplish. Then they pick one of three occupations dealt to them. You want to make sure your occupation and trait goals align in some way.

Then each player is dealt five feature cards, from which they select three to give to the other player. These are the traits each one noticed about the other when they first met.

Between the players sits a personality dimension track, on which they place personality tokens. For each trait that the players have they need to place one of their personality tokens onto the top or bottom of each of these tracks. Each of them represents personality traits and are used as positive and negative indicators of that character's actions throughout the game. At the end of the game the players determine what kind of people they are based on these traits and see if they've accomplished their hidden objectives. Each trait has an opposite trait across from it, one moving up and the other moving down. The opposite of disciplined is disorganized; curiosity versus closed-mindedness; extroversion versus introversion; sensitive versus thick-skinned; gentle versus rough; and sincere versus deceitful.

On their turns, players try to add more of these trait tokens to the board in an attempt to accomplish their goals. Some of their goals are shared and others are individual. If a player is attempting an individual goal, she adds up her total for that personality dimension. There are positive and negative personality traits for each personality dimension. For example, if disciplined is the personality dimension, a positive trait would be organized while a negative trait would be disorganized. The smaller of the two positive and negative personality trait tokens is subtracted

COOPERATIVE GAMES

from the larger one and what's left is that player's score for that personality trait. For shared goals the players' tokens are added and subtracted collectively. This can lead to some conflicting views and situations for the two players.

If players fail to complete these goals, they get negative happiness at the end of the game. If they achieve it, they gain positive happiness points. During each round players are given a prompt and then they put a token facedown in front of them, indicating their choice for the scenario. Sometimes they get bonuses or punishments for having the same choice. Each chapter has a number of scenarios played out each round depending on the story being played. Keep in mind that all of the decisions are determined in part by the characters' motivations. The players get to place personality tokens onto the board based on the decisions they made in each scenario. Sometimes the scenario cards can also activate other scenario or secret cards that need to be resolved immediately and will have an impact on the storyline.

There are also secrets within the game that change the characters' motivations during the game play. Secrets are played facedown and aren't revealed until activated either during the game or at the end. Finally, there is a final card to resolve the story and the players reveal their destinies then compare to see if they chose the same destiny at the start of the game. Destiny cards also determine whether you stay in the relationship or break up based on each player's happiness.

ESSENTIAL

For added fun, instead of choosing three traits for the other player based on cards dealt to you, you can deal them the actual first three traits you noticed about them and then play your relationship as yourselves. This is called Nightmare Mode and was suggested by board game reviewer Eric Yurko in his blog *What's Eric Playing?*

EXPANSIONS

- It Will Never Last
2018

- Paranormal Romance
2018

- Trouble with the In-Laws
2018

TRAITOR!:
HIDDEN ROLE GAMES

Hidden role games typically include bluffing, deduction, and negotiation. Bluffing games don't always require deception but oftentimes encourage players to use it to accomplish their goals, and most of the time this means that not all information in the game is visible to the other players. Deduction games require players to narrow down information similarly to games like Clue by giving the player small bites of truthful information that they use to solve the puzzle in front of them. Negotiation games typically involve making deals with other players but not always having to stay on the righteous side of the agreements that have been made.

These games all share one thing in common: the tension in the air between the players. When a player can't trust even his closest family and friends, he spends a fair amount of time wondering who he can trust long after the game is over. Hidden role games are unique in tabletop gaming as well because they alter the players' relationships with each other every time a game is played. If a player lies often, the other players grow increasingly likely to accuse that player of lying in future social deduction games. To make matters worse, much like in poker, players quickly catch on to other players' "tells" that give them away.

Especially for folks on the more introverted side, in the right setting hidden role games can be one of the most captivating experiences in tabletop gaming. The feelings of the game stick with players hours after playing.

VILLAGER

ROBBER

TROUBLEMAKER

TANNER

DOPPELGÄNGER

WEREWOLF

SEER

VILLAGER

One Night Ultimate Werewolf

Difficulty: ✳ ✳ ✳ ✳ ✳

Age Recommendation: 8+

Number of Players: 3–10

Play Time: 10 minutes

WHEN TO PLAY:

- When you have a spare ten minutes

- When you want something fun and easy

- When the whole family is around

Release Date: 2014

Publisher: Bezier Games

Designers: Akihisa Okui and Ted Alpach

 ## THE GOAL

Win the game by either finding the werewolves and killing them or by simply surviving the passing nights as one of the townsfolk. Some roles given to players have special objectives.

 ## LET'S PLAY!

One Night Ultimate Werewolf is a simplified and streamlined version of a famous role-based game, Mafia (also known as Werewolf). This game was first published in 2014 and took the board game industry by storm thanks to its easy travel-sized box and companion app that makes the game even easier to set up and get to the table. The goal of the game depends on the role that each player is playing, which is hidden from all of the other players.

In this version of the game, there are many roles available for players to play. Players may use any combination of cards they want, although it's recommended that players first play a more basic game with simpler roles before introducing a bunch of new roles.

Before each round, each player is given a token that corresponds to one of the cards in the center of the table. This ensures that everyone knows the available roles but doesn't

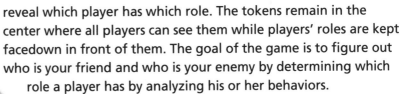

reveal which player has which role. The tokens remain in the center where all players can see them while players' roles are kept facedown in front of them. The goal of the game is to figure out who is your friend and who is your enemy by determining which role a player has by analyzing his or her behaviors.

Each of the roles has effects that change the nature of the game. Some roles clearly help the village team while others clearly help the werewolf team. Due to the game's short nature, even if the werewolves seem to be triumphant several times in a row, that's okay because the game is going to be over in just ten minutes and a new day begins.

The app tells all players to close their eyes. Then it wakes up players one by one in a specific order. If players choose not to use the app, they elect one person to play the role of Game Master, who calls players to wake up in the proper order. When a player wakes up, she opens her eyes and does exactly what is stated for that role.

The werewolf team is made up of just two types of characters, the werewolves and the minion. The werewolves wake up and look for other werewolves on their turn. After that the minion wakes up to see who the werewolves are. The werewolves stick their thumbs up, identifying their roles to the minion while all other players keep their heads down, unable to see who the werewolves are. The werewolves won't know who the minion is. If the minion dies and no werewolves die, the werewolves still win. If no players are werewolves, the minion wins as long as one other player other than the minion dies. Players die during each round.

The villagers' team is made up of many roles and their goal is to survive and kill all of the werewolves before they kill them!

Two mason tiles are always placed into the game together. The mason wakes up and looks for the other mason. If there isn't a second mason at the table, it's in the center not being used by another player. When the mason is told to open her eyes, the seer may look at one other player's card or at two of the center cards, but she does not move them. The robber may choose to rob a card from another player and place his robber card where the other player's card was. The robber is now on the team of whatever his new role is. If he chooses not to rob a role, he remains the robber on the village team. When told to open his eyes, the troublemaker may switch the cards of two other players without looking at them. The players who receive new cards are now that role even if they don't know what role that is until the end of the game. The insomniac wakes up to look at her card to see if it has changed. The villagers have no special abilities, and thus all werewolves claim to be them. Finally, the hunter, if shot, shoots and kills whoever he is pointing at as they both fall to their death!

The more players in the game, the more chaotic things become. While One Night Ultimate Werewolf simplifies a much more intense game like Werewolf, this version of the game became more popular due to its accessibility features like the companion app. This version of the game also moves fast enough that no player feels slighted. Knowing the game is only going to last ten minutes also allows you to take revenge on another player in a future game. One of the best things about short games is that if someone in your group doesn't love the game, you can always move on to something else.

ESSENTIAL

The tanner wants to die and he only wins if he does. If the tanner dies and the werewolves do not, then the werewolves do not win. If the tanner dies and a werewolf also dies, the village team wins too. This is the only role within the game that is on neither team!

EXPANSIONS

- One Night Ultimate Werewolf Daybreak **2015**

- One Night Ultimate Vampire **2015**

- One Night Ultimate Alien **2107**

- One Night Ultimate Super Villains **2018**

WHEN TO PLAY:

- When you love solving puzzles
- When you have a spare ten minutes
- When you're just getting started with tabletop games

Release Date: 2014

Publisher: Cryptozoic Entertainment

Designer: Alexandr Ushan

Spyfall

Difficulty: ★ ★ ★ ★ ★

Number of Players: 3–8

Age Recommendation: 10+

Play Time: 15 minutes

THE GOAL

Spies: Guess everyone's location.
Everyone: Guess the spy before the spy figures out everyone's location.

LET'S PLAY!

Spyfall is a tabletop board game of deduction. In this game, players are all attempting to deduce either what location they are at if they are a spy, or who is deceiving them if they are not a spy. By cleverly asking just the right questions of the other players, non-spies do their best to provide just enough information to ensure the other players know they know where they are, but not so much information that the spy figures out where the players' shared location might be, as this information is kept from each spy.

Each location deck has seven location cards, and on top of those cards is an eighth card, a spy card. One of the players shuffles each of the decks, which are inside of small baggies. Then, she selects one of the baggies randomly and takes the cards equal to the number of players off the top of the deck. She shuffles those cards and deals one facedown to each player. Players may only look at their card.

If you have received a location card, it's up to you to give just enough information to the other players so they know you are not a spy. However, each location card also has a role in the bottom left-hand corner, and the players in the game must answer the questions asked of them honestly, keeping that role in mind. For example, if you're located on a boat, perhaps your role is that you are the ship's captain. You must answer questions as if you were, in fact, the ship's captain. Be careful not to forget your role either, because once you put your card down, you cannot pick it back up. Once the last card is placed, start an eight-minute timer.

The dealer takes the first turn. She asks one person a question and must address him by name. You are not allowed to clarify your question or ask it again, and you cannot ask follow-up questions. Here are a couple examples (the person answering the question is playing the specified role):

- **Location:** Casino
- **Role:** Dealer
- **Question:** Hailey, how was work today?
- **Answer:** You know, I've really been dealing with a lot this week.

- **Location:** Cruise Ship
- **Role:** Passenger
- **Question:** Hey, I found this antique car, do you want to check it out with me?
- **Answer:** Sure, but I'm worried about the door.

- **Location:** Space Station (but you don't know this)
- **Role:** Spy
- **Question:** Hey, I've got a question for you. Can we step outside for a quick chat?
- **Answer:** Sure!

Of course, if you answered that last question like that, you would immediately be outed as the spy because someone in a space station wouldn't be headed outside to have a chat. At that point all of the other players would get points, so it's important to be vague enough that the other players don't catch on to you! At any time during a round a player may accuse another player of being a spy. If all other players agree with the accusation, the round ends and the accused player is forced to reveal his identity. If he really was the spy, all other players score a point. The spy can also choose to end a round by announcing that he understands where the secret location is! If he guesses correctly, he scores points.

Spyfall is an excellent party game; at least four players are needed to make the game interesting. It's no wonder that this game has been nominated for many awards due to its innovation. The game's low price point makes it additionally appealing and accessible, not to mention it makes a great gift.

EXPANSIONS

• Spyfall 2

The Resistance

Difficulty: ★ ★ ★ ★ ★

Age Recommendation: 12+

Number of Players: 5–10

Play Time: 30 minutes

WHEN TO PLAY:

- When you want to play on a team

- When you want something fun and easy

- When you're at a dinner party

Release Date: 2009
Publisher: Indie Boards and Cards
Designer: Don Eckridge

 ## THE GOAL

Your team either sabotages three missions (if you're spies) or succeeds at three missions (if you're the resistance).

 ## LET'S PLAY!

The Resistance is a game inspired by Mafia (Werewolf). However, it has unique mechanics that increase the resources for informed decisions, intensify player interaction, and remove player elimination entirely. In the game, some players are resistance operatives and others are imperial spies. Each player's role is kept a secret from the other players.

In this game, players carry out between three to five rounds. The resistance must depend on each other to carry out the missions against the evil empire; meanwhile the empire will stop at nothing to undermine the resistance. While they do this, they must attempt to identify the other players' true identities and gain their trust. Each round begins with a discussion, determining who is the leader for the round. When players have decided who is the leader, they vote to approve or deny that vote. This gives important information to the other players. A spy might want to intentionally agree with the resistance players simply for the sake of staying undercover.

HIDDEN ROLE GAMES

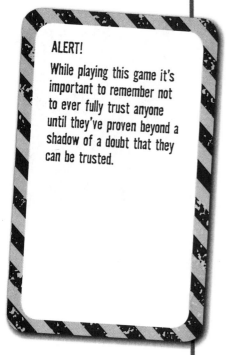

While you are technically on teams in this game, it truly feels like everybody is out for themselves because no players can reveal their true identities to the other players. The leader of that round chooses a number of players to accompany him on the mission, as specified on the board under the mission they are taking on. Then all players vote on whether or not to approve the assignment, also revealing important information about themselves. Once a team has been approved for a mission, it begins, and the players selected must decide if they would like to support or sabotage the mission.

There are two scenarios that can occur:

1. The mission can pass, in which case all players vote to support the mission and it is achieved. The resistance team gets the mission token on this round.
2. The mission can fail, in which case at least one player has chosen to sabotage the mission. If this occurs, then the spy team gets their token on this round.

When a mission fails, it becomes apparent to the other players that at least one other player is a spy and is out to get the resistance. It's up to the players at the table to deduce exactly who that person is before he or she is able to do any more damage. Be wary, though, because there's never just one spy at the table and you need to keep an eye out for any suspicious characters sitting next to you at the table.

One popular technique in this game for many people who have the spy role is to play along with the resistance team, all the while sabotaging missions and blaming it on someone else. If two spies end up on a mission with the same resistance player in two separate rounds, it's likely advantageous for them to sabotage the resistance player, but they have to be careful that only one of them votes to tank the mission. If both players tank the mission, the resistance will know for certain that at least one of them, if not both, could be a spy. It's also important to not be too obvious about sabotaging the other players, so start the game off letting the resistance think you're a good guy.

If either team has three of the same tokens on the board at any given time, they win the game. The Resistance is a modern classic board game that took hold in the community and is now seen nationwide in small retailers as well as big-box stores. Thanks to its simple but epic rules, the game is easy to teach and more fun to play a second time.

EXPANSIONS

- Avalon

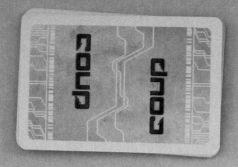

Duke

Take 3 coins from Treasury. Blocks Foreign Aid.

Contessa

Blocks assassination.

Coup

Difficulty: ★ ★ ★ ★ ★

Age Recommendation: 8+

Number of Players: 2–6

Play Time: 15 minutes

WHEN TO PLAY:

- When you're having a game night

- When you're just getting started with tabletop games

- When you want a game you can carry with you

Release Date: 2012
Publisher: Indie Boards and Cards
Designer: Rikki Tahta

 THE GOAL

Be the last player standing by having at least one card left.

LET'S PLAY!

Coup is a game of deception where players attempt to assassinate each other. There are five total roles that they might be playing but because their roles are hidden, they don't have to be honest with the other players. There are three roles in the deck and five total roles. They all play off of one another in unique ways, so it's important to understand every role before starting the game.

At the start of the game each player is dealt two cards, facedown in front of them. They may look at them at any time. There are five total roles available to the players:

1. The ambassador.
2. The assassin.
3. The duke.
4. The captain.
5. The contessa.

HIDDEN ROLE GAMES

The ambassador can exchange two cards for two cards from the deck and can block assassination attempts from the assassin. The assassin can pay three coins to attempt to assassinate another player. She can also be blocked by the captain, who can block or steal two coins from another player. The duke can take three coins from the treasury, and finally the contessa can block all assassination attempts.

On their turn, players can take any of the previously mentioned actions, regardless of what roles they actually have in front of them. In addition to those actions, players can also take one basic action of income, foreign aid, or they can perform a coup. When a player takes income, she takes one coin from the treasury. When she takes foreign aid, she takes two coins from the treasury, but a captain or ambassador can block it. Finally, if the player decides to perform a coup, she may pay seven coins and force another player to immediately lose one of her cards. If a player ever has more than ten total coins, she must take this action for her turn.

Any time a player takes any action on his card, any other player can choose to challenge his action. If the player was being honest and did have the role, the player who accused him of being dishonest loses one of her two character cards. However, if the other player was deceiving the other players, he must be honest about his deception after being accused. Then he must reveal one of his two roles to the other players.

While playing the game it's important to remember to never make yourself too much of a target for the other players. Any time a player gets close to seven coins, it's likely that she ends up being stolen from to prevent her from performing a coup. If the player is quickly approaching seven coins, it might be a good call to block steals by claiming the captain or ambassador role.

An early strategy that tends to work well is claiming the duke, regardless of whether or not you have it. But be wary: other players are likely to follow suit, making your claim to dukedom increasingly suspicious.

Coup is one of those games that sounds simple but when you and your friends start to get into each others' heads, the game becomes increasingly difficult and your friends grow increasingly unpredictable. Social deduction games like Coup, The Resistance, and One Night Ultimate Werewolf helped forge a path for a resurgence of hidden role games like Dead of Winter and Dark Moon. Now when you look for social deductions games there is more of a selection than ever on *BoardGameGeek*, and there are more coming out every week on *Kickstarter* and in retail.

ESSENTIAL

While all players in Coup have exact roles in front of them, those roles are only known to them. They don't ever have to tell the truth about those roles if they don't want to.

EXPANSIONS

There are currently no expansions for this game.

WHEN TO PLAY:

- When it's time for a little competition

- When you're at your local game store

- When you want to play something challenging

Release Date: 2011
Publisher: Stronghold Games
Designer: Evan Derrick

Dark Moon

Difficulty: ✶ ✶ ✶ ✶ ✶

Age Recommendation: 12+

Number of Players: 3–7

Play Time: 60–75 minutes

 THE GOAL

Survive.

 **LET'S PLAY!**

Directly inspired by cult horror movies *Alien* and John Carpenter's *The Thing*, Dark Moon is all about isolation and paranoia in a down-and-dirty science fiction setting.

Players are employees with special skills working for a major corporation on a remote mining base on Titan, Saturn's largest moon. During a routine mining operation an accident exposed certain members to an unknown pathogen and they have begun to act strangely. As the base's important operational systems start failing one by one it has become clear no one can be trusted.

Players are either one of the uninfected employees working together desperately trying to keep the base running while they wait for help, or one of the infected who are sabotaging the base in hopes of plunging it into cold and unforgiving darkness.

Players use a pool of dice with a range of negative and positive outcomes to complete actions, hold votes, and complete events and tasks. There are weak dice with more negative outcomes than positive, and strong dice with opposite effects. At the beginning of your turn you pull from the used pool of dice from the previous turn up to your dice limit (usually five), and what is left is what you get.

The twist is these dice are always rolled behind a screen so the other players cannot see the outcomes, but the dice they submit to complete the task are shown openly. This means that if you commit to rolling dice you have to submit them and are expected to explain yourself to the other players. Having to lie or explain your suspicious behavior when you submit a bunch of negative dice you either did or did not have control over is what ramps up the paranoia more than other hidden traitor games.

The heavily stylized board displays all the major functions of the base that need to be maintained and tracked to ensure the uninfected player's survival and the parts of the base the infected sabotage. The board also has event cards that need to be completed and tasks that add the successes to complete those events.

After retrieving dice up to their dice limit, players use their dice to take an action. First and foremost, players can attempt to repair one of those damaged systems. The player rolls up to three dice and submits one after declaring which system he wants to repair. If the die he submits is positive, the repair is successful and the damage token from that system is removed. Keep in mind that the player doesn't have to declare how many dice he actually rolled or what he rolled, but no matter what, anyone who attempts this action has to submit. Other actions are possible: there's a risky way to help complete the event card, or you can call a vote to decide if a player needs to be quarantined because you suspect her to be infected.

After the player's action is resolved she draws two task cards and places them on the board for everyone to see. She discards the other one without anyone seeing it. Get ready again to explain yourself if you pick a really bad one! If it's a malfunction task, it states which system on the base this affects, the difficulty, and the consequence.

FACT

Dark Moon uses the hidden traitor mechanic in a way most other games in the genre do not: your actions are largely public rather than secret.

EXPANSIONS

• Dark Moon:
  Shadow Corporation
  2017

Starting with the current player and going clockwise, each player will decide if they want to try to complete the task. If they choose not to, they get to retrieve dice from the pool up to their limit. This is how the game gives the uninfected players a legitimate reason to not help with the task, and the infected players a way to tank the results and make sure the bad stuff keeps happening.

Each player who wants to help complete the task now takes turns rolling his dice and then submitting at least one to beat the difficulty number of the task. You can submit as many dice as you want each time, but every time you re-roll your remaining dice you are required to submit at least one until you either pass or run out of dice. The infected are trying to contribute just enough to not look suspicious but still fail the task. Uninfected who roll poorly have to plead their case. Either way, nobody trusts anyone by the time everyone has rolled and submitted dice. If the sum of the dice in the pool is equal to or higher than the difficulty, the task is successful and a cube is placed on the current event card.

While the infected have all these avenues to destroy this base, the only way the uninfected can win is simply to live through the ordeal. Cards are drawn and have a certain number of spaces for event cubes. They remain in effect until all the spaces are completed. Once three events and one final event are completed, the uninfected players have prevailed.

Dark Moon ramps up the metagame found in other hidden traitor cooperative games by increasing the difficulty and paranoia with every action and decision the player makes.

Dead of Winter

Difficulty: ★ ★ ★ ★ ☆   **Number of Players:** 2–5

Age Recommendation: 13+   **Play Time:** 1–2 hours

 **THE GOAL**

Complete your personal player objective.

 **LET'S PLAY!**

Zombies have invaded earth, and while it would be nice if you were the hero who could save the world from them, in this scenario you are lucky to make it out alive. The food is running out and there are only a few locations remaining with any goods worth fighting for. Your team needs to cautiously sneak away. Do your best to protect your colony, gather the necessary resources, and fight off the impending horde of zombies that threaten your friends, allies, and known or unknown enemies.

Dead of Winter charges players with the simple task of surviving. Each player is tasked with scavenging the hospital, police station, school, library, grocery store, and gas station for food, weapons, and fuel, and occasionally they even bump into other survivors, who may ask to join their colony. The colony is shared among the players so any survivors found will end up being one more mouth everyone needs to worry about feeding, so it's important to be careful how many people you welcome into your home. As they make their way around, players need to be careful to not make too much noise, as the noise attracts

Release Date: 2014
Publisher: Plaid Hat Games
Designers: Isaac Vega and Jonathan Gilmour

WHEN TO PLAY:

- When you want to play something challenging
- When you have a few spare hours
- When you're in a table-top game marathon

HIDDEN ROLE GAMES

> **HOW DO I KNOW IF SOMEONE IS A TRAITOR?**
>
> You don't, but you can pay attention if his actions align with the goal of the colony.

additional zombies to whichever location they happen to be at, and navigating those zombies is no easy task.

In front of each player sits a reference sheet where the players keep their followers, their used and unused dice, as well as their secret objective, none of which are visible to any other players. Between all of the players sits the colony as well as six locations the players may choose to travel to. It's important to watch where the other players are headed. Each location has a set number of resources available, and at the start of the game, a mission is revealed, usually involving survival or gathering of resources. Each player needs to work toward completing that mission, as well as her own personal mission. In order for the players to find out who the traitor is, if there is one, they need to pay close attention to where the other players are traveling, noting the kinds of resources available at those locations.

During the game, there are high tensions as the players must keep up the morale of the colony, which means making sure everyone is fed, clothed, and not negatively impacted by the loss of other colony members. Should a colony member lose his life, however, the morale of the colony may decrease. If the morale tracker ever reaches zero, the game ends immediately and all players, other than the traitor, lose the game. The traitor, however, still might not win the game as his hidden objective still needs to be completed in order to win.

Designer Isaac Vega does an excellent job of telling a story by introducing the characters' personalities slowly through the use of crossroads cards. While players are given a fairly in-depth description of the characters they are playing, when crossroads cards come up, depending on what characters are playing in the game, more of their stories, or traumas, may be revealed as strengths or weaknesses. They positively or negatively impact the game as well as the other players. The hidden traitor mechanics leave the players paranoid and unable to trust anyone until the true traitor is revealed.

If you have a group of people you've known, loved, and trusted for many years, this is a great experience to share because even if one of you sabotages the mission, there won't be too many hard feelings at the end. That said, this is not the game to play with your friend who has a hard time losing because many times a number of the players in the game are going to lose. Dead of Winter is also fairly lengthy; however, different missions can be selected to change the length and scenario of the game. This can change the number of rounds in the game, making it longer or shorter. It also serves the purpose of changing the challenges the players are up against. Perhaps the zombies are stronger than ever or maybe the colony is facing a food shortage.

Dead of Winter is an experience every person who enjoys board games should have. It's engaging, an edge-of-your-seat experience, and something no one who plays it soon forgets, thanks to its in-depth character narrative and adventurous atmosphere. Each revealed card is read aloud to the table so all players know what's going on at all times. This means that there's never a dull moment for anyone during the game play.

EXPANSIONS

- Warring Colonies
  2017

Battlestar Galactica

Release Date: 2008
Publisher: Fantasy Flight Games
Designer: Corey Konieczka

Difficulty: ✴ ✴ ✴ ✴ ✴

Age Recommendation: 14+

Number of Players: 3–6

Play Time: 2–5 hours

 THE GOAL

Win the game as the Cylons by sabotaging the ship or as the humans by keeping *Galactica* in one piece long enough to make it home to earth.

 LET'S PLAY!

The Cylons have attacked, and it's up to you and your crew to accomplish one simple goal: survive. This tabletop game is based on the widely acclaimed Syfy channel series, *Battlestar Galactica*, and it vaguely follows the show's story and stars everyone's favorite characters. Each of these characters has his or her own abilities and weaknesses. All players are tasked with working together to save humanity. However, this isn't as simple as it might seem. After the Cylons attacked, the battered remnants of the human race went on the run searching desperately for earth. Cylons, however, have developed perfect androids—so perfect that they look human, which means anyone could be a Cylon, even you, and you wouldn't even know it until it's too late.

This semi-cooperative board game puts three to six players inside *Battlestar Galactica* as it attempts to make its way home to earth. Players choose from a number of roles needed on the ship, including everything from pilots and engineers to military and political leaders. Each player is also dealt a loyalty card, which informs her if she is working with the humans or attempting to sabotage the ship as an incognito Cylon. Any player could be the Cylon, so it's up to the other players to figure out which player is sabotaging the ship.

On her turn, each player can choose to move around the ship and take actions or jump in a viper and head off to battle as the Cylon relentlessly attacks the ship. Some players are far superior in piloting these ships due to their skill set. On each player's turn she draws cards according to her character sheet. The cards are skill (color) based. After that players get to move. They can move to any location on the same ship as their action. They might instead choose to discard a card and move to any location on another ship. Finally, if the player is in a viper, she can move to an adjacent space or discard a card to move to any location on a ship. After she moves, she gets one action. Each location on the board has an available action. Some characters also have actions. If the player is in a viper, she might choose to spend her action moving or shooting. After their actions, players draw a crisis card, which is where things get interesting.

Some crisis cards add Cylons to the board. Others include a skill check with a target number. One by one, facedown, players add any number of skill cards they want into a central pile plus two random skill cards from the deck. Then they are all flipped over and counted up:

- If the cards add up to beat the target number, the players pass.
- If the cards fail to meet that target number, they fail and bad stuff happens.

All players need to collect skill cards to deal with the problems that arise throughout the game, and sometimes they simply won't have what the ship needs to complete tasks, putting them at risk for being called out as a saboteur, or worse: being attacked and obliterated by the Cylons.

Halfway through the game, in a twist, each player is dealt a second loyalty card. As in the show, you never know who is actually a Cylon and who is not. The Cylons could be anyone, even you. This means that during the first half of the game there is only one Cylon who knows they are a Cylon, but in the second half of the game, there could be two.

If the players can work together and keep up their food stores, fuel levels, morale, and population long enough to get *Galactica* to earth, the humans win the game. However, if the Cylon players reveal themselves at just the right time, they may be able to bring down the ship entirely.

CONTROL WHAT YOU CAN:

AREA CONTROL

8

Area control is a genre of tabletop game that is typically rife with violence, blood, and gore. Of course, since we're talking about tabletop games, none of this is ever depicted, and all the players ever see are tiny figures and chits moving about a board. This gives these games a generally pleasant and cheerful mood even if you are destroying each other with magical powers. Other area control games can be completely free of violence! Perhaps they are about building a city or a public transportation system, or even simply being leaves in the fall making their way across a gorgeous meadow.

Under these glorious tales of honor, control, and war lie math-filled puzzles to be solved by the players one at a time. The game is constantly changing and affected by the other players, so players need to adjust and act accordingly. The difficulty of the games skews a little high, so be prepared to learn more than a few rules in this genre.

Small World

Difficulty: ✶ ✶ ✶ ✶ ✶

Age Recommendation: 8+

Number of Players: 2–5

Play Time: 40–80 minutes

WHEN TO PLAY:

• When you need to relax

• When the whole family is around

• When you're in a table-top game marathon

Release Date: 2009
Publisher: Days of Wonder
Designer: Philippe Keyaerts

 ## THE GOAL

Be the player at the end of the game who holds the most victory coins, which are gained by taking over territories on the map. In short: world domination!

 ## LET'S PLAY!

Small World takes a very contentious type of game—area control—and mixes it with the whimsy of fantasy creatures such as elves, dwarves, ratmen, and orcs to provide a cutthroat experience that's palatable for families and players new to gaming.

The core of Small World is the set of unique and variable combinations of races and powers to create civilizations with which to conquer the world. Fourteen races are combined with twenty powers to make different pairings every game. On the first turn of the game, players select one of these pairs and choose a territory on the map from which to start their first civilization. They then expand out from this region, earning victory coins for each region they occupy at the end of their turn. If a player finds herself in a position where she is unable to expand further, she can choose to spend her turn sending her civilization into decline instead and choose a new race/power pair for

AREA CONTROL

her next turn. Choosing the optimal moment(s) to switch civilizations is one of the keys to victory in Small World.

There are, of course, limitations to spreading your civilization across the map. Expansion is costly, especially when you're trying to take over regions that are already occupied or contain difficult terrain, such as mountains. As your numbers dwindle, you are unable to keep expanding and may even lose ground as more powerful civilizations start invading your hard-won territories. But choosing a new civilization is actually kind of exciting as long as you don't wait too long to do it!

Each race comes with its own ability (skeletons, for example, give you extra tokens whenever you conquer a region that isn't empty), and each race is paired with a power that grants some other advantage (mounted allows you to conquer hill or farmland regions for one token less than usual). Some of these pairings can prove to be incredibly powerful, and because of this each race and power has a number on it that determines how many tokens you're allowed to have. In the example here, skeletons always give you six tokens, and mounted gives you five, so you'd be able to take eleven skeleton tokens from the tray when you choose this combination.

Sending your civilization into decline forces you to flip over your tokens that are on the board, which means you can no longer use them to take over new territories, but you *can* still score any territories where they remain at the end of your turn. Ideally, you choose a moment when they are still fairly widespread so that you can score them for another couple of rounds before they're wiped out. You can only have one civilization in decline at a time, however, so you also need to make the most of your active race as possible.

Once the round marker has reached the final spot on the track, and players take their final turns, everyone adds up all of the coins each player earned throughout the game, and the player with the most points wins!

AREA CONTROL

Bosk

WHEN TO PLAY:

- When you're having a game night

- When you're at a gaming convention

- When you're at your local game store

Release Date: 2019
Publisher: Floodgate Games
Designers: Daryl Andrews and Erica Bouyouris

Difficulty: ★ ★ ★ ★ ★

Age Recommendation: 13+

Number of Players: 2–4

Play Time: 20–40 minutes

 THE GOAL

Control the most parts of a forest.

 LET'S PLAY!

In Bosk players watch the life cycle of trees over a year in a national park as they vie to control first the grid and later the various regions of the park. It's a codesign from Erica Bouyouris and Daryl Andrews, who previously collaborated on another area control game, Roar: King of the Pride. The game is played over four seasons; in two of the seasons (spring and fall) players play to the board, and in the other two seasons (summer and winter) they score the board they built up in the previous round.

The game starts with spring, and in spring players plant their trees by placing them on various intersections of rows and columns on the board. Each tree is numbered one through four, which represents the tree's height; taller trees are more imposing and result in a more impressive view for various tourists that also visit the park during the summer.

In summer, players score the rows and columns that they control with their trees, as those values also represent points of control on the grid. If a player completely controls a row or column with no challengers, she gets a bonus.

In fall, the trees shed their leaves (and, occasionally, their squirrel occupants). Players are each given eight leaves valued two to eight (and one squirrel); then they check the wind movement and spend one of these leaves on their turn in order to place leaves in lines emanating from trees of their choice. The wind blows the leaves in that direction. After they place on trees one through four, they place on the other four trees in the order of their choice. If needed, they may cover leaf piles with their own leaves in order to remove their opponents' control from a space. They may also play a squirrel, which helpfully always ends up on top of a pile and cannot be covered by other leaves. This cements the player's control of one square in the grid.

In the final phase of the game, winter, players score the regions that they now control with their leaves; whoever has the most leaves in a region controls it, and again, if a player completely controls a region with no challengers he gets a bonus. The player with the most points after the winter season is the winner of the game.

The game is striking (as is generally the case with Kwanchai Moriya's artwork), as it moves from a beautiful board to a vibrant forest to a colorful assortment of leaves over the course of the game, always leaving players with a sense of accomplishment. Many area control games tend to be intense (and aggressive) games of strategy and planning. While Bosk is certainly a game where it helps to plan ahead, the theme (and the ability to cover the leaves of other players) allows the game to seem more pleasant, peaceful, and forgiving than other games in the genre.

EXPANSIONS

There are currently no expansions for this game.

Tokyo Metro

Release Date: 2018
Publisher: Jordan Draper Games
Designer: Jordan Draper

ESSENTIAL

Tokyo Metro is one game in a twelve–series set that can all be mixed together to play new games and expansions.

Difficulty: ★ ★ ★ ★ ★

Age Recommendation: 14+

Number of Players: 1–5

Play Time: 90 minutes

 THE GOAL

To earn the most yen by the end of the game.

 LET'S PLAY!

Tokyo Metro is a unique mash-up of worker placement, area control, and investment economics. Players are investors moving on a background grid juxtaposed against the real Tokyo Metro map, in an attempt to build stations at ideal locations for income as trains pass through them. The fun of the game comes from the timing of station investments (area control) against the many other stock investment opportunities, which all arise from a semirandomized worker placement action system.

There are four phases to the game that repeat a set number of times based on the player count. Each round of the game new cards are drawn that players can use as actions. First, six rows of cards that contain available actions for the round have a card discarded, and a new one drawn in its place in an effort to always keep the cards fresh each round so the game doesn't stagnate. Next, players bid on turn order, paying their bid to the bank. Thirdly, players use action discs in turn order to take one of twelve actions in the game. These actions range from paying to build a station next to your player meeple to buying stock in a train line, or receiving a bicycle that allows you to move faster on the map. Finally, all of the trains that have received investment from players travel five stations on the map, triggering payouts for stations that they pass along their route to players and the train's income. Rinse and repeat five to eight times depending on the player count, and then all of the private train line income earned during the game pays out to investors, at which point the richest player will claim victory over Tokyo's transport!

Similar to Japanese martial arts, Metro has simple foundations that lead to complex strategy from the balance of efficiency, area control on the map, and opportune timing of investments. There are three main paths to take with the available actions: setting up your empire of stations on the map, which gets you instant income to use for leveraged investments; spending yen to get more action discs and using those discs to receive further efficiencies; and investing in private train lines to build up a monopoly and crush your opponents at the end game payout. It's simple to pick up and learn, with only three categories of actions to take on your turn, yet the overlapping aspects of player interaction make every game unique and special.

FACT

The box contains two double-sided maps to accommodate different player counts, as the dynamics really change a lot for two, three, four, and five players. This is pretty unusual for games like this but essential in this case to create a balanced experience.

EXPANSIONS

- Because this is one of twelve games offered in the Tokyo series by Jordan Draper (nine more games are to be released by **2021**), Metro can be mixed with all of the other titles for new games and expansions.

- Tokyo Jidohanbaiki **2018**

- Izakaya **2018**

Five Tribes

WHEN TO PLAY:

- When you want to play something challenging

- When you're at your local game store

- When you have a few spare hours

Release Date: 2015
Publisher: Days of Wonder
Designer: Bruno Cathala

Difficulty: ✶ ✶ ✶ ✶ ✶

Age Recommendation: 13+

Number of Players: 2–4

Play Time: 1–2 hours

 **THE GOAL**

Have the most victory points when you've placed your last camel or no more meeple moves are possible!

 **LET'S PLAY!**

At the start of the game the player receives his camels and turn order markers, depending on the number of players. Each player is given twelve camels and fifty gold coins, which he uses to accomplish things within the game. However, these are kept facedown and are secret until the end of the game because money is victory points! All thirty tiles are mixed up and placed into a 6-by-5 tile grid to form the sultanate and they should all be oriented in the same way. Then all ninety meeples are put into a bag and three randomly drawn meeples are placed on each tile.

The turn order markers are placed on the board in bid order, as the starting positions are bid on at the start of the game. The resources and djinn cards are shuffled and their stacks are placed facedown. Nine resource cards and three djinn cards are put faceup to form a display. The palm trees and palaces are put out along with the remaining gold.

The game takes place in three steps: bidding for turn order, the action phase, and the clean-up phase. The players all make a bid for the turn order and then pay the bank the gold shown and order their player markers appropriately. The more money you pay, the more likely you are to go first, but at what cost? After turn order has been established the players enter into the action phase.

On their turn the players take the following six actions in order. First they move the turn marker from the turn order track and place it on the first empty space on the bid order track. Then each player selects a tile that contains at least one meeple and picks up all of the meeples on that tile. Then he chooses an orthogonal pathway from the select tile of the same length as the number of meeples he has, dropping one meeple in each space. He cannot backtrack and his final meeple must be placed on a tile that already has that color of meeple. Once they've all been placed the players check tile control. The active player takes all of the meeples of that color from the last tile in the path. If he happens to remove all meeples of the selected color from that tile, then the player places one of his camels there and he now controls that tile. At the end of the game, he gains victory points for that tile!

Each of the meeples collected have different effects on game play. Some are worth victory points, some allow players to activate abilities and tiles, some allow the players to take resources from the faceup resource cards, collect gold from the bank, or even remove other meeples from other tiles or players' collections. This can even include eliminating a final meeple and taking control of a tile for points at the end of the game.

In addition to the points gained on the tiles, players also get to use the actions on the tile they ended on, which allows the players to gather resources, place palaces and palm trees, and collect djinns that provide victory points and give special abilities.

The resources the players gather can be discarded to collect gold. They are worth exponentially more gold for each different resource discarded. The game ends when one player has placed his last camel or when there are no moves left to make!

ESSENTIAL

Five Tribes is set in the world of 1001 Arabian Nights. The sultan has died and control of Naqala is up for grabs. The oracles foretold of strangers who would maneuver the Five Tribes to gain influence over the legendary city-state. In this game players are tasked with cleverly maneuvering meeples over villages, oases, and the sacred palace tiles that make up the city.

EXPANSIONS

- The Artisans of Naqala **2015**

- The Thieves of Naqala **2016**

- Whims of the Sultan **2017**

Kemet

Difficulty: ✶ ✶ ✶ ✶ ✶

Age Recommendation: 13+

Number of Players: 2–5

Play Time: 1.5–2.5 hours

 THE GOAL

Be the first player to gain 8 or 10 victory points through any means possible.

LET'S PLAY!

In Kemet, players deploy troops of an ancient Egyptian tribe and use the mystical power of the gods in Egypt to conquer their enemies. Players score points by building their armies, fighting in glorious battles, and invading rich territories in attempts to control their temples and pyramids, and to make sacrifices to the gods. Between all of the players sit detailed miniatures and a map of ancient Egypt along with a slew of tiles the players vie to control throughout the game.

Each turn takes place in two phases, day and night. Players choose one of nine actions during the day. Once all players have taken five actions then the night phase begins and the players gather prayer points from their temples, draw cards, and determine the turn order before beginning the next day. As the game goes on, they gain new tiles that recruit magical creatures and additional troops, and grant them special powers.

Each player starts by choosing a side of the board, depending on the number of players. Then she chooses a player color and is given action tokens, an ankh marker, a turn order tracker, twelve units, and six battle cards. She is then given one random divine intervention card, which does not count as an action. These cards can be played in the same phases with the same effects, and their effects can stack.

Players gain victory points by controlling temples, sacrificing units at sanctuaries, withdrawing units back into their pool, gaining a victory point power tile, raising pyramids, and winning battles. They also gather prayer points, which can be used to take various actions and buy tiles within the game. The players can take a wide variety of available actions. They can pray to gain prayer points, which they can later use to buy a power tile. There are restrictions on how many of these a player can buy, and a player can only ever have one of each kind. The player can also spend prayer points to recruit units from her pool and put them into districts in cities, provided that she has control of the city at that time. Players may also choose to move and attack, which allows them to move one troop, positioning themselves for a war. They can also teleport troops from any pyramid to an obelisk space at any time, provided they have the prayer points to do so.

When engaging in combat the players add divine intervention cards to their fights, which add strength to the battle at hand. These can be played very carefully and can even steal things from another player even if that player manages to win the battle.

Perhaps the most important thing that any of the players do, though, is acquire power tiles. These have a wide range of abilities. The red tiles tend to add to the player's movement and combat strength. The blue tiles allow the players to recruit additional units, increase their troop sizes, save their battle cards from sacrifice, and take additional actions. White tiles allow the players to gain additional prayer points through using actions, discarding cards, and winning battles.

Kemet is a huge game, and it takes you multiple hours to play. It's also not for the faint of heart: one wrong turn could cost a player the game. With all of that said, if you have just the right competitively spirited group, this might be the perfect game for game night.

EXPANSIONS

- Kemet: Ta-Seti **2015**
- Kemet: Seth **2018**

AREA CONTROL

Blood Rage

Difficulty: ✴ ✴ ✴ ✴ ✴

Age Recommendation: 14+

Number of Players: 2–4

Play Time: 90 minutes

Release Date: 2015
Publisher: CMON
Designer: Eric Lang

 THE GOAL

Find a home in Valhalla.

 LET'S PLAY!

In Blood Rage, players are each leading their own Viking clans, leaders, warriors, and ships. The world is ending and your sole objective is to go out in a blaze of glory, securing your spot in Valhalla. There are, of course, plenty of ways to accomplish this quest by fighting in epic battles, either by dying with honor or succumbing to the inescapable doom of Ragnarök.

To start the game each player chooses a clan, which comes with figures and a leader along with his player board and ship figure. Then each player takes his glory marker and places on the gigantic board sitting between all players, ripe with battleground and destruction. Depending on the player count, some provinces in the game are already destroyed. The map is divided up into nine provinces, eight of which have a random Ragnarök token placed on it. If they are destroyed they are placed destroyed-side up.

WHEN TO PLAY:

- When you feel like adventure
- When it's time for a little competition
- When you're having a game night

AREA CONTROL

The center province is Yggdrasil, and the other eight provinces are divided into three regions. Each province has three to five villages, and each village can hold just one figure. Each round players move figures into these spaces, moving them from region to region, taking actions, completing questions, and dying in a blaze of glory and honor.

Each player starts the game with a number of cards from which they draft, and they will do this a total of three times as the game is played over three total ages. They use these cards

as their actions, provided they can pay the required cost in rage from their rage track. There are more of these given out at the start of ages two and three as well. When this track runs out, the players' turns for that age are done and they cannot perform any more actions, not even one that costs zero rage to use. The action phase ends when all players have zero rage. The actions the players take do not have to be cards played from their hand, however. Each player has in front of her a player board with actions that may be taken. A player can choose to invade, moving a figure onto the board and paying rage equal to its strength. She might also choose to march, paying one rage to move any number of her figures from that province to empty villages in another province anywhere on the board. She could decide to upgrade her clan, in which case she chooses an upgrade card from her hand and pays rage equal to its strength and places it into her clean sheet, knowing she only has room for eight upgrades.

Players quest by taking a quest card and placing it onto the board facedown to be revealed later in the game after its conditions have been satisfied. This costs no rage, and there are no limits to the number of these that can be placed, but they may only commit to two quests of each type available in the game. If they manage to fulfill the demands of the quests, they reap the rewards listed on them. They might also choose to pillage, in which case they choose a province that has at least one of their figures that has not yet been pillaged this round. It costs no rage to do this. Once a player has decided to pillage an area, it is resolved in three steps.

First the players are called to battle. In this step, starting with the person to the fighting player's left and going clockwise, each player may, if he wishes, choose to move one of his figures from an adjacent province into an empty village in the province his is in. It doesn't cost rage. Once all of the villages are filled up, or no one else wants to join in, the battle begins. Each player participating in the battle must choose a card from his hand and hold it facedown in front of him. If he reveals a strength card it's added to his overall strength. If he reveals an upgrade or quest card, nothing happens. If he has the highest total strength, he wins the battle, and in a tie, everyone loses. The winner discards his played cards, and the losing players take theirs back. The losing players destroy all of their figures in the battle and place them on the Valhalla sheet! This might be a good thing for the player, depending on the quests that he played. The winning player is rewarded with the pillage token that typically results in glory or permanent upgrades for his player board, which also reward him with glory near the end of the game.

At the end of each age all figures in Valhalla are returned to their respective owners, and the pillage tokens are returned to their reward sides. Players are rewarded glory for a whole mess of things within the game, and the player with the most glory wins.

EXPANSIONS

- Gods of Asgard
  2015

- Blood Rage:
  5th Player Expansion
  2015

- Blood Rage:
  Mystics of Midgard
  2015

AREA CONTROL

Ethnos

Release Date: 2017
Publisher: CMON
Designer: Paolo Mori

Difficulty: ★ ★ ★ ★ ★

Age Recommendation: 12+

Number of Players: 2–6

Play Time: 60 minutes

 **THE GOAL**

Gain influence in a region to gather victory points.

 **LET'S PLAY!**

Welcome to Ethnos! This is a realm steeped in mythology, filled to the brim with creatures and teetering on the brink of destruction. In Ethnos, an age of war and revolt has just ended and the inhabitants of all the monster tribes as ready to move back into these open territories and begin to rebuild. But unlike the past, the giants, dwarves, elves, and centaurs are fractured and looking for a new leader to take them into an age of prosperity. Over three ages, players pick a leader, gather followers, and carve out a new territory. At the end of each age, the players with the most influence in a region score for that region.

This game is shockingly simple, plays a large group in under one hour, and provides enough strategic options to keep even the most experienced gamer satisfied. Do you love Small World but found it too cartoony? Do you like Blood Rage but found it too dark? Ethnos sits right in that happy middle space.

In Ethnos, the board is divided into six different regions. When the game is set up, each region receives three randomly placed glory tokens ordered from lowest to highest. These are the points players who control the region score at the end of each age. For the first age, the first glory token is scored, in the second age the second glory token is scored, and so on.

There are twelve tribes in Ethnos, and each tribe is represented by a small tribe deck of cards printed with its name and special ability. To determine the allies deck used for a game, six of the twelve tribe decks are chosen and shuffled together. Each time you play the game, a different combination of tribes is used, providing a new and exciting game experience. No game of Ethnos is like the last!

At the beginning of each age, each player draws one card from the allies deck into her hand. The players form a market of cards from the allies deck equal to two times the number of players. The deck is then split into two equal halves, and the three dragon cards are shuffled into one half of the deck with the other half placed on top. When the third dragon card is drawn from the deck, the current age ends, and scoring for that age begins.

On a player's turn she can recruit an ally by taking one card from the market or drawing a card from the allies deck. Empty spaces in the market are not refreshed from the allies deck, leaving open spots and the possibility that the market may become depleted. If one the first two dragon cards is drawn on a player's turn, it is placed to the side of the board, and a new card is drawn.

Instead of recruiting an ally, players can play a band of allies. When playing a band of allies, all the cards played need to share the same border color (belong to the same region of the board) or come from the same tribe of creatures (all dwarfs or trolls, etc.). One card from that grouping is designated as the leader and placed at the top of the set. The player can then place an influence marker in the region designated by the leader and use that leader's special ability. Remember, the band of allies played has to be greater than the number of markers from that player already in the region in order to place a marker. After playing a band of allies, any cards still in the player's hand get discarded into the market, leaving the player with an empty hand and clean slate for her next turn.

This continues until the third dragon is drawn and the current age ends. Then players score points for highest influence in each of the six regions on the board and points for the size of each band of allies played for that age. For the first age, only the first player in each region scores, in the second age the players coming in second score, and in the third age the player coming in third gets to score as well.

EXPANSIONS

There are currently no expansions for this game.

DEXTERITY GAMES

Dexterity games refer to games that require players to compete using their physical reflexes and coordination. This means that they bring a different kind of puzzle to solve, one that brings your body into play. They present to you a challenge that you must solve using your body. These games tend to be easy to learn, have a quick play time, and are fun to play because they always require some degree of skill.

The very first dexterity games date back to the year 1000. Palet is a French game in which cast-iron, slightly convex discs are thrown onto a wooden board from about five meters away. The goal is to be nearer to the jack, a heavy token in the center of the board, than your opponent to gain points, and the first person to get 12 points wins the game. It's easy to draw similarities from ancient dexterity games to our modern games of horseshoes, ladder ball, or croquet.

Plenty of folks grew up playing games like pick-up sticks, Jack Straws, and tiddlywinks. Most wouldn't believe that all of those games were actually designed before 1900. Since then there have been thousands of dexterity games designed, published, and made popular, although few have stood the test of time. Jenga was first released in 1983 and is one of the best-selling dexterity game in modern history.

Companies like Restoration Games aim to solve this by remaking older games like Fireball Island and showing just how fun they can be by making them readily available. The biggest barrier to entry in tabletop gaming is acquiring the games themselves, and if we can solve the accessibility issues by making them more readily available in schools, libraries, and community centers, we make the world a happier place, one table at a time.

Klask

Difficulty: ★ ★ ★ ★ ★

Age Recommendation: 6+

Number of Players: 2

Play Time: 10 minutes

WHEN TO PLAY:

- When the whole family is around

- When you have a spare ten minutes

- When you want something fun and easy

Release Date: 2014
Publisher: KLASK
Designer: Mikkel Bertelsen

 THE GOAL

Be the first player to score 6 points.

👥 LET'S PLAY!

Klask is a competitive game that feels like a cross between foosball and air hockey. It comes fully contained in a large box, which holds a board with plenty of space above it to play the game and below it for the players to move the components on top using innovative magnetic pieces. These are designed to be moved around the top of the board to smash into the small wooden ball that is whizzing around the board. You do so by moving player-controlled magnets below the board that control the Klask paddles on top of the board. If one player gets the ball into her opponent's goal, then she scores a point

Making goals is not the only way to score points though! If any player gets too close to the three magnetic tokens in the center of the table the magnet attaches itself to him, and if two of them manage to attach onto a single player's piece, his opponent scores a point because of it!

If your player piece ends up in your own goal instead of the wooden ball, your opponent also scores a point for your general clumsiness.

While the game seems simple when playing it for the first time, the more time you spend with your opponent, the more easily you will be able to predict his play style and the better you get at throwing him off.

EXPANSIONS

There are currently no expansions for this game.

Animal Upon Animal

Difficulty: ★ ★ ★ ★ ★

Age Recommendation: 3+

Number of Players: 2–4

Play Time: 10–20 minutes

WHEN TO PLAY:

• When you need to relax

• When you want something fun and easy

• When the whole family is around

Release Date: 2005
Publisher: HABA USA
Designer: Klaus Miltenberger

 THE GOAL

Be the first player to get rid of all of your animals!

 LET'S PLAY!

Sometimes a game is so simple that its simplicity makes it even better. In Animal Upon Animal players stack animals, as you might have guessed, upon other animals. The goal of the game is to be the first player to get rid of all of your animals.

Setting up the game is critical. First, you need to make sure you are playing on an even and level surface. A wobbly crocodile won't help anyone. Then, place the crocodile in the center of the table. It's the first animal of the animal pyramid. Each player takes seven different animals from the pile of animals and puts them in front of him. The extra animals go back in the box.

Then the first player takes his turn and the other players follow in a clockwise order. The first player is determined in a flamingo off. Whichever player can stand on one foot like a flamingo the longest starts the game. We do not recommend playing this game with any yoga masters, as they always get to go first.

At the start of each turn, the player rolls a die. If she rolls a one, she takes one animal and places it carefully onto the stack of animals. If she rolls a two, she may take two animals from her pool and place

ESSENTIAL

HABA Games specializes in games for young people, but they're as much fun for kids as they are for many adults. With My Very First Games Animal Upon Animal, you can play with kids as young as two years old!

them carefully one after the other, using only one hand, onto the pyramid. If the player rolls a crocodile, she may take an animal from her pool and place it next to the crocodile's mouth or tail so that both animals touch! If the player rolls a hand, she may choose any one of her animals and give it to another player who then has to place the animal on the pyramid. If she rolls the question mark, the other players decide what she has to put on the pyramid.

This is the kind of game that requires patience, skill, and tact despite seeming so simple, and it's as easy to lose to a three-year-old as a forty-year-old. Unfortunately, all good things must come to an end, and when the pyramid collapses, there are several things that can happen:

- **The whole pyramid collapses:** Stacking ends immediately, the player takes two animals into his pool, and all remaining animals are put back in the box.
- **One or two animals fall off:** The player who tried to pile them on has to put them back into his pool to use in a future round.
- **More than two animals fall off:** The player who tried to pile them on takes two of them into her pool.

Luckily for players of this game, the game doesn't end when the pyramid collapses. The game only ends as soon as a player is left without any animals! That player is deemed the best animal stacker of the day and is given a +1 to his rolls for the rest of the game when he attempts to pet animals.

If you find yourself getting *too* good at the game, you can always try the challenge rules, which include distributing all of the animals in the box evenly among the players. If an animal falls off, the player must take five animals, and if the player only has one animal left she can stack it immediately onto the pyramid without rolling the die.

Animal Upon Animal is one of those games that you want to play over and over again as well as something you can't resist showing your friends who haven't played before.

FACT

There are more than eight different editions of Animal Upon Animal, and some of them even have boards that rotate!

EXPANSIONS

There are currently no expansions for this game.

Hop!

Difficulty: ★ ★ ★ ★ ★

Number of Players: 3–6

Age Recommendation: 6+

Play Time: 30 minutes

 **THE GOAL**

 **THE GOAL**

Be the player with the most points when one player reaches level seven on the cloud platform in the center of the table *or* any one player loses all of his balloons.

 **LET'S PLAY!**

At times, it's very important to be clear on what the core audience for a game is. Hop! is a ring-toss game that's very specifically for two core audiences: children and drinking adults, preferably not at the same time.

The premise of the game is that a young boy found a book in his grandparents' attic about an entire realm in the sky where rainbows were used to climb through the clouds, and, with the power of friendship, nothing could be stopped! Each challenge in the game gives the active player a new objective to climb higher in the sky. However, players can only meet these challenges by helping each other to gain levels. As soon as one player hits level seven, the game is over, and the player with the most points at the end of the game wins!

Before the game starts players need to set up the cloud board, which holds all of the gorgeous painted miniature figurines that represent a wide variety of young kids with unique hobbies and

WHEN TO PLAY:

- When you're just getting started with tabletop games

- When you want something fun and easy

- When you're having a game night

Release Date: 2016
Publisher: Funforge
Designers: Marie Cardouat and Ludovic Maublanc

DEXTERITY GAMES

interests. Then someone spreads these figurines along the bottom row of the cloud on the "1" spaces. Next, the bird tokens are arranged around the board and the dare cards are shuffled to form a facedown deck. Each player should be given a player card, a cloud token, and five balloons.

Players make a throw with the rainbow throwing ring and then pass the rainbow throwing ring to their left for the next player to take his turn. There are four roles to be played in Hop!:

- **Hurler:** The person taking her turn who must throw the rainbow ring.
- **Skewerer:** The person who places his elbow on the table and his pointer finger in the air.
- **Assister:** The person who helps the Hurler achieve her mission as designated on the card!
- **Turbulator:** A player who helps ensure the Hurler's failure by interfering!

In addition, there's the Gambler. Any player who is not one of the four roles above may make bets on the player's success in her throw. If they think it will be a success, they put the cloud token happy cloud up. If they think it will be a failure, they put the cloud token angry cloud up. The bets remain secret, and the rewards are collected after the throw.

If the throw succeeds and the dare is fulfilled:

- **Hurler:** Advances one level on the game board
- **Skewerer:** Gains a cloud token (victory points at the end of the game)
- **Assister:** Gains a cloud token
- **Turbulator:** Nothing happens

If the throw fails, the following happens:

- **Hurler:** Loses a balloon
- **Skewerer:** Nothing happens
- **Assister:** Nothing happens
- **Turbulator:** Gains a cloud

No matter how the throw goes, the following happens:

- **Gamblers:** If they bet correctly, they gain a bird token dove-side up.
- **Gamblers:** If they bet incorrectly, they gain a bird token crow-side up.

When a player reaches three dove tokens, he returns all of his birds to the pool of bird tokens around the game board and advances one level up! When a player reaches three crow tokens he returns them to the pool and loses one of his balloons.

After a player has reached the seventh level or a player has lost his last balloon, the game comes to an end. If you lost all of your balloons, you cannot stay in the sky, so your token is pushed to the side of the board. All players gain the value of their level plus the total value of their cloud tokens. The player with the highest score wins the game!

FACT
Hop! is a beautifully made, readily available party game. There's a lot to be said for games with gorgeous art-work, fun game play, and silly actions to be taken that make everyone just a little more goofy for the day.

EXPANSIONS

There are currently no expansions for this game.

WHEN TO PLAY:

- When the whole family is around

- When you need to relax

- When it's time for a little competition

Release Date: 2011

Publisher: HABA USA

Designers: Scott Frisco and Steven Strumpf

Rhino Hero

Difficulty: ★ ★ ★ ★ ★

Age Recommendation: 4+

Number of Players: 2–5

Play Time: 5–15 minutes

 **THE GOAL**

Be the first player to get rid of all of your roof cards.

 **LET'S PLAY!**

Rhino Hero is a dexterity game for children from one to ninety-nine. This hilarious and thrilling tower-building game challenges players to stack a tower as high as they can, all the while climbing up it and making sure they don't knock it over. As a superhero from the animal world, you fearlessly scale the highest houses looking for burglars and rogues! The rhino hero is as strong as a lion and as smart as a fox, but also as heavy as a rhinoceros. Unfortunately for our hero, even the most robust tower may start to wobble. It's up to the players to help the rhino hero accomplish his mission.

In the center of the table sits a tower. The players collectively build the tower, which is made up of walls and ceilings, just like a real house. The marks on the roof determine how the walls are placed on each level. Some are in the center of the floor with just a single wall, and others have multiple walls in the corners of the card. The cards are always folded at a 90-degree angle.

On their turn, each player places wall cards on the last floor placed and then folds her walls to a 90-degree angle and places them on the spaces in the floor. Then, she adds another floor on top of them, doing her best to not knock it over. Some of the roof cards being placed have special symbols that allow players to manipulate the game play:

- **Change direction:** Continue playing but switch directions from clockwise to counterclockwise or vice versa.
- **Take a breather:** The next player in turn order loses his turn.
- **Additional card:** The next player has to draw a new roof card from the provisions before starting to build.
- **Double roof:** The player is allowed to place a second roof card on top of this one. No more than one of these cards can be played together.
- **Super rhino:** Our rhino hero climbs to the next floor of the building with the super rhino symbol on it.

There are several ways to win the game. If a player plays his very last roof card, he wins the game. If a player makes the house collapse, he loses the game. The player who has the fewest roof cards at that point of the game wins. If all of the walls have been built then all players win the game together.

Rhino Hero shines because it's one of the few games on the market designed specifically with kids in mind. However, it happens to be as much fun for adults. When the game is over, most of the time you find yourself setting it right back up to play again. Rhino Hero is a delightfully simple dexterity game that keeps everyone on their toes through the whole game. If you want to cheer each other on or shout each other down, either way, you're certain to have a howling good time with Rhino Hero.

ESSENTIAL

Rhino Hero has a more advanced version called Rhino Hero: Super Battle that allows players to build on a bigger player board and has walls of varying sizes! The rules are more complex, but the game play is just as fun!

EXPANSIONS

There are currently no expansions for this game.

Loopin' Louie

WHEN TO PLAY:

- When you have a spare ten minutes

- When you're having a game night

- When you need to relax

Release Date: 2015
Publisher: Hasbro
Designer: Uncredited

EXPANSIONS

Standalone:

- Loopin' Chewie
- Buzz to the Rescue
- Looping Bumblebee

Difficulty: ★ ★ ★ ★ ★

Age Recommendation: 3+

Number of Players: 2–4

Play Time: 10–15 minutes

 **THE GOAL**

Be the last player standing with all of your chickens left.

 **LET'S PLAY!**

Nothing is more exciting than flying through the sky, and in this game players use a lever to move a small plane that is bouncing haphazardly around the board! Between all of the players sits a weighted, battery-powered vehicle, and in it sits Louie. Louie and his plane bounce around toward four arms, and attached to them are the players' barns and chickens they are attempting to protect.

Each player has to do her best to protect her chickens by skillfully knocking Louie a certain direction with her arm, which is used to anxiously tap away at Louie as he soars through the sky. However, it's not as simple as it sounds. Louie is moving quickly around the board, and with enough practice many players can figure out trick shots like making him do a loop or jump directly across the board. Players are required to be their own offense and defense. They need to be prepared to knock Louie away from their chickens using an arm that only moves up and down. However, they also need to figure out how to time Louie just right to knock the other players' chickens down.

Louie can be somewhat difficult to predict, but if you're up for a challenging, mostly skill-based game, this might be for you. Conventions and game stores are known to have tournaments for the game. In addition to the Star Wars–themed version of Loopin' Chewie, other ones feature characters like Buzz Lightyear, and there is even a version called Bobbin' Bumblebee that features a bee.

Thanks to the invention of 3-D printing, some fans have gone as far as modifying their versions of the game to play more players by combining two sets of the game and then installing adapters to the other player arms. Games can last anywhere from sixty seconds to thirty minutes, which is usually the point that someone gives in and lets the other player win. This is a great game to play with young kids and an equally good way to settle a bet with an old friend.

WHERE, OTHER THAN THE UNITED STATES, HAS LOOPIN' LOUIE BECOME POPULAR?

Germany. But not quite in the way you might think. Loopin' Louie is one of Germany's more popular drinking games. Every time a German playing the game loses, he has to take a swig of schnapps.

FACT

Loopin' Louie was initially published in 1992 under the name Loopin' Louie but was reimagined in 2015 as Loopin' Chewie. There have been other themed or licensed versions of the game as well, which is a testament to its quality.

Ice Cool

Release Date: 2016
Publisher: Brain Games
Designer: Brian Gomez

EXPANSIONS

• Ice Cool 2

Difficulty: ✶ ✶ ✶ ✶ ✶

Age Recommendation: 6+

Number of Players: 2–4

Play Time: 20–30 minutes

 ## THE GOAL

Be the player with the most points after each player has played the catcher once.

 ## LET'S PLAY!

In Ice Cool the penguins sneak out of class and slide through the halls to grab something to eat: the fish! But watch out for the hall monitor, who is known as the catcher. He's certain to catch you if you're not careful. Sneak your way around the halls and gobble up all of the fish of your color by sliding through the doorways beneath them.

Between all of the players sits a gorgeous icy blue school that all of the penguins attend. The Ice Cool school board is made out of the game box itself. There are connected rooms whose archways line up to form a breathtaking board with walls the penguins can't slide out of and doorways with plenty of room for them to slip through. If players get stuck in a doorway they may not eat the fish; however, they can move their penguin to the red line on either door. They still need to slide through it to collect their fish. If a player jumps over a doorway, he cannot collect his fish above the doorway.

Each player is given a player card as well as a penguin, who functions a bit like a Weeble. The penguin sits on a round base and in it sits a weight, which causes it to wobble back and forth. This allows players to perform trick shots, flicking the penguin on the head or flicking the penguin on the right or left side to make it curve around doorways and into other rooms. Don't flick your penguin too hard though—you don't want him jumping out of bounds.

The catcher earns points each round for every hall pass confiscated. The values of these fish cards are between 1 and 3 points. The 1-value cards have ice skates on them, and when a player has two of these, she may use them to take another turn immediately.

The runners (students) gain points each round by avoiding the catcher and by collecting fish by sliding under the doorways. Above these doorways sit fish of the runner's colors. The catcher's fish does not go above doorways, and only runners can take a lunch break. Players draw one fish card for every fish they ate as well as one if they managed to keep their hall pass.

A round ends when any one player has collected all of her fish or the catcher has caught all of the runners and taken their hall passes. The game ends after each player has been the catcher at least once. Some players might want to play a game twice as long, and since Ice Cool 2 is now available, many Ice Cool fans have combined the two to play giant games of Ice Cool with up to eight players.

Ice Cool is a novel game that causes people to stop and stare, so taking it to a game night at work or even the local library can be a great way to make new friends. One of the best things about board games is that they bring people together—in this case, literally.

FACT

Brian Gomez is a pen name for the team that worked on the game. The name is a fun little play on the name of the company, Brain Games.

ALERT!

Any time a player is too close to the wall of a room, she may also move her penguin to the red line inside the room.

Fireball Island: The Curse of Vul-Kar

WHEN TO PLAY:

- When you feel like adventure

- When you're at your local game store

- When you're in a table-top game marathon

Release Date: 2018

Publisher: Restoration Games

Designers: Chuck Kennedy and Bruce Lund

Difficulty: ✶ ✶ ✶ ✶ ✶

Age Recommendation: 8+

Number of Players: 2–4

Play Time: 45 minutes

 ## THE GOAL

Be the player with the most points once all three Vul-Kar marbles are activated in a cataclysm.

 ## LET'S PLAY!

Is it hot in here or is it just me? In Fireball Island players navigate an island, collecting treasures, gathering souvenirs, and, hopefully, stealing the slippery heart of the ancient idol, Vul-Kar. Proceed with caution though, because angering Vul-Kar causes him to spew vicious lava all over the island. If you're not careful, it barrels you over and you lose treasures to whoever shot the marble out of Vul-Kar. There are other times that players are able to flick the marbles sitting on the game board directly at other players. As players make their way around the board, they also take snapshots of Vul-Kar and earn points as they go.

The island is lush with beautiful palm trees that can block the way.

At the start of the game, each player is given one souvenir card and two action cards. Souvenir cards all say when you can play them, and after playing them you put them into the discard pile.

There is no limit on the number of these you may hold. Each player always has two action cards in his hand every round. He must move the exact number of spaces stated on the card, and he may move in either direction but may not change directions. No player is ever allowed to be on another space with another player.

Snapshots spaces are scattered around the board, and there are two different spots for each color that are placed in different regions of the board. Each player may only gain one of each color. There are only two cards available for the whole table of each snapshot, so get them while they're hot!

When a player has three different-colored snapshots she can summon the hello-copter and make her escape and bring the heat! Once the first player escapes the island, she activates the end of the game and the other players have just two turns to get to the helipad and get out of there.

Treasures are scattered around the board, and they are gained when you enter or start a turn in a space on the board with small red arrows pointed toward these treasures. These never refill, so it's best to get them while you can. They're worth more points if you have more than one type. There are three types:

- **Cataclysm Cards:** When three of these action cards have been played, the deck gets shuffled with them back in and an additional fireball is added to the board. When all four marbles have been added to the board, the players have two turns to get off the island or else they perish!
- **Fireballs:** Cards in the game activate fireballs. The player who activates them takes all of the ones in the board track that are not in the cataclysm tracker and then drops them into Vul-Kar to wreak havoc down the island.
- **Ember Marbles:** Some cards activate ember marbles. These are flicked or pushed by the player who activated them, and they are sitting precariously around the board.

HOW OLD IS THE FIREBALL ISLAND GAME?

The original Fireball Island was published in 1986 and was restored and funded on *Kickstarter*. They raised more than $2.8 million in the campaign.

FACT

Fireball Island was hand-sculpted in clay before it was scanned in to be made of plastic.

The cataclysm tracker holds the additional fireballs that are used as Vul-Kar's rage increases; these are placed into the scar of the island. Each time three cataclysms fill up the cataclysm track, another fireball marble is added to the scar.

If you start or land on a cave, roll the die. Then proceed to move to any cave whose number matches the dice roll.

Bridges and ladders are not stable, so if you move onto one, you must stop moving until your next turn unless you have a card that states you may do otherwise.

The fiery heart of Vul-Kar is picked up like any other treasure, and when it is, you immediately add a fireball to the scar, but be careful because other players can steal the heart from you.

The first player to escape the island receives bonus points for doing so, and then the other players have just two turns to get off of the island or else! This is the kind of game that keeps everyone at the table tense—although still having fun. No matter which player is in the lead, the other players never feel that sense of despair that some games can bring when you see yourself falling behind.

Fireball Island is the kind of game that catches everyone's eye, and to make matters even better, this reimagined version of it makes it easier to teach than ever. This is the kind of game that you need on your shelf out of sheer novelty, and your friends who are fans of Indiana Jones will thank you after they play it with you!

EXPANSIONS

There are currently no expansions for this game.

Tokyo Highway

Difficulty: ✴ ✴ ✴ ✴ ✴

Age Recommendation: 8+

Number of Players: 2–4

Play Time: 45 minutes

WHEN TO PLAY:

• When the whole family is around

• When you're at a dinner party

• When it's time for a little competition

Release Date: 2016

Publisher: Asmodee North America

Designers: Naotaka Shimamoto and Yoshiaki Tomioka

 THE GOAL

Be the first player to place all of your cars.

 **LET'S PLAY!**

Tokyo Highway is an odd dexterity game in which players construct pillars on which they build roads and place tiny cars. When placing roads, players must always place them on a pillar that's one higher or one lower than the one they are currently building the road from.

During a player's turn she may take three actions:

• **Construct a pillar:** Pick a location to construct a pillar. It can be based anywhere as long as it's reachable from your base point where you placed your first pillar, car, and road. Any time you are placing a pillar you must place it one above or one below the one you are currently moving from.

• **Construct a road:** A new road must rest between the base point and the pillar constructed in the first phase. If a player needs to adjust the pillar to place the road, they may.

• **Place a car on a highway:** Any time a road goes over or under an opponent's road, the player who placed it may place a car on that road. Thankfully, the game comes with handy tweezers, which can be used to get your car into the most precarious of positions.

When crossing over a road, a player may only place a car on it if there are no other roads over the opponent's road. When crossing under a road, players may only place a car if there are no other roads crossing under that road. If the road crosses multiple roads, they may place multiple cars as long as it meets these requirements. It's also important to note that players may not place a car when crossing over or under their own roads, and they may not place a car on constructed roads later in the game.

Players also have the ability to branch two ways from their highway from a junction at any time. In addition to that, players may also ground a road safely to the table and create an exit to their highway, and they are able to place an extra car when doing so.

When players fail to successfully place their cars, roads, or pillars and knock them over, they suffer consequences for every one that gets dropped. The number of pieces dropped are the number of pillars or roads the offending player must give to their opponent. If any player runs out of construction materials, they immediately lose the game and then they must fix the parts that were dropped. In a two-player game that player simply loses.

Tokyo Highway is a game that is simple on the surface but can evolve into a deeply strategic game. In addition to having a breathtaking table presence, this game has quality components and beautiful bright colors that are sure to make your day.

EXPANSIONS

There are currently no expansions for this game.

COLLECT 'EM ALL!:

SET COLLECTION

Set collection is a staple of tabletop gaming. Most people would recognize it from Monopoly. In that game the players are tasked with collecting sets of properties of the same color in order to build hotels on them. Believe it or not, lots of set collection games in tabletop gaming are even simpler than that, although others are far more complex. The oldest-known popular set collection game is also a game most people have heard of: bingo, which, of course, still has its place in 2018, a true testament to the game's staying power. We have the mechanic pop up again in popular games like Old Maid, rummy, mah-jongg, poker, and pick-up sticks. There are even popular set collection games like Pit that date back to 1903 but are still being reprinted to this day.

It's safe to say that set collection helped make tabletop gaming what it is today. There are more than 10,000 games listed on *BoardGameGeek* as set collection games. The satisfaction that players are given from successfully collecting things never fades! Just look at the Pokémon franchise. It shows no signs of slowing or stopping any time soon, and collecting things is literally what the franchise was built on.

Jaipur

Difficulty: ✶ ✶ ✶ ✶ ✶

Age Recommendation: 10+

Number of Players: 2

Play Time: 20–30 minutes

WHEN TO PLAY:

- When it's time for a little competition
- When you're having a game night
- When you're at a gaming convention

Release Date: 2009

Publisher: Asmodee & Gameworks

Designer: Sebastien Pauchon

 ## THE GOAL

Obtain two seals of excellence for winning the round by having the most points at the end.

LET'S PLAY!

Jaipur is set in the capital of Rajasthan, which is a state in the northwestern region of India.

In Jaipur, each player plays one of the two most powerful traders in the city, and each competes to be the richest merchant in the land. Players trade in their starting goods, using the assistance of helpful camels to carry goods near and far. But they want to pay close attention to the marketplace, where some goods are worth far more than others depending on the timing of the sale.

Between the players sits a marketplace where they sell the goods they gather from the colorful market made up of a deck and five faceup cards. There are fifty-five goods cards and on them are various goods, some more scarce than others and some more valuable. There are also camels, which help players carry their goods from place to place. The more camels a player has, the more goods she can swap out in the market. Players can also swap out these cards during the game for any other cards in their hand, bearing in mind they must trade a card for every card they take, leaving what they put in the center up for grabs by their opponent.

Each player has a land limit of seven total cards, and they each start the game with five cards. If they have any camels in their hand, they place them onto the table. These always go faceup in front of the player. Any time a camel is taken from the center row, the player must take all of the camels into his herd. However, on any future turn, rather than taking a single card from the marketplace, he may then trade any number of his camels for the same number of cards in the market, keeping in mind that players still may not have more than seven total cards in their hand.

On their turn, each player can either take cards or sell cards. A player may never do both on her turn. When a player goes to take a card from the center, she may only take one unless she trades them for the camels in her herd, keeping in mind that the next player then likely has access to a whole lot of camels he can take and use later. When a player's opponent does take the camels, he's in luck because more shiny goods are revealed after the camels are taken because, if there are fewer than five goods in the market, they are replaced by the market deck.

When a player decides to sell his cards he gains victory point tokens two ways. The players take goods tokens, which decrease in value as they are taken, with the highest on the top of the stack. The sooner the players sell goods they have, the more they are worth. Each good is balanced in value based on the total number of those goods cards in the deck. The first one earned is worth the most points, and the last one in that stack is usually worth a very small amount. There are, of course, exceptions to this rule.

Players also gain bonus points based on the number of goods they sell at a time. Players may not sell fewer than two goods; however, if they sell three, four, or five cards they receive a bonus

IS THERE A MINIMUM NUMBER OF GOODS YOU HAVE TO SELL AT A TIME?

Yes! You must sell at least two goods in order to sell on your turn.

number of points increasing by the number of goods they sell. The round ends when three token stacks are completely depleted. Then the player with the most camels gets the bonus camel token, and then the players add up their total points, revealing their bonus tokens.

Jaipur is a delightful two-player game, and while there is a great deal of depth and strategy to the game, it's buried under gorgeous artwork, easy to understand mechanics, and a delightful back and forth antagonism between the players. It's a game that rarely leaves someone's collection after being purchased, and its low price makes it even more appealing.

EXPANSIONS

There are currently no expansions for this game.

Sheriff of Nottingham

Release Date: 2014

Publisher: Arcane Wonders

Designers: Sergio Halaban and André Zatz

WHEN TO PLAY:

- When you're in a table-top game marathon

- When you want something fun and easy

- When you're having a game night

Difficulty: ✶ ✶ ✶ ✶ ✶

Age Recommendation: 8+

Number of Players: 3–5

Play Time: 60 minutes

 ## THE GOAL

Have the most gold at the end of the game.

 ## LET'S PLAY!

Prince John is coming to Nottingham, and you are one of the merchants in town looking to turn a quick profit by selling goods in the city as it fills with people hoping to see him! That said, the sheriff is keeping a close watch on the goods coming in and out of the city, so it's up to you to decide if it's worth the risk to sneak illegal goods into the city. Contraband is frowned upon, and you could end up with a hefty fine if you're caught with any goods you didn't tell the sheriff you were bringing in.

To start the game, each player is given a player board where they keep all their goods after sneaking, err, *bringing* them through the gate and into the city. One player is handed a sheriff marker; she acts as the sheriff for that round. There are three kinds of goods in the game. Every card has a value on it inside a shiny gold icon, as well as a penalty cost below. If players successfully bring their goods through the gates past the sheriff, they score the gold value on them, and the player with the most of each legal good at the end of the game receives a bonus. Royal goods aren't legal goods. However, they typically count as two or three of a legal good at the end of the game, so it's advantageous to sneak them through in your bag of goods. Finally, contraband is downright illegal. However, if successfully snuck past the sheriff, contraband goods are worth lots of gold, which can make them tempting when filling your merchant bags with goods. Each player starts the game with fifty gold coins, which he uses to pay fees or even bribe the sheriff.

Each turn takes place over several phases. It starts with the market phase. During this phase, players may discard any unwanted cards and draw new ones in hopes of finding the perfect hand. After that, everyone who is not the sheriff this round picks the number of goods they are going to put into their bag. They must select one good and state the number of goods inside of the bag. Players must be truthful about the number of goods, but they don't have to be truthful about the type of goods, because they can mix and match as many goods as they like. For example, a player could say, "My bag has three apples in it." His bag might have three apples in it, or it could have one apple, one adult cider, and a chicken in it. The only way to find out for certain is for the sheriff to open his bag.

Once all of the players have filled their bags with goods and snapped them close, they are all handed over to the sheriff and players state what's in their bags while making direct eye contact with the sheriff. The sheriff can then decide to let the players pass through or he can take a peek inside of their bags for contraband. If the snap is undone at any point, the sheriff must open the bag, and if there are any goods not stated in players' initial statement to the sheriff, they must pay the penalty cost to the sheriff. However, if they were being truthful in their statements to the sheriff and he opens their bag, the sheriff must pay the players their penalty cost, making for an interesting table dynamic as players take turns being the sheriff each round.

If a player chooses to, she may bribe the sheriff into not checking her bag, which leads to an interesting negotiation between the merchants and the sheriff. It's important for players

ESSENTIAL

Once the button on a bag is undone, the sheriff must open it and find out if the merchant was lying or not. If the sheriff was wrong and the merchant was telling the truth, the sheriff player needs to pay the merchant for the trouble!

- Merry Men
  2017

to keep in mind that they are always free to offer the sheriff coins or even goods inside of the bag to convince him to not open their bags, keeping in mind that deals made are only binding until the end of that sheriff's turn.

Sheriff of Nottingham is a delightfully charming game that will have most of the table laughing, shouting, and lying through their teeth. The game was ahead of its time not only in its quality of artwork but also its innovative and clever design.

Hanabi

Difficulty: ★ ★ ★ ★ ★

Age Recommendation: 10+

Number of Players: 2–5

Play Time: 20–30 minutes

 ## THE GOAL

Create fireworks in order to get as high a score as possible, a perfect score being 25 points.

 ## LET'S PLAY!

In Japan fireworks are known as *hanabi*. In this cooperative game, players try to create the most stunning fireworks show by placing the cards in their hand onto the table. However, they cannot see their hands, so they need to rely on the hints from the other players to figure out the best cards to play, noting that it's equally important to remember the clues the other players have given. It's up to you to cooperate with each other to put on the greatest fireworks show ever seen!

Between all of the players sits an open space and a limited number of clue tokens, which players spend as they give clues to each other. Because these are a shared and limited resource it's important for all players to use them wisely, giving as much information as possible. The players hold their hand of cards facing away from them so that the other players can see the cards and the player cannot. On her turn, a player can either give a clue, discard one of the five cards in her hand to gain a clue, or play one of the five cards in her hand using the information she gained from

WHEN TO PLAY:

- When you love solving puzzles
- When it's time for a little competition
- When you're at your local game store

Release Date: 2010
Publisher: R&R Games
Designer: Antoine Bauza

SET COLLECTION

EXPANSIONS

There are no expansions for this game in English.

previous clues given to her. Clues may only consist of one bit of information. The player may either give the other players a color clue or a numerical clue; the clue tells the player all of one color or number in another player's hand, keeping in mind that it's up to the person she is giving the clues to, to remember them.

In between all of the players sit five spaces for fireworks to be placed. There are five colors in the game and numbered cards in each color from one to five. There are three of each one; two of each two, three, and four; and just one of each five. Each of these cards must be played in order, so if you want to play a white two, you must first play a white one. If you have already played a one and play another, that too would get rid of a fuse because you are only trying to go up in numerical order and never want to play a duplicate. If any of the cards are played out of order then the team loses one of their fuses. They only have three of these, and if they lose all three of them the game ends immediately and the fireworks show is a total flop.

The objective of the game is not to win; it's to achieve a better score than you did the last time you played. A perfect score is 25 points, meaning you played one of each numerical card of each color in order. Inside the game is a rating sheet that tells you how well you did on a scale from horrible to legendary, but due to the game's difficulty and lack of permitted communication outside of clues, it's probably best to just aim to do marginally better than you did in the last game you played.

Arboretum

Difficulty: ★ ★ ★ ★ ☆   **Number of Players:** 2–4

Age Recommendation: 10+   **Play Time:** 30 minutes

 THE GOAL

Score the most points at the end of the game by creating the best arboretum.

👥 LET'S PLAY!

Arboretum is a deceptively tricky game about planting trees and creating your own park. Originally released in 2015, it went out of print and remained so for a surprisingly long time despite strong interest from the gaming community. Finally Renegade Game Studios acquired the license and re-released it in 2018. Arboretum requires that you plan for both what you are placing in front of you and what you keep in your hand at the end of the game, as well as being very aware of what your opponents are placing.

Players are dealt seven cards for their initial hand and one card faceup; that serves as the first card in your discard pile. The remaining cards are placed in the middle of the table to serve as a draw pile. A turn is very simple: draw two cards, play one to your arboretum in front of you, and discard one to your discard pile. However, you can draw your cards from any combination of the draw pile *or* any faceup discard pile on the table! The game ends when there are no more cards in the draw pile.

Release Date: 2015

Publisher: Renegade Game Studios

Designer: Dan Cassar

WHEN TO PLAY:

- When you're ready to explain rules
- When the whole family is around
- When you want to play something challenging

SET COLLECTION

Scoring is where things get a bit tricky, and that's why thinking about the end of the game is important even from the very beginning. There are several colors of trees (the exact number varies by player count) and only the player with the most value in cards of a color in his hand at the end of the game is able to score for that type of tree. What you are actually scoring is paths in your arboretum, which are sequences of cards of increasing value, where the first and last cards are the same color.

It seems pretty simple and straightforward, but it's also entirely possible that you could have an amazing path in your arboretum that would give you a bunch of points, but you don't have enough in your hand at the end of the game to actually score it. Or you could have the highest value of cards for a color in your hand, but you didn't put any of those trees down in your garden, so you have nothing to score for it. Throw in the added wrinkle that if you have an eight in your hand, and someone else has a one, it makes your eight worth a one. Having a good memory of what has been played and discarded is a huge asset in trying to determine whether or not you are able to score what you think you can.

SET COLLECTION

EXPANSIONS

There are currently no expansions for this game.

7 Wonders Duel

Difficulty: ★ ★ ★ ★ ☆

Age Recommendation: 10+

Number of Players: 2

Play Time: 30 minutes

 **THE GOAL**

Develop your civilization by constructing buildings and wonders to win via a military, scientific, or civilian approach.

 **LET'S PLAY!**

7 Wonders is one of a few strategic games that plays up to seven players, so it's a handy one to have on your shelf if you have a lot of friends coming over for a game night.

However, 7 Wonders is not fantastic at two players. Enter 7 Wonders Duel, a distillation of the original in a new structure that suits the two-player experience much better.

As in the original 7 Wonders, the game takes place over three ages, using different decks of cards for each age. Every card represents a building you can add to your civilization, and each provides resources, military strength, scientific knowledge, trading abilities, or points. The cards in the three ages are tiered to get more powerful as the game goes on and allow you to get discounts based on cards purchased in previous ages.

In each age, cards are laid out in a pyramid shape, with some faceup and some facedown. The starting player chooses a card and does one of three things with it: pays the cost listed on the card to play it in front of them, discards it to gain money, or uses it to

WHEN TO PLAY:

- When it's time for a little competition
- When you're at a gaming convention
- When you're at your local game store

Release Date: 2015
Publisher: Repos Production
Designers: Antoine Bauza and Bruno Cathala

SET COLLECTION

construct a wonder. Only cards that are not in any way covered are available to choose. If a card is revealed when one player takes the remaining card on top of it, that new card is available for the next player. If it was facedown before it was made available, the card is flipped faceup. Each age continues, with players taking turns taking one card from the pyramid until all cards have been taken.

There are seven different types of building cards that come out during the game:

1. **Raw materials (brown):** basic resources (wood, stone, and brick) needed for building most of the structures and wonders
2. **Manufactured goods (gray):** advanced goods (paper, glass) also needed for some buildings and wonders
3. **Civilian buildings (blue):** these provide just straight victory points and no other benefits
4. **Scientific buildings (green):** points and symbols, which can be used to gain bonuses and possibly a scientific victory
5. **Commercial buildings (yellow):** these can be a mix of things, including resources, coins, better trading rules, and sometimes points
6. **Military buildings (red):** increase your military strength and can lead to a military victory
7. **Guilds (purple):** these cards are only available in the third age and give you bonus points based on specific criteria

Players also start with four wonders each. These are cards that grant the player large amounts of points, money, or abilities (or some combination) and have fairly high costs to build. Only seven wonders can be built between the two players, so the first to build their four ultimately forces the other player to discard one of hers. Players don't have to build these to win the game, but they can provide huge advantages.

The most straightforward way to win is by having the most points at the end of the game. Points are a combination of your different buildings and wonders and anything gained from scientific or military achievements. In addition, there are two other ways that the game can end. If one player collects six out of seven scientific symbols available in the game, she immediately wins. Likewise, if a player is able to push the conflict pawn via their military strength into their opponent's capital (on a small track that sits above the pyramid of cards), they immediately win. Shrewd players do their best to ensure that their opponent is not amassing enough military or scientific prowess to win in this way, but it's very easy to sneak up on you.

EXPANSIONS

- Pantheon
  2016

Above and Below

Difficulty: ✶ ✶ ✶ ✶ ✶

Age Recommendation: 8+

Number of Players: 2–4

Play Time: 90 minutes

WHEN TO PLAY:

- When you feel like adventure
- When the whole family is around
- When you're having a game night

Release Date: 2015
Publisher: Red Raven Games
Designer: Ryan Laukat

 THE GOAL

Tell stories in such a way as to have the most points at the end of the game.

 LET'S PLAY!

Adventure games are a special genre of their own because they go beyond rolling dice and collecting things. Adventure games tell stories, and part of what makes Above and Below so special is the way in which it tells stories, rewarding the players for their good or bad decisions along the way. This game comes with a huge story module and prompts players to experience new adventures along the way, as well as giving them an overwhelming number of other actions they can take. Always keeping in mind that having fun, not winning, is the most important part of playing any game.

Above and Below is one of those games that people play for the first time and their faces light up. The adventure bug has bitten them, and they can't turn away; most of the time, they're sad when it's over. While exploring the land you run into a variety of creatures ranging from painfully cute to mildly horrifying. During these encounters, you gather resources that help fuel your other endeavors. Each player starts the game with four gold coins, and they need to use them wisely.

ESSENTIAL

Players want to lock in as many different types of goods as possible. However, if they think they are going to have many of them, they may want to wait to lock them into their advancement track because the higher up the track you go, the more victory points each good of that type is worth at the end of the game.

Between the players sits a reputation track and a wide array of various cards that can be gathered and used if purchased for the right price. Players gain victory points through these cards. They gain points at the end, courtesy of their reputations' final placement. As players gather goods and lock them into the player board in front of them, each turn their income grows, allowing them to purchase increasingly expensive cards. These facilitate more successful adventures each round. Once a good is locked into this track it may not be moved; duplicate goods are stacked on top of each other.

The advancement track sits on each player's board, and as the game progresses, each player gathers resources and then locks them into his or her advancement track. When players do this that good type is locked into that space, and any goods added to the track are worth the number of victory points listed on the space they locked that good into. These increase in value with each different type of good for the number of victory points each good is worth, or it increases the player's overall income from round to round.

Gathering goods can be quite the conundrum. There are five different actions a player can take on his turn.

1. A player may choose to **day labor** and exhaust one of his limited workers to gain a coin.
2. He may also **recruit another character** by paying its cost listed below them on the recruitment board, which allows him to take more actions in future rounds.
3. The player can also **build a building** either above or below if he has the cave space.
4. The player could choose to **harvest a good** from one of the buildings he's already acquired if it has goods on it.
5. The player can choose to **go on an adventure**.

When a player chooses to go on an adventure he selects at least two characters to take on his adventure. Then he draws an adventure card and rolls a die. The die matches up with a story from the book, which a different player reads aloud to the active player.

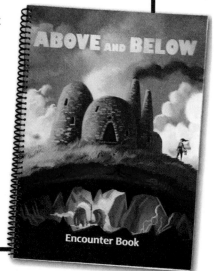

The player is then given a decision to make. If his characters have the required skills or strength, he succeeds at the mission. While the player is always rewarded for his actions, only the strongest and bravest adventurers will reap the best rewards.

Each character rolls a die and is granted a number of adventure points based on the die results. If he has enough adventure points, he may select different story options. There are even some cards in the game that allow the player to reroll during these adventures.

Above and Below combines storytelling and worker placement mechanics for a thrilling experience that works for all ages. It's a perfect family game.

EXPANSIONS

- Groves
  2016

LUCK-BASED GAMES

11

Everyone wants to win the lottery. However, you're more likely to be struck by lightning. In push-your-luck dice games, the odds are a bit better when it comes to accomplishing goals and objectives, but caution may be required. These kinds of games are typically fairly easy to teach but require just the right balance of luck and strategic planning to win.

Testing your opponents is important, as is stopping them from accomplishing their goals or objectives. Thanks to this dynamic, players tend to be more engaged on the turns of other players in an effort to better anticipate their actions and better thwart their plans. Sometimes gambling is involved, but that's not always the case. At times players are simply trying to protect their people from drowning or being eaten by sea serpents.

Risk versus reward is no easy thing. One of the most important but unspoken aspects of push-your-luck games is baiting or antagonizing your opponents to make a mistake. Tempting your opponents to push further than they should can oftentimes result in a full-on loss, which can be very advantageous for you. However, make sure to account for your opponents' ability to stop while they're ahead. Not everyone is as gullible as one might be led to believe.

There have been many games famous for their push-your-luck mechanics. Poker games like Texas Hold 'Em and Blackjack are perfect examples of this genre. Some players enjoy press-your-luck games because while there can be some strategy, the aspect of luck makes for a more fair and well-rounded game for all of the players. It makes it slightly more difficult for one player to run away with the win, unless that day they just happen to be incredibly lucky.

Exploding Kittens

Difficulty: ★ ★ ★ ★ ★

Age Recommendation: 8+

Number of Players: 2–5

Play Time: 15 minutes

WHEN TO PLAY:

• When you want a game you can carry with you

• When you have a spare ten minutes

• When you want something fun and easy

Release Date: 2015
Publisher: The Oatmeal
Designers: Matthew Inman, Elan Lee, and Shane Small

🎯 THE GOAL

Be the last living player at the end of the game.

LET'S PLAY!

Exploding Kittens is exactly what everyone thinks it's about—it's a game about kittens who explode if they are not defused. Kittens may only be defused with the right cards, which must be discarded after they're used. After a kitten has been defused the player who defused it may put it back in the deck wherever they like, in secret.

In Exploding Kittens you are pushing your luck not only against the kittens that could explode on you but also the other players, who manipulate the deck in hopes of thwarting your grand plans.

Turns consist of two phases. During the first phase, you play any number of action cards in order to discard cards, look at future cards, or change your hand. After playing an action card, you draw a card and hope it's not an exploding kitten. After that card is drawn, your turn is over. However, there are special cards!

- **Nope cards:** These stop players from taking their action and can be played as a reaction to any other player's card. These are great cards to mitigate dangerous plays by your opponent.

The only cards they don't work on are defuses and exploding kittens. These are very good cards to save in case of an emergency.

- **Cards without actions on them:** Some cards don't have instructions on them. These cards can be used to steal cards from other players. If a player has two of a kind, he may take a card at random from a player's hand. If he has three of a kind, he may name a card and a player to give that card to. If the other player doesn't have that card, he gets nothing. Stealing from the right person is critical.

With that said, players can steal cards from other players with *any* two cards that have matching upper left-hand corner symbols. The cards without actions on them are not the only cards that can be used to thwart a player's opponents. Be wary of those ominous nope cards. If a player has one, she's certain to stop you from stealing her other cards.

The person who wins the game is the last person living in the end. (No actual cats were hurt in the making of the game Exploding Kittens.)

Exploding Kittens is an incredibly quick game that can be taught as it's being played, which makes it accessible, easy to learn, and easy to move on from. If you're looking for a great game to introduce players to pushing their luck, this is a perfect introductory game for players who have never played one before.

EXPANSIONS

- Imploding Kittens
  2016
- Streaking Kittens
  2018

Survive: Escape from Atlantis

Difficulty: ★ ★ ★ ★ ★

Age Recommendation: 6+

Number of Players: 2–4

Play Time: 20–30 minutes

Release Date: 1982
Publisher: Stronghold Games
Designer: Julian Courtland-Smith

 ## THE GOAL

Escape from the island and save your meeples!

 ## LET'S PLAY!

The island is sinking and the volcano is active! There are limited rafts to escape the island, and the rest of the meeples may just have to swim their way to safety all while navigating the dangerous waters that are filled with sea serpents who devour everything in their path, whales who gobble up boats, and sharks who are hungry for meeple blood!

Between the players sits a randomized island board with all tiles facedown. The players collectively build the board together at the start of the game and then add their meeples to the island one by one, carefully placing their more valuable meeples closer to a safe escape. Then the players take turns placing the boats nearby to help rescue their meeples. Four sea serpents are placed on the board to start, and whales and sharks make their appearances as well.

Each turn takes place in three phases. Players move their meeples or boats, remove land, and then roll the die to move a creature.

WHEN TO PLAY:

- When it's time for a little competition

- When you're having a game night

- When you need to relax

The player starts by moving a meeple or boat with one of his 3 action points. He can move one space for any meeple or boat he chooses to use for the cost of a single action point. He moves his meeple one space on the island or onto a boat, provided that the tiles are adjacent. Moving one space costs 1 action point. If the player has majority control of the boat (more meeple than any other player), then he may move the boat in a direction of his choice.

To remove land, the player flips a tile over and performs the action on the back of it, keeping in mind that she must remove the land in order. Sandy beaches first, then more sturdy land, and finally stone. There are two kinds of actions that can be on the back of these land tiles.

When it is an instant action, the player immediately places whatever monster or item is indicated on the back of this tile. If it is a whirlpool, it gobbles up the surrounding tiles, boats, monsters, and meeples.

If it's an ability action, the player keeps this facedown until a future turn when she can use it at the start of her turn. Ability actions typically consist of the ability to move monsters, meeples, and boats.

Finally the player rolls the die and moves a creature. She rolls the six-sided die onto the table. It may land on any of the three animals that can move a number of spaces depending on their species. If she rolls a sea serpent, she can move it one space and it devours meeples and boats. If she rolls a shark, she may move two spaces. Sharks devour only meeples in water. If the whale is rolled, it may move three spaces and it only devours boats.

On the bottom of each meeple is a value between 1 and 6 points. Players may only look at these values at the start of the game when placing them onto the board, and after that they must have their values memorized. There's a strategic advantage to putting all of your valuable meeples on one side of the island and your less valuable meeples on the other side: it reminds you who to save. However, if the other players identify this kind of behavior, it can be risky. The other players can take action against you with their special tiles as well as the monsters of the ocean.

Survive: Escape from Atlantis is an excellent family game that can be played with kids as young as six years old (although the official age recommendation is eight and up).

This is a game for the lighthearted who aren't sore losers. If you thought your friends and family loved you, you might reconsider after playing Survive.

EXPANSIONS

- Dolphins & Squids & 5–6 Players Oh My!
  2015

Dairyman

WHEN TO PLAY:

- When you want something fun and easy

- When you need to relax

- When the whole family is around

Release Date: 2016
Publisher: Homosapiens Lab
Designer: Chi-Fan Chen

Difficulty: ★ ★ ★ ★ ★

Age Recommendation: 6+

Number of Players: 2–4

Play Time: 25–30 minutes

 THE GOAL

Make dairy products and be the player at the end of the game with the most dairy points.

 LET'S PLAY!

Have you ever wanted your own cow farm? In Dairyman, all players saddle up for the wild ride of making cheese and ice cream! On the board sit three dairy farms that players use to acquire additional milk, which they eventually turn into cheese and ice cream. Doing this grants them special abilities to help mitigate their bad luck in dairy farming.

To start the game, three dairy farms are put onto the board along with three milk-side-up dairy products that each have a value between ten and forty. This is how many points each one of them is worth at the end of the game unless they are flipped to the opposite side, which can only be done by fulfilling the tiles requirement in the upper right-hand corner. These consist of either a freeze token or a yellow die. When flipped over they increase by a number of points depending on what's on the back of that tile. There are various cheeses worth between 25 and 45 points, which are flipped with yellow dice, and ice creams worth between 10 and 30 points, which are flipped with freeze tokens.

Players then take turns rolling all eight of the dairy dice, seven white dice and one yellow die. Then they use a combination of either two or three dice total that add up to ten total. Each time a player assigns dice to a specific farm she has the opportunity to buy a dairy product from the board. These come in tens, so if a player has assigned two fives to the first dairy farm, she may take a ten-value milk product. If she assigned four fives to the first dairy farm, she may take a milk product with a twenty value. After a player assigns at least two dice to the first dairy farm she may then move onto the second dairy farm. If she also manages to assign dice adding up to ten using only two or three dice total, she may also buy an item adding up to her total number of assigned dice on all of her dairy farms.

If the player fails to roll any working combination of dice adding up to ten, she busts and is given a -5 points card that only counts against her at the end of the game. Luckily, to mitigate those potential negative effects, the player is also given an extra red die to roll on her turn for as long as that -5 card is in her hand. The number of these cards that can be in play at one time depends on the player count.

When any player rolls on the final diary farm location, and any roll after that, he is given a freeze token that may be used in one of two ways. He may use a freeze token to turn milk into ice cream or he may use it to keep a die the same from one round into the next. In either case the freeze token is discarded.

When a player rolls her yellow die with her white die, she may choose to assign her yellow die to a dairy product in order to turn it into cheese. This die may not be used to purchase more dairy products, and it must be the exact number listed in the corner of that tile.

When dairy products are flipped to their cheese or ice cream side, players are given a special ability listed in the bottom right-hand corner that allows them to reroll dice once per turn. Some of these state any die, others list only specific numbers, and others might even allow the player to reroll all of a certain number.

ESSENTIAL

Dairyman takes push-your-luck games and simplifies it in a lactose-free kind of way. It's easily digestible and quick to play. It's one of those games that you learn once and teach to a table who wants to play again and again. With its short play time, it's hard not to play it a few times in a row.

EXPANSIONS

There are currently no expansions for this game.

WHEN TO PLAY:

- When you're at a dinner party

- When you're just getting started with tabletop games

- When it's time for a little competition

Release Date: 2014

Publisher: Asmodee North America

Designer: Steffen Bogen

Camel Up

Difficulty: ✶ ✶ ✶ ✶ ✶   **Number of Players:** 2–8

Age Recommendation: 8+   **Play Time:** 20–30 minutes

 THE GOAL

Have the most coins at the end of the game. The game ends when a camel crosses the finish line and then the players finish the leg of the race.

 LET'S PLAY!

Far away in the desert sits a stunning pyramid, and around it the camels are racing away as noble folk make bets on who wins the race. Camel Up is a wild betting party game for two to eight players in which players bet on camels in a race. Along the way they make bets on legs of the race for different-colored camels. They do this by taking betting tiles off the table and placing them in front of them. They also gain coins by rolling dice to move the camels around the board and reap the benefits. Between all of the players sits an arena in which camels will be racing around, circling a stunning pyramid doubling as the device that will randomize the rolling of the dice.

 Each player gets to take one of several actions on his turn. He may take a better tile, place a desert tile, move a camel, bet on the winner, or bet on the loser. If the player decides to take a betting tile, he acquires one of the many faceup betting tiles for the leg of the race. Each one gives the players coins at the end of the round if the player has one of those cards in his possession, but only if the camel he bets on comes in first or second place. If the camel comes any later in the race, the player loses a coin. A leg is over once all camels have moved this round.

If the player decides to place his betting tile, he takes his desert tile that is double-sided and places it on a space in the middle of the game board. It must be at least two spaces away from any camels. If you place it faceup, when a camel lands on it, it moves one space forward. If you put it facedown, then when a camel lands on it, the camel goes back one space. Either way, the player who placed the tile gains 1 point.

If the player decides to move a camel, he picks up the pyramid contraption and presses the lever. That drops one die out of the pyramid. Whatever color shows up is the color of camel that moves. The number that shows up on the die is always between one and three. The camel moves forward on the sixteen-space race track. If he lands on a desert tile, he moves forward or back as specified and the desert tile is returned to the player who placed it.

If a player decides to bet on the overall winner, she takes one of the camel cards from her hand and places it facedown in the win pile. These are only revealed at the end of the game, and players acquire more coins the sooner they place their accurate bet. If their bet is wrong then they lose one coin. If a player instead bets on the overall loser, she takes one of the camel cards from her hand and places it facedown in the lose pile. These are only revealed at the end of the game, and players acquire more coins the sooner they placed their accurate bet. If their bet is wrong then they lose one coin.

Camels move differently around the board. When one camel is stacked on top of another camel, if the bottom camel moves, all camels on top of them also move with them. The camel on the very top of the stack of camels is always considered in first place ahead of the other camels. When all dice inside the pyramid have been rolled out of the pyramid, the leg of that race ends. After a camel has passed the finish line, the end of the game is activated and the

EXPANSIONS

- Supercup
  2015

leg is finished. Then all of the win and loss cards are revealed, coins are given out, and the player with the most coins wins the game.

Camel Up is a delightfully fun game that captures the magic of family gaming in a way that leaves people having fun no matter their luck in the game. It's a game that inspires passionate voice raising, boisterous laughter, and fierce competition!

Kanagawa

Difficulty: ★ ★ ★ ★ ★   **Number of Players:** 2–4

Age Recommendation: 10+   **Play Time:** 45 minutes

 THE GOAL

Be the player with the most harmony points when one player has at least eleven total cards in her print.

 LET'S PLAY!

Kanagawa takes place in 1840 in the great bay of Tokyo. The great master Hokusai decided to open a painting school to share his art with his disciples. As one of them, you must prove yourself worthy. Follow his teachings and expand your studio while you paint all he wishes to see. This work becomes the work of your lifetime as you compete to be the best art student of Master Hokusai.

The objective of Kanagawa is a simple one: to be the best art student in a painting school taught by Master Hokusai. As one of his disciples you need to prove yourself worthy of his teachings by expanding your studio and painting your preferred subjects, whether they are animals, humans, trees, or buildings. Make sure you pay attention to the changing seasons. Each card has a season icon in the upper right-hand corner. The more consecutive season icons in a row, the more victory points each painter scores at the end of the game.

In between all of the players sits a school board, and on it there are spots for cards that are flipped over one row at a time. On his

WHEN TO PLAY:

- When you're at your local game store

- When it's time for a little competition

- When you're at a gaming convention

Release Date: 2016
Publisher: Iello Games
Designers: Bruno Cathala and Charles Chevallier

or her turn, each player flips over a number of cards equal to the number of players onto the school board. Any cards being placed onto a white square are faceup. Any cards flipped onto a red square are placed facedown. Starting with the player to his right, the first player offers one of the columns to take. If the player does not take a column of cards, the next player is allowed to take a card. If she also refuses, then the next player decides if he takes the card or not. Eventually the play returns to the player whose turn it was. If he also chooses not to take any of the columns, the next row is filled with cards and the process repeats. The most cards any column can ever have in it are three total lesson cards.

There are several different ways to score points from the lesson cards. Players may gain pure points, earn points from lesson cards, gain points from sequences of seasons, gain points from diploma tiles, and gain points for having the grand master pawn. To gain pure points, the lesson card has an end-of-game bonus in the upper right-hand corner of the print or studio. When earning lesson card points, each player scores one card for each card in her lesson card print.

When scoring seasons, players score 1 point for each card in the print that is a part of a consecutive season. Any awkward single season blocking the way of your beautiful run can be mitigated by placing a storm token over it. This token acts as wild so your season's bonus can flourish.

As the game play moves along, players receive reward tiles for each color of diploma tile they have acquired. These are acquired by meeting the tiles requirements below it. Each player may only take one of each color of these tiles, and she must decide when she meets those requirements if she takes that tile or if she pushes her luck and holds out for the next tile in hopes that her opponents cannot accomplish the requirements before she can.

The player with the grandmaster pawn receives 2 points for having him at the end of the game.

When players take the paintings they decide if the cards go into their studio or into their print. Cards may *always* go into the studio, on the bottom half of their board. However, in order to paint a card into their studio, players must pay the cost from their studio. Each player starts the game with two brushes. Along the way she may gain more by either adding them to her studio or by acquiring diploma tiles that provide them to the player. Brushes act as the player's workers, which can be placed on the resource tokens in the studio (the bottom row) of the player's board. Only one brush can be moved to a different resource per turn unless the player has a special ability in her studio allowing her to move more brushes.

Kanagawa has deep strategy with light game play and simple rules. While the game might be a tad challenging to explain to a first-time player, it goes fast enough that a Game Master can explain the game as she goes along with the other players. A newcomer might not win her first game, but by its end she should have a fully formed understanding of the game.

EXPANSIONS

- Kanagawa: Yokai Expansion

FACT

The game's elegant design work makes for a breath-taking table presentation, and its complex strategy makes for engaging game play that keeps the players invested and attentive when playing the game.

Abyss

Difficulty: ★ ★ ★ ★ ★

Age Recommendation: 10+

Number of Players: 2–4

Play Time: 45–60 minutes

 **WHEN TO PLAY:**

- When you're ready to explain rules

- When you want to play something challenging

- When you're in a table-top game marathon

Release Date: 2014

Publisher: Asmodee North America

Designers: Bruno Cathala and Charles Chevallier

 THE GOAL

Have the most points when any one player has at least seven lords from the court. Then each player is allowed an equal number of turns before the game ends.

👥 LET'S PLAY!

In the Abyss power is once again vacant, which means the throne is up for grabs! Use your cunning to win or buy votes and recruit the most influential lords to abuse their powers and take control of the depths of the sea so that you are the one true ruler of the Abyssal people.

Abyss takes place in a magical underwater kingdom where players compete to appeal to the lords of the court. Players accomplish this by recruiting lords, affiliating allies, and fighting eels in the deep under the sea. The end of the game is activated when any one player has recruited at least seven lords from the court or when the council deck runs out.

Each player, on his turn, takes three actions. He may delve, recruit from the council, or influence the court. When you delve you flip over cards one by one onto your track. Each time one of these ally cards is flipped, the player to your left gets the first opportunity to purchase that card. The first player who decides to

In Abyss players can earn special underwater locations, which are unlocked through recruiting lords with keys on them. Any time three keys appear in front of a player, she acquires a location and can no longer use the special abilities of the lords recruited with keys on them.

buy a card can buy it for one pearl. However, the next player has to pay two pearls to buy a card, and the third must pay three pearls. If there were additional players in the game the price of the cards would continue to rise. The catch is that once all players have refused a card, if the bidding gets back around to the player whose turn it is, that person may then decide to take that card for free and stop delving. If the cards ever reach this space while delving, the delve ends automatically and the current player must take that card as well as a bonus pearl. At the end of a delve, any cards not taken are sorted by color and discarded facedown into the council area.

When recruiting from the council, you take one of the facedown stacks of allies and add them to your hand. The allies you acquire through delving or recruiting are used to complete the next action, influencing the court. To influence the court, players must pay the cost in allies. The cost to influence a council member is located in the bottom left-hand corner of the card. The payment must include the color of the first bubble; any additional bubbles must be paid with additional cards of any other color.

In total they must equal at least the number determined on the card. While players can overpay in value, they cannot add cards simply to throw them away. They may also choose to spend pearls in order to reduce the cost by the number of pearls spent, though they must still use the required amount of differently colored allies.

Each time you influence a court member, you must affiliate one of your lowest-cost cards you used and place it into your affiliated allies pile. At the end of the game you are given points for the highest number card in each color of affiliated allies.

If taking a court member reveals a two-pearl symbol on the board, the player refills the board with court members in addition to collecting two pearls. At any time before a player takes his action, if there is space available in the court, he can choose to pay one pearl and add a court member to the court from the top of the deck to help open up his purchasing options.

While influencing various court members, he gains the points shown in the upper left-hand corner. Players also find that some of them have ongoing special abilities, while others have instant effects that are signified by the arrow on the card. These abilities are largely what makes the game interesting, as they can grant additional points, pearls, board manipulation, and superpowers that allow the player to do things like taking two stacks of cards from the council.

Instant abilities happen when a player influences that court member. Ongoing abilities, however, stay in play until the player has three or more keys. At that point he must draw one to four locations from his stack and choose one to put into play, covering up three keys and negating those court members' effects. These locations grant the player bonus points at the end of the game. The locations the player doesn't choose are now left faceup next to the stack. On future turns when a location would need to be chosen, players can choose to take one of these faceup locations instead of drawing.

The keys players need to build locations can also be won from battling. Sometimes when delving, a player comes upon an eel and must decide whether or not he would like to fight it. If he chooses to fight it, he takes the reward that is currently listed on the eel track. Should he choose to pass, he then increases the reward on the eel track to further tempt the next player who would run into an eel in battle. If a player flips an eel on the last location in the delve deck, however, he then immediately has to fight the eel and take whatever reward is available on the track. This can make for a sticky situation if he's already at two keys and has two ongoing abilities he is attached to. Only the player currently on the delve is able to fight or avoid the eels.

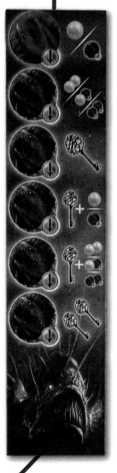

The game ends when a player has recruited his seventh council member or when the council deck runs out. Each other player takes one more turn, and then everyone adds up their scores. The player with the highest total wins!

Abyss is very simple and easy to teach. Unfortunately, its box can make the game seem more forbidding than it actually is. The strategy can be surprisingly deep thanks to the variety of lords available in the game. The game plays best with three to four players, but it's entirely playable with just two players.

THE FIRST DRAFT:

CARD-DRAFTING GAMES

Gone are the days of having a single hand of cards dealt out randomly at the beginning of the game. Instead, players start with a hand of cards or tiles but then build their hand by picking one card to keep and then pass the rest to their left or right. This continues until everyone has a hand of cards (and some advance knowledge about what other cards are out there). Thus the "pick and pass" game was born! There are many variations on this mechanism. In Cat Lady, players draft from a grid of cards displayed on the table and take more than one card at a time. In Azul, players draft from groups of colorful tiles but are only permitted to take one type and have to take all of that type. Sushi Go and 7 Wonders are simpler drafting games in which you pick one card to play and then pass the rest. By eliminating traditional turns, these games are quick, variable, and engaging for everyone with very little downtime. You never catch a person checking her smartphone during a drafting game. Drafting can take place either from a hand of cards or from a central location available to all players.

Drafting is often combined with set collection or tile placement, opening a whole universe of possibilities. What makes these games special is they give the players the power to make decisions that not only impact them but often impact the other players.

Drafting games have been around for many years. However, when 7 Wonders was released in 2010 the mechanic really started to gain notability in board gaming and not just in collectible card games such as Magic: The Gathering. Following up in 2013, Sushi Go's release made the genre even more accessible with its simple rules set, inviting the mass market into the fold of drafting games. This allowed players who understood Sushi Go to step easily into other more complex drafting games.

Azul

Difficulty: ★ ★ ★ ★ ★

Age Recommendation: 8+

Number of Players: 2–4

Play Time: 45 minutes

WHEN TO PLAY:

- When the whole family is around

- When you're having a game night

- When you want something fun and easy

Release Date: 2017
Publisher: Next Move Games
Designer: Michael Kiesling

 THE GOAL

Place tiles on the game board in such a way as to have the most points at the end of the game.

LET'S PLAY!

Azul was yet another smash hit that was initially published by Plan B Games. This stunning game mimics *azulejos*, or tiles, which were fully embraced by the Portuguese when their king Manuel I went on a visit to the Alhambra palace in southern Spain. Awestruck, he ordered that his own palace in Portugal be decorated with similar tiles. In this game, players are tasked with drafting colored tiles from suppliers to their player board and later in the game, tasked with scoring them in specific patterns while they attempt to complete sets.

Azul is what some would call an abstract strategy game. In the game, players take turns selecting tiles from sets of factory displays. On each player's turn, they pick a factory display and remove one type of tiles. Players must take all tiles of that color and place them on their player board. All tiles left in the factory display are then placed in the center of the board where the first player token is located. From this point, players may also select tiles from the center of the table instead of a factory display, and

the first player to do so acquires the first player token and places it on the floor line at the bottom of her player board. She goes first in the next round at a cost of -1 victory point during end-round scoring.

With their chosen tiles, players must select one of their five pattern lines into which the tiles are to be placed. Players may only ever have one type of tile in a pattern line at any given time, but more than one line may contain tiles of the same type. If a player takes more tiles than fit in the selected pattern line, leftovers must be placed in her floor, which costs her points at the end of the round. It's important to not have too many extras at the end of each round, as losing those points really does add up.

Players continue taking tiles in turn order until there are none left on the table. Players then score points by shifting tiles from their completed pattern lines onto their wall of tiles. Each row on the wall has only one space for each type of tile; all remaining tiles from the completed line are removed and set aside to a community discard pile, and players must pay careful attention to not put them back in the bag. Tiles in pattern lines that were not completed remain on the player's board and can be completed in future rounds.

Scoring is where the game gets especially interesting! Any tile, when placed, is always worth at least 1 point. However, with some planning, players have the potential to score many more by connecting them to other tiles. Check to see if there are one or more tiles linked either vertically or horizontally to the placed tile. Any tiles linked horizontally score 1 point for each linked tile. Then proceed to do the same for tiles linked vertically. If a tile links to others both vertically and horizontally then the player scores both of them.

Remember the floor line we talked about earlier? The floor line is a big old mess that each player has to spend time picking up at the end of each round. The more tiles a player has on his floor, the more points he loses. Players lose points for each tile in each spot in the floor line.

After scoring, players set up the next round by refilling the factory displays with random tiles drawn from the bag. The player who collected the first player marker that round returns it to the center of the table, and she begins the new selection phase.

Rounds continue until any one or more players have completed at least one horizontal line of five consecutive tiles on their wall during the scoring phase. At the end of the final round scoring, players collect additional points if they have achieved any of the bonus goals listed on their player board: +2 points for each row completed, +7 points for each column completed, and +10 points for each color of which they have placed all five tiles on their wall.

There is also a variant mode where players can flip over the game board to the gray side. The rules are exactly the same except that when a player moves a tile from a completed pattern line to his wall, he may place it on any space so long as no single tile type appears more than once in each of the five vertical lines on his wall.

ESSENTIAL

You might think that getting the most tiles is always the best move, but it's not! If you aren't able to place all of your tiles in one row, you might end up losing points for some of them!

EXPANSIONS

- Joker Tiles
  2017

Sushi Go

Release Date: 2013
Publisher: Gamewright
Designer: Phil Walker-Harding

Difficulty: ★ ★ ★ ★ ★   **Number of Players:** 2–5

Age Recommendation: 7+   **Play Time:** 10–20 minutes

 THE GOAL

Eat sushi to wind up with the most points.

 LET'S PLAY!

It's several hours past dinnertime and you are starving. What better to hit the spot than some scrumptious maki rolls, sashimi, and tempura? In Sushi Go, you take your favorite sushi delights and gobble them up. Players score points for each type of sushi in a different way. Some score more for having more of them; others need a certain number of sushi rolls; and in other cases, cards allow players to take more sushi rolls on a later turn.

To start the game, shuffle all of the cards together and then deal each player a number of cards based on the total number of players in the game, ranging between seven and ten total cards. Players hold the cards in their hand, secret from their opponents. Each turn players select a card and place it facedown in front of them. When all of the other players have selected the cards they want to draft, all players turn their hand faceup and leave it faceup in front of them.

Each of the cards scores in a unique way, leaving the players with plenty of tough decisions for the players to make, but once the players understand how each of the cards works, the pace of the game picks up dramatically. Maki rolls only score points for the two players at the end of the round with the most of them. The player with the very most Maki Rolls scores 6 points, and the player with the second most scores 3 points. Tempura scores in sets of two. If players only have one, they don't score. Sashimi scores in sets of three, and if players don't have at least three they are worth nothing. Dumplings score exponentially in that one is worth 1 point, two are worth 3 points, three are worth 6 points, four are worth 10 points, and five or more are worth a whopping 15 points! While there are many types of nigiri, they score between 1 and 3 points each, and their scores can be tripled if placed with a wasabi. Chopsticks aren't worth any points, but when a player has one in front of them on his turn he may yell, "Sushi Go!" and exchange it for an additional sushi card in his draft hand. There are also special cards that only score at the end of the game, like puddings. The player with the most of these at the end of all of three rounds gains 6 total points.

At the end of each round, players count up their points and the cards are discarded faceup beside the draw pile, excluding the pudding cards, which are kept until the end of the game. Each player is dealt a new hand of cards, and the drafting direction is reversed. It is reversed again at the end of each round played.

ALERT!

Hang on to the chopsticks until something awesome comes along, but don't hang on to them too long! They aren't worth any points at the end of a round. At the end of each round, the players tell the scorekeeper their scores, and at the end of three rounds, they are all added together along with the pudding points, and the player with the most points wins the game.

EXPANSIONS

- Sushi Go Party
2016

Cat Lady

Release Date: 2017

Publisher: Alderac Entertainment Group

Designer: Josh Wood

Difficulty: ✶ ✶ ✶ ✶ ✶

Age Recommendation: 8+

Number of Players: 2–4

Play Time: 15–30 minutes

 THE GOAL

Earn the most points by having the happiest, most well-fed cats.

 LET'S PLAY!

Some people love cats and others love dogs, but it takes a special kind of person to become a full-blown cat lady. The kind of cat lady who dresses them up, gives them all of the toys they could dream of, and feeds them until they can eat no more! Beware, though, the other players vie for the cats' affection as well, and the local strays have extra powerful abilities that score the best cat lady tons of points.

Before starting the game, it's important to know the different kinds of cards that you encounter throughout the game. In the game, there are cats, food, toys, catnip, spray bottles, costumes, and lost cat flyers. Cats score points at the end of the game, but only if they are properly fed with tuna, chicken, or milk. These can be moved from cat to cat during the game at any time as they only matter at the very end of the game. Toys score in sets, and there are five different kinds of toys. In order to complete a full 12-point set, you must gather each of the different kinds of toys. If you have fewer than that, you score fewer points. If you have multiples of the same toys, they count as a different set of toys entirely. It's possible but very difficult to have more than one complete set of toys. Catnip scores points based on the number of cats the player has fed with that catnip. If you only have one catnip, you lose points because the cats fight over the yummy kitty drug. The player with the most costumes at the end of the game gains 6 points because he has the best *Instagram* in town. If a player has no cat costumes, he loses 2 points at the end of the game. The lost cat flyers allow the players to adopt stray cats. Any time a player has at least two lost cat flyers, he may adopt one of the three faceup lost cats. These cats have special abilities that score based on the amount of food they are fed, the number of fed cats of a specific color, or even the types of food other cats have been fed. There are other special scoring mechanics, but let's not spoil all of them. After all, the exploration of games is half the fun!

To start the game, put out a 3-by-3 card grid with all nine of these cards visible. Give the first player the cat token and allow her to place it facing one row or column. The row or column of cards that the cat token is facing may never be taken, and any time a row or column of cards is taken, the cat is moved to facedown in that row or column. Thus a player cannot take all three of the freshly replenished cards. The exception to this is if you use the spray bottle, which allows you to spray and move the cat to any other row or column.

After the cat has been placed, the first player must take a row or column that the cat is not facing. She then takes those three cards and puts them in front of her, unless they are food cards, in which case the player should discard them and exchange them for food cubes to place on her cats.

After all of the cards have run out, the players arrange their cat food on their cats for optimal points. Any cats that are not fed run away and find better homes with the appropriate resources to take care of them. Players add together all of their cat points, toy points, catnip points, and costume points, and then trade in any two extra lost cat cards for 2 victory points each. The player with the most points is the most glorious cat lady and gets first dibs on cat pets for the rest of the evening!

DO I WANT TO GET ALL OF THE CATS?

No! It's important to strike just the right balance between having many cats and having enough food to feed them all. Cats at the end of the game who are not fed don't score the player any points.

EXPANSIONS

There are currently no expansions for this game.

7 Wonders

Difficulty: ★ ★ ★ ★ ★

Age Recommendation: 10+

Number of Players: 2–7

Play Time: 45 minutes

 THE GOAL

Have the most points at the end of three rounds.

 **LET'S PLAY!**

Short of Magic: The Gathering, 7 Wonders might be the most popular card-drafting game ever made. Not only have there been multiple official expansions but there is a two-player version called 7 Wonders Duel as well. There are even fan-made expansions for the game created by people who love the game so much they were inspired to add on to it themselves. On the surface, the game seems simple, but as the game unfurls, players start to realize the importance of their actions and the ways their decisions impact the other players. 7 Wonders might seem like a nice fun game at first until one of the players starts taking cards simply to spite others, giving the game an additional layer of complexity and entertainment value. Table talk is highly encouraged during a game of 7 Wonders.

The game starts in age one and is played through the end of age three. At the start of each age, players are dealt a hand of seven cards each from the appropriate age deck. Over the course of six game turns, the players select one card from their hand and place it facedown in front of them. Once all players have selected their card, players simultaneously reveal their selections.

WHEN TO PLAY:

- When you're just getting started with tabletop games

- When you're at your local game store

- When you're at a gaming convention

Release Date: 2010

Publisher: Repos Production & Asmodee

Designer: Antoine Bauza

CARD-DRAFTING GAMES

These selections can consist of one of seven total categories of cards, and each of them allows the players to benefit and score points from them in different ways. Raw materials doesn't give the players any points directly; however, it does give them resources that can be used to build other cards in the game. If ever a player is short on resources, she must pay her neighbor to use his resources at a cost of two coins. There are some commercial structures that allow the players to pay less for these resources. The manufactured goods work the same way, only they are far more scarce. The civilian structures typically have a higher cost but score many more victory points. There are also many of these that allow players to build future structures for free during the second and third ages. The military structures give the players points if they have a strength greater than their neighbors at the end of each age, and the rewards increase with each passing age. Scientific structures score victory points based on the three scientific fields; players will gain points for each set they have of these, and they'll gain even more points for having more of each scientific category. For one symbol in each set they'll score 1 point. For two they'll score 4 victory points. For three they'll gain 9 victory points, and for four they'll score a whopping 16 victory points. Finally, there are guilds, which score points according to very specific criteria listed on each individual card that players discover as they draft them. These are usually based on the cards in front of the players and reward them with either victory points or coins.

In front of each player sits a wonder, which players build in stages. The player takes the card of their choice from the hand of card's given to them and keeps it secret, then places it facedown underneath the section of the wonder he wishes to build. The cards text has no effect but the card itself serves as the foundation of the wonder. The wonder must be built in order from left to right. Each stage has a cost listed on it, and it must be paid before placing a card under that section of the wonder. Each stage gives the player a reward as a result of paying its cost. If building a part of the wonder doesn't appeal to the players they can always discard any card on their turn to gain three coins.

EXPANSIONS

- Leaders
  2011

- Cities
  2012

- Babel
  2014

- Armada
  2018

Century: Spice Road

Difficulty: ★ ★ ★ ★ ★

Age Recommendation: 10+

Number of Players: 2–5

Play Time: 45 minutes

WHEN TO PLAY:

- When it's time for a little competition

- When you're having a game night

- When you feel like adventure

Release Date: 2017
Publisher: Plan B Games
Designer: Emerson Matsuuchi

 THE GOAL

Have the most points after a player has claimed his fifth victory point card.

 LET'S PLAY!

Century Spice Road surprised everyone with its success in 2017 as the first game debuted by Plan B Games, who went on to create a series of increasingly successful games. They have consistently impressed gamers with their quality production value, well-designed games, and stunning artwork by Fernanda Suárez, a famed artist who worked on highly successful games such as Dead of Winter. Following the first game came a second, Century: Eastern Wonders, and a third game that is expected to debut sometime in 2019–2020. All of these games are designed to use an engine-building system, which leads to endless possibilities with strategies and decisions to be made.

Between all of the players sits a flourishing marketplace ripe with trades to be made for the goods that players barter for. At the start of the game, each player is given two cards to form her hand, and players are given appropriate resources depending on their starting position. The bowls of cinnamon, cardamom, saffron, and turmeric are placed within arms' reach of all of the players

CARD-DRAFTING GAMES

so they can easily exchange their goods for better ones in the future. Of the two cards, the players start with one that allows them to upgrade their goods one tier twice, meaning they can either upgrade two goods once, or they may upgrade one good twice. Players upgrade their goods throughout the game or simply acquire new ones by playing the cards from their hand, which produces goods for them.

On their turn, a player can take one of four actions:

1. Play a card from her hand.
2. Acquire a merchant card from the available faceup cards.
3. Take all of her previously played cards back to her hand.
4. Exchange the goods in her caravan to acquire a point card.

Each player has a caravan in front of her, which is only capable of holding a total of ten goods. The player may never exceed ten total goods in her caravan, and if she has more than ten at the end of her turn she must return spices of her choice into the bowls until her limit is reached.

When a player uses a card from his hand he simply takes the goods listed on the card unless it's an upgrade card, in which case he may exchange the goods listed on the card for another type of good. This is made clear by a one-way arrow between the two goods. Most importantly, the player can exchange any number of goods this way. If the card lists two turmeric for two saffron, he may do this as many times as he likes provided he has the turmeric to make the exchange. When the player chooses to acquire a card from the center of the table he may acquire the card on the far left for free. Every card placed right of the far-left card costs one additional spice of any kind, and they are placed on the card passed by. The players who take those cards in the future also gain any spices on top of the card they are taking.

If the player doesn't see any cards on the table he is interested in, he might choose to rest. Any time someone plays a card from his hand, it's placed faceup in front of him until he chooses to take the rest action, at which point all of those cards are placed back into his hand. If they find themselves with enough spices to claim a card for points, players must return all of the listed goods from their caravan to the supply and then take the point card, placing it facedown in front of them. After claiming it, they refill the space with another card from the deck. If a player claims the leftmost or second-leftmost point cards, he gains bonus points accordingly.

Once any one player has claimed her fifth or sixth card, depending on the player count, the game ends and the players add up all of their points. Each non-yellow cube left in their caravan is worth 1 point as well. The player with the most points wins the game.

Century Spice Road looks simple on the surface but is the perfect game to introduce new players to engine-building games after they've been introduced to the idea of card drafting. This is a perfect next step after a game like Sushi Go or Cat Lady.

EXPANSIONS

- Century:
  Golem Edition
  2017

- Century:
  Eastern Wonders
  2018

- Century:
  A New World
  2019

Fields of Green

WHEN TO PLAY:

• When you want to play something challenging

• When you're having a game night

• When it's time for a little competition

Release Date: 2016

Publisher: Stronghold Games & Artipia Games

Designer: Vangelis Bagiartakis

Difficulty: ✷ ✷ ✷ ✷ ✷

Age Recommendation: 12+

Number of Players: 2–4

Play Time: 60 minutes

 THE GOAL

Build up your farm so you're the player at the end of the game with the most points.

 **LET'S PLAY!**

Fields of Green takes place on a luscious green farm in the second half of the twentieth century. Players take on the roles of farm owners trying to expand their property and businesses by adding fields, livestock, and facilities in an attempt to build a viable economic engine. The game takes place over four years, during which players draft cards and add them to their farm. The placement of the cards is everything because come the harvest season the players' fields must be watered and their livestock fed. Players compete to be the most wealthy and successful farmer in this card-drafting and engine-building game.

Fields of Green is far from a simple game. However, it brings a short play time, easy-to-explain rules, and complex game play together to form a delightfully well-rounded gaming experience. In this game players draft cards for their farm: buildings, constructions, crops, and livestock. Each type of card offers something unique ranging from money, wheat, water, or points. These cards interact heavily with the cards around them so their placement is of the utmost importance.

Players begin the game with fifteen coins, a full water tower, and a grain silo with two wheat tokens. At the start of each round after the first, players receive one wheat token, two water, and three coins. Then each player takes six cards total from at least three different categories of cards. In a game with three or more players each player selects one card from his hand and then passes it to his left in rounds one and three, and to his right in rounds two and four.

In a game with just two players, at the start of each round, all of the cards the players have selected are shuffled together without looking at them and six are placed faceup on the table. Players take them one at a time from the available cards. When there are four or fewer cards, the players add in two additional cards from the ones they shuffled together.

It's important to keep careful track of the number of coins, water, and wheat each player acquires during the game. For example, water towers in the game only have a reach of two fields unless they've been upgraded with a tool. This means they can only water fields two cards away from them. The placement of cards in the game is critical.

Tools can be used on a variety of cards, and each tool card states on it exactly what kind of card it can be played on and when it activates. These add special bonuses such as additional resources, money, points, or special abilities. When a card allows a player to take a tool, she draws three tools off the stack and selects one of them to add to her farm. Tools show the type of card they are placed on and can either be placed immediately or held onto and added as the player puts down a new card. Each card can only hold one tool at a time. It's important to read them carefully and not forget to apply their effects, especially if they grant the players points.

If players don't like any of their card choices, they can also choose to throw a card away and take two coins for selling a card

ESSENTIAL
Some cards have instant effects that come into play immediately, requiring players to pay their cost right away to receive the benefit of that card.

- Fields of Green:
  Grand Fair
  2018

FACT

The rise of Magic: The Gathering beginning in 1993 led to a wave of other collectible card games. One of the more popular was Vampire: The Eternal Struggle, published by White Wolf. It concerned a conflict between a group of vampire clans and was later made into a short–lived TV series.

instead. Players can also sell up to two wheat for two coins each at the same time. Alternatively, players can spend two coins and throw a card away to build an empty grain silo or a full water tower, which players need, as growing a farm is no easy task.

At the end of each round is the harvest phase. This means players need to pay water, wheat, and money to upkeep their buildings and use their abilities. If they fail to activate their abilities, that card is then flipped over and cannot be used again until they repair it.

The player at the end of four years who gathers the most victory points is the winner.

TAKE THAT!:

DIRECT ATTACK GAMES

Vengeance. It feels splendid but isn't right for every occasion—unless, of course, that occasion is over a friendly rivalry in a board game. In this chapter, you're going to learn all about the perfect games to settle squabbles with good friends and family members. These games walk a line between skill and luck but still give the players just enough power to really mess with each other. Direct attack games are often referred to as "take that" games because one might say, "Ha! Take that!" while performing actions within the game play.

The games covered in this chapter tend to be on the simpler side. However, they cover a wide range of other mechanics and genres from party games like Cash 'n Guns to strategy games like Battle Line. The one trait they all share is the way that players interact with each other: viciously! These games can be highly confrontational and are not for the faint of heart. Expect that you attack others and that you are being attacked by the other players, so brace yourselves for some playful antagonism.

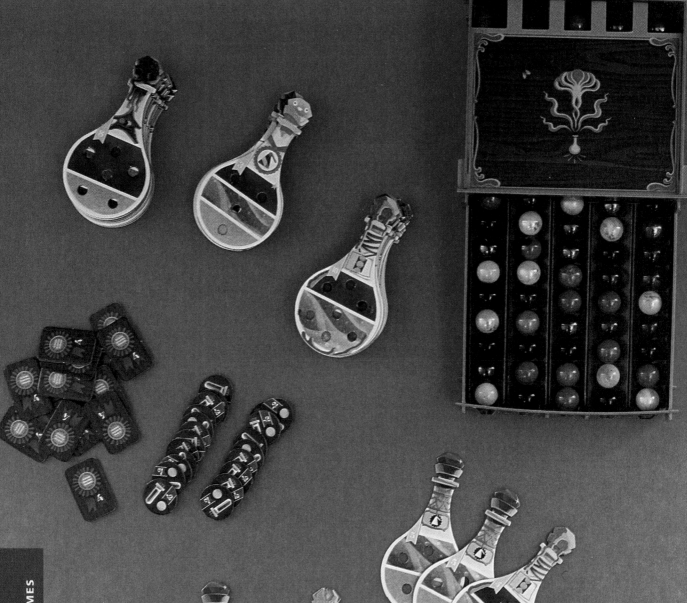

Potion Explosion

Difficulty: ✶ ✶ ✶ ✶ ✶

Age Recommendation: 8+

Number of Players: 2–4

Play Time: 45–60 minutes

 THE GOAL

Be the player with the most points after one player has the required number of skill tokens causing the game to end.

LET'S PLAY!

Many board games have great game play, but fewer board games have innovative and captivating mechanics along with experimental components. Potion Explosion was quite the game changer when it came on the scene with its highly original marble dispenser. The marble dispenser consists of five marble columns and players take marbles from it, causing wild explosions of other marbles and gaining ingredients to concoct their potions, which they use for their own gain or even their opponents' downfall!

To set up the game, put the marble dispenser between all of the players, as they all need to be able to reach the dispenser to take their ingredients off it. Each player starts the game with two potions and a desk board. His goal is to gain as many points as possible by completing the potions in front of him and then replacing them with new ones.

Each potion has specific ingredients that it needs to be completed. The players gain these ingredients by taking a single

WHEN TO PLAY:

- When you're at your local game store

- When the whole family is around

- When you're at a dinner party

Release Date: 2015

Publisher: CMON

Designers: Stefano Castelli, Andrea Crespi, and Lorenzo Silva

DIRECT ATTACK GAMES

ingredient marble from the dispenser. Their goal is to take more than just the one ingredient by making other ingredients of the same colors collide with each other, making them explode so that they may be taken too. Any time two marbles of the same color run into each other in the marble tray they "explode," allowing the players to take them along with any other marbles that also explode as a result of the marbles being removed from the tray. The bigger the explosions, the faster the players are able to brew their potions. There are eight different kinds of potions, and each of them has its own powers. No explosions are triggered because of any of these potions being used.

1. The **Potion of Wisdom** allows the player who made it to take an ingredient from the dispenser.
2. The **Potion of Magnetic Attraction** allows the player to take two vertically adjacent ingredients of different colors from the dispenser.
3. **Abyssal Draft** allows the player to take one ingredient of each color from the bottom row if they are available. They may only take one ingredient from each slide track.
4. The **Balm of Uttermost Sickness** allows the player to take two or more adjacent ingredients of the same color from the same slide track of the dispenser.
5. The **Elixir of Blind Love** allows a player to steal all of the ingredients from an opponent's extra pool of ingredients, which is a three-marble space on the players' desk board positioned for holding extra ingredients they cannot yet fit in their potions.
6. The **Potion of Prismatic Joy** allows the player to place all of his ingredients in that pool onto any holes of his incomplete potions, ignoring the color restrictions.
7. The **Sands of Time** allow a player to activate again the effect of one of his used-up potions.

ESSENTIAL

Each potion requires between four and seven ingredients. These are represented by holes in the potion tiles and are filled with the corresponding ingredient color needed.

8. The **Filter of Lavamancing** allows a player to discard up to five ingredients of one color from the same slide track of the dispenser and throw them back into the tank! Remember, once a potion is used, it's flipped upside down and then only used again if activated by the Sands of Time. It's only worth points after being used.

Each potion is worth a certain number of points, which depend on the ingredients needed to complete it and the strength of the ability it grants. As the players complete these potions they are also granted bonus points based on the kinds of potions they acquire. If they complete three potions with the same power or five potions all with different powers, they receive a skill token, which is worth four additional points that be added to their total score at the end of the game. There are a limited number of skill tokens placed in the game. When they are gone, the beginning of the end is here. There are between four and six skill tokens, depending on the player count. When the last one of these is taken, the players get an equal number of turns and then the game is over.

EXPANSIONS

There are currently no expansions for this game.

Cash 'n Guns

Release Date: 2005
Publisher: Repos Productions
Designer: Ludovic Maublanc

WHEN TO PLAY:

- When it's time for a little competition
- When you're having a game night
- When you want to learn more about your gaming friends

Difficulty: ★ ★ ★ ★ ★

Age Recommendation: 13+

Number of Players: 4–8

Play Time: 30 minutes

 **THE GOAL**

Have the most wealth at the end of the game.

 **LET'S PLAY!**

The more the merrier, they say, and in Cash 'n Guns we mean it! In this game players are tasked with splitting the loot. That's because between the players sits a fat stack of goodies: gemstones, cash, artwork, and more. Players fight over the loot, and those who survive reap the rewards and stacks of stuff. Be careful who you tick off; it might come back to shoot you in the cash.

At the start of the game, each player is given five click cards and three bang cards. Throughout the duration of the game, you point your foam guns at another player, giving her the choice to either walk away, or potentially take a bullet in the name of hijinks and heists! These cards are limited and once used they are discarded, so it's important to keep that in mind when pointing your foam gun at another player. Each player selects one of them, places it facedown in front of her, and then points her foam gun at another player. The player who currently has the desk in front of him is the boss, and he gets to point one person's gun away from a player—usually himself, but it could be anyone. He doesn't get to choose whom the player picks as the new target; he simply gets to tell that player to move it.

After everyone has their target, each player who has a foam gun pointed at him decides if he lies down and is out of the round, or is brave and stays in the game, risking being wounded by another player's gunshot! Any player who has her gun pointed at another player who chooses to be brave reveals his bullet card! If it's a click, nothing happens; however, if a boom is revealed, the player who has the gun pointed at him receives a wound and is put out for the round, unable to receive any of the treasures. If a player ever has three total wounds, he is eliminated from the game.

All surviving brave players, whether they had no guns pointed at them or simply clicks pointed at them, split the loot in the middle. Starting with the boss player sitting behind the desk, each player takes one loot in clockwise order.

There is straight cash worth between $5k and $20k, there are diamonds worth between $1k and $5k, and there is art that is worth more money if you have more art starting at $4k and going all the way up to $500k, and last there is the desk card, which allows a player to take the boss role during the next round if you flip the desk and it lands desk-side up. The player with the most diamonds at the end of the game receives a $60k bonus. The player with the most money at the end of the game is the winner!

EXPANSIONS

- More Cash 'n More Guns
  2015

- Team Spirit
  2016

Unstable Unicorns

WHEN TO PLAY:

- When you want a game you can carry with you

- When you want something fun and easy

- When the whole family is around

Release Date: 2017
Publisher: Breaking Games
Designer: Ramy Badie

Difficulty: ✶ ✶ ✶ ✶ ✶

Age Recommendation: 10+

Number of Players: 2–8

Play Time: 30–45 minutes

THE GOAL

Be the first player to gather six or seven unicorns, depending on the player count, and become the righteous ruler of all things magical!

 LET'S PLAY!

Start the game with an adorable baby unicorn, but don't get too attached because no unicorn is safe in this game! Collect as many unicorns as you can, but be wary because your friends are out to destroy them. Seek revenge on your friends, all while working hard to protect your own stable.

Each player is given a baby unicorn to start her unicorn army. Each magical unicorn has special powers, and is not to be underestimated! Players use unicorn upgrades and downgrades to protect and build their stable or attack the other players. The instant cards in their hand helps them stop other players from messing with them. The first person to complete his unicorn army wins the game.

To set up the game, the players gather all of the baby unicorns, shuffle them, and then deal one out to every player. The starting player is the one who is wearing the unicorniest colors.

On each player's turn he starts by checking the cards in his hand to see if any say, "At the beginning of your turn." If they do, he may use the effect on that card at this time. If he forgets to do it before he draws, he misses out on using its effect this turn. He draws one card from the draw pile. Then he enters the action phase and decides if he should play one card from his hand or draw an additional card from the draw pile. He may only do one of these two things. At the end of his turn, he must discard down to seven cards in hand if he has more than that.

There are three different kinds of unicorns within the game. There are baby unicorns, with which everyone starts the game. During the game, they can only be summoned by using special cards. There are basic unicorns, which are placed in a stable on a player's turn and don't have any special powers. They are still special despite loving pumpkin spice lattes. Finally, there are magical unicorns, which come with a special power that can aid the player in her efforts to win the game.

There are other cards that go far beyond unicorns. Magic cards can be played on a player's turn to create mayhem. These are sent to the discard pile after they are used. Upgrades allow players to give unicorns in someone's stable a positive effect, while downgrades give someone's stable a negative effect. There are also instant cards that can be played at any time to stop another player from playing a card, and these do not need to be played on a player's turn; they are played in response to other players' playing cards.

There are specific words you need to be aware of in the game. Cards currently in a player's stable are "in play," and if a player brings a card directly into play, it does not count as her action! If a player sacrifices another unicorn, she sends a card from her stable to the discard pile. If she destroys a unicorn, she sends a card from another player's stable to the discard pile. If she discards a unicorn, she sends a card from her hand to the discard pile.

FACT

Unstable Unicorns raised more than $1,800,000 on Kickstarter.

In a two- to five-player game, the players only need seven unicorns at the end of their turn to win the game. In a six- to eight-player game, the players only need six unicorns at the end of their turn to win the game. With all of that said, there are special rules for players if no one wins the game before running out of cards.

If you are a stickler, the game ends when there are no cards left and nobody gets to be the righteous ruler of all things magical! If you are a rule-breaker, you can reshuffle the discard pile back into the deck. If you are a baby unicorn, the game ends when you flip the table. Nobody likes a baby unicorn.

Battle Line (Schotten Totten)

Difficulty: ✳ ✳ ✳ ✳ ✳   **Number of Players:** 2

Age Recommendation: 10+   **Play Time:** 30 minutes

 **THE GOAL**

Be the first player to claim three flags in a row or five total flags on the battlefield.

 **LET'S PLAY!**

Between the players sit nine flags waiting to be claimed in glorious battle. Players create formations of cards in an effort to claim the flags in front of them. The catch is that in order to claim a flag they must prove beyond a shadow of a doubt that they are beating the player's formation and not using the cards in their hand but solely using the cards currently on the battlefield. Players take turns playing cards onto the battlefield one card at a time. After they've played a card on their turn, they draw to replace the card. They may either draw from the troop deck or the tactics deck.

The troop deck is made up of sixty cards. There are six different-colored cards, and each color has numbered cards from one to ten in them. These are the cards that players are playing to create troop formations on the board. The highest value is ten and the lowest is one. The players only create three card formations unless otherwise specified by tactics cards. The best card formation is a wedge using three cards of the same color and consecutive values; for example, three blue cards made up of a seven, eight,

WHEN TO PLAY:

- When it's time for a little competition

- When you're at your local game store

- When you're at a gaming convention

Release Date: 2000

Publisher: GMT Games (Iello Games)

Designer: Reiner Knizia

DIRECT ATTACK GAMES

and nine. The only formation that could beat that formation would be a wedge of a higher value consisting of an eight, nine, and ten. The second-highest card formation is a phalanx: three cards of the same value; for example, three cards that are all nines of three different colors. The third-highest formation is three cards of the same color. After that is three cards of consecutive values but not necessary matching values. Any other formation is fine, but the higher the cards, the higher the ranking.

Players may only claim cards at the start of their next turn. In order to claim a flag, they must compare their card formation to the other player's current cards and cross-reference it with the other cards on the table. If a player can prove beyond a shadow of a doubt that her card formation is better than the other player's card formation, she may claim that flag. When she does, the flag moves over to their side and it is claimed. It can no longer be taken by the other player. No player may play any more cards on that formation, which means at times it might be a good idea to dump dead cards in your hand onto a card formation that you know is soon going to be claimed.

The tactics deck is made up of ten cards that should be played strategically. A player can only ever play one more tactics card than his opponent has played, so it's important to not fill your hand with tactics cards. There are three kinds of tactics cards: guile, environment, and morale.

Morale cards consist of two leaders, Alexander and Darius, as well as companion cavalry and shield bearers. The leaders act as wild cards and can be any card even if that card is already in play. However, each player may only play one, meaning that if one player draws both of them, he is out of luck and stuck with a dead card in his hand for the rest of the game. The color and number are defined as the flag resolves. The companion cavalry can be played like any troop card, but it always has a value of eight. Its color is defined as the flag resolves. The shield bearers play like any troop card, but their color can be anything, and their value cannot be larger than three when the flag resolves.

The environment tactics cards are played faceup on the player's side near an unclaimed flag, leaving enough space for tactics cards. When played, an environment card stays in its place until the end of the game. There are two of these, fog and mud. Fog disables all card formations and merely decides the winner of that flag based on the total value on each side of the flag. Mud cards are based on four cards on either side, meaning the card formations are based on four cards instead of three.

Guile tactics are played faceup on the player's own side next to the tactics card deck. All cards played must be visible and remain there until the end of the game. There are four of these: the scout, redeploy, deserter, and traitor. The scout allows the player to draw a total of three cards from either or both decks. Then the player chooses two cards from his hand and places them facedown on top of his respective deck or decks. Redeploy allows the player to choose any troop or tactics card from her side next to an unclaimed flag and place it faceup into another of her available slots, or discard it faceup on her side next to the tactics deck. Deserter allows the player to take any one troop or tactics card from the opponent's side next to an unclaimed flag and place it faceup on the opponent's side next to the tactics card deck. The traitor card allows the player to choose any one troop card from the opponent's side next to an unclaimed flag and place it into an empty slot on his own side.

The first player to gather five total flags or three consecutive flags wins the game.

FACT

Battle Line was published in 2000. It was later republished by Iello Games under the title Schotten Totten using fewer cards with similar formations. The game play is identical; however, in Battle Line the cards run one through ten instead of one through nine and the players hold seven cards in their hands instead of six. The tactics cards in Schotten Totten have iconography. The tactics cards in Battle Line spell out the actions.

EXPANSIONS

There are currently no expansions for this game.

URSULA'S LAIR

ERIC'S SHIP

THE SHORE

OBJECTIVE
...r turn with the
...and the Crown
...rsula's Lair

MALEFICENT

FORBIDDEN MOUNTAINS

BRIAR ROSE'S COTTAGE

THE FORES...

MALEFICENT'S
OBJECTIVE
Start your turn with a Curse
at each location.

JAFAR

SULTAN'S PALACE

STREETS OF AGRABAH

Villainous

Difficulty: ✶ ✶ ✶ ✶ ✶

Age Recommendation: 10+

Number of Players: 2–6

Play Time: 60 minutes

Release Date: 2018
Publisher: Wonder Forge
Designer: Prospero Hall

 ## THE GOAL

Complete your character's specific winning condition to win the game immediately!

 ## LET'S PLAY!

Take on the role of a Disney villain! To win the game you must explore your character's unique abilities and discover how to accomplish your story-based objective. Each villain guide gives the players hot strategies and tips. There are six villains, meaning there is plenty to explore and tons of playability.

First, select one of the six main villains: Captain Hook, Jafar, Maleficent, Prince John, the Queen of Hearts, and Ursula. Each player is then given his villain deck, consisting of thirty cards, and his fate deck, consisting of fifteen cards. The cauldron is set in the center with the power tokens, lock tokens, and fate token. Each player is given a reference card and a villain guide to match the character he selected. Then each player puts the lock token on the right-most location in front of him that has a lock symbol in its corner. Each player's player board has four locations on it, which he moves to and from throughout the game in order to take his actions.

WHEN TO PLAY:

- When you feel like adventure
- When the whole family is around
- When you need to relax

SCIMITAR

Attach Scimitar to an Ally.
That Ally gets +1 Strength.

Item

Effect

Each player starts the game with a hand of cards, as specified in his villain guide according to the character he chooses. Each player has a unique objective as well, and none of the universes interact with each other.

On his turn, a player moves his villain and then performs the actions at that location. Each player has a chunky, transparent villain pawn that cannot be moved to a locked location. On his turn he moves it to a different location and performs the actions listed on it. At times, actions are covered by cards like heroes, causing them to be unusable, meaning the player moving his pawn may only take two of the four actions listed on that location. That's okay, because not all of them are needed all the time. After completing his actions if the player has fewer than four cards in hand he draws cards from the villain deck. Then the turn passes to the next player.

There are eight different types of actions and they appear appropriately on different players' boards depending on the villain's objectives:

1. The first one is **gain power**, which allows the player to take a number of power tokens from the cauldron.
2. Next up is **play a card**, which allows the player to play a card from his hand.
3. **Activate** allows the player to choose one ally and activate a symbol on it after paying the cost shown, then he performs the ability.
4. The **move an item or ally action** allows the player to do just that, move an ally from one unlocked location to an adjacent unlocked location.
5. **Move a hero** allows the player to move a hero from one unlocked location to an adjacent location.
6. **Vanquish** allows the villain to discard a hero in his realm by discarding any number of allies and item cards below the same location.

7. **Discard cards** allows the player to get rid of as many cards as he likes from his hand but not draw up immediately.

8. Finally, there is the **fate action** that allows the player to choose one opponent and then reveal two cards from his fate deck and play one of them to his realm. If neither can be played, they are simply discarded. These are designed to thwart the players and cover up valuable action spaces at various locations.

Captain Hook's goal is to defeat Peter Pan at the *Jolly Roger*. In order to accomplish this he must unlock the Hangman's Tree location by playing the Neverland Map, then Peter Pan must be played by him or an opponent to Hangman's Tree. Then Peter must be moved to Mermaid Lagoon, then Skull Rock, and finally to the *Jolly Roger*, where he must be defeated for Hook to win the game. Hangman's Tree starts out as locked so it has to be unlocked before Peter appears.

Maleficent needs to start her turn with a curse at each location. A curse is a type of card unique to Maleficent, and these cards are played to location. Each one has an ability that affects heroes at that location. However, each curse also has an action that causes it to be discarded, so the player needs to strategize when and where to play each curse. They can be moved using items or ally actions.

Prince John needs to start his turn with at least twenty power because he's oh so greedy! Just remember, in order to make money, one must spend money. Heroes can hinder John's ability to gain power, so it's a good idea to play allies, even before any heroes have been played. By doing so, Prince John is more prepared to vanquish a hero that is impeding his progress.

Jafar wants exactly what you'd expect him to want, to become an all-powerful genie. To win the game, Jafar must start his turn with the magic lamp at the Sultan's Palace and the genie must be under his control. To achieve this, Jafar must unlock the Cave of

> **ESSENTIAL**
>
> At no point in this game do the Disney characters' words interact with each other directly. Instead, players play "fate" cards that take place in that character's universe, thwarting their plans and covering up the actions they can take.

Wonders with the scarab pendant, which can be found in his deck. Then, the magic lamp must be played to the Cave of Wonders, which brings the genie to the same location. Then Jafar must hypnotize the genie to put him under a spell and then move the magic lamp to the Sultan's Palace.

The Queen of Hearts needs to successfully have a wicket at each location and successfully take a shot to win the game. She has some cards with activated abilities that make this easier for her by giving her more power, and thus more ability to manipulate the board state.

Ursula is tasked with starting her turn with the trident and the crown at her lair. To win, the trident and the crown must be on the player's side of the board. The palace starts locked, so that will need to be unlocked before the player can complete her objective.

EXPANSIONS

- Villainous: Wicked to the Core

Smash Up

Difficulty: ★ ★ ★ ★ ★

Age Recommendation: 10+

Number of Players: 2–4

Play Time: 45–60 minutes

Release Date: 2012

Publisher: Alderac Entertainment Group

Designer: Paul Peterson

 THE GOAL

Destroy bases and earn points! Earn 15 points and you win the game!

 LET'S PLAY!

Rather than a deck-building game, where you start with a small deck and add cards to it to customize your experience as you play, Smash Up uses two premade faction decks, which the player combines into one. You then use this new deck to play actions and send minions to bases (cards with thresholds and point values that everyone is competing over) to try to score the most points, in an area-control style.

The original Smash Up comes with eight factions—aliens, dinosaurs, ninjas, pirates, robots, tricksters, wizards, and zombies— each with different play styles and abilities that are thematically linked to their character. For example, the dinosaur deck has a lot of high-strength minion cards but not a lot of sneaky abilities, while the zombies have a number of action cards that allow discarded cards to come back into your hand (risen from the dead, if you will). Before the game begins, each player chooses two factions from these eight, which she shuffles together to make the forty-card deck she plays for the game. The base cards are shuffled

EXPANSIONS

- Awesome Level 9000
  2013

- The Obligatory
  Cthulhu Set
  2013

- Cease & Desist
  2016

- Big In Japan
  2017

- That 70s Expansion
  2018

- Oops, You Did It Again
  2018

together and dealt to the table—one more than the number of players. Each player draws five cards from her deck, checks to make sure she has at least one minion (if not, she can discard it and draw a new hand), and the start player begins.

On every turn, you may play one minion and/or one action, in any order. Minions are played in front of bases and count toward a threshold value that eventually triggers the scoring of a base. At that point the value of the base is scored by the players who contributed to its destruction. Many minions also have abilities that may augment your own minions, affect other players' minions, or affect the bases at which they are played. Action cards vary in effect but are generally not attached to specific bases. They may let you draw more cards, or mess with other players, or allow you to retrieve cards from your discard pile.

Play continues until a base reaches its threshold value. At the end of a player's turn when this happens, evaluate who contributed the most to that base. There are first-, second-, and third-place points that are doled out by contribution. There are no points awarded for fourth place. That base is discarded and a new one replaces it from the base deck. Once one player has reached 15 points, the game is over and she is declared the winner!

The different combinations of factions can lead to some really crazy combo opportunities. Some decks are very action-focused, and others have more minion-based powers, so combining one from each can lead to a pretty strong deck. Some factions favor certain play styles over others, like the ninja and pirate factions; both have a lot of manipulation abilities in the bases and the other players themselves. There is a very large degree of variability in terms of the experience due to all of the different pairs of factions in the base game, and even more once you start to add in expansion factions!

FUN FOR EVERYONE:
PARTY GAMES

Everyone seems to have played a party game, whether it's charades (1550), Pictionary (1985), or Scattergories (1988). Charades is one of the most well-known party games unless you count games like bingo or lotto. Liar's Dice (1800) is still popular today and was even recently given a simplified reprint called Fluff by the Bananagrams company. What sets party games apart from everything else is their ability to get people riled up, moving around, having gut-busting conversations, and making idle threats to each other in jest.

Party games can likely be credited for tabletop gaming having any visibility. They tend to have simplified rules, which are as easy to learn as they are fun to play. The game play is typically incredibly fast, under an hour, and due to their lack of time commitment they really are perfect for bringing out at any occasion. Party games are perfect for everything from holiday gatherings to conventions. Do you have a company party you're really dreading attending? Bring a party game. Be the hero that everyone needs and give them something to do that isn't dreadful small talk. Here are the perfect games to bring to your next family gathering, birthday party, or social situation that no one was prepared for.

Dixit

Difficulty: ✶ ✶ ✶ ✶ ✶

Age Recommendation: 8+

Number of Players: 3–6

Play Time: 30 minutes

WHEN TO PLAY:

- When you're at a dinner party
- When you love solving puzzles
- When you're in a tabletop game marathon

Release Date: 2008
Publisher: Libellud/Asmodee
Designer: Jean-Louis Roubira

 ## THE GOAL

Be farthest on the scoring track at the end of the game.

 ## LET'S PLAY!

Dixit is a game about telling stories, but it is not really a storytelling game. Players need to have a vivid imagination, an appreciation for whimsy, and a penchant for mind reading. It's a game about making associations, but they can't be too obvious or too obscure. Playing Dixit is a little bit like walking a tightrope, only instead of being suspended dozens of feet above the ground, you need to come up with something clever to say about a picture of a bride and groom in a birdcage being dangled above a cat.

To start the game, six cards are dealt to each player. Each player chooses a colored wooden rabbit to use as her score-tracking pawn and places it on the zero space of the score track. One player is chosen as the "Storyteller" for the turn, looks at her hand of six cards, and chooses one of them for the round. Without showing the card to the other players, she makes up a sentence or phrase about the card and says it aloud. Every other player chooses a card from their hand that they think best matches this sentence and slides it facedown to the Storyteller, who shuffles them up with her own and then lays them faceup in a row. The other players

EXPANSIONS

- Dixit: Quest
  2010

- Dixit: Odyssey
  2011

- Dixit: Journey
  2012

- Dixit: Origins
  2013

- Dixit: Daydreams
  2014

- Dixit: Memories
  2015

- Dixit: Revelations
  2016

- Dixit: Harmonies
  2017

now choose from their numbered tiles which card they think was the Storyteller's (the cards being numbered one, two, three, etc. from left to right). Once all players have chosen a number tile and placed it facedown in front of them, all players flip and reveal their choices.

Scoring depends on how many people correctly guess the Storyteller's card. If all players have figured it out or none of them managed to, then the Storyteller scores 0 points and all other players score 2. She was clearly not a very good Storyteller. If one or more (but not all) players guess the correct card, the Storyteller scores 3 points, as does every player who correctly guessed it. Any player who was not the Storyteller but who managed to secure guesses from other players gets 1 point for each vote for his card. Players move their adorable wooden bunnies along the score track equal to the points they earn for the round.

Everybody draws a new card (so they once more have six in their hand), and the player to the left of the previous round's Storyteller becomes the new Storyteller. Rounds continue until the last card has been drawn from the deck, and the player whose bunny is farthest along the track wins!

Pantone: The Game

Difficulty: ✶ ✶ ✶ ✶   **Number of Players:** 2–20

Age Recommendation: 8+   **Play Time:** 15–30 minutes

 ## THE GOAL

Create iconic characters in order to be the player at the end of the game with the most points!

 ## LET'S PLAY!

In the 1990s Scott Rogers worked in video game design and video game art. His first games were for the Super Nintendo and the Sega Genesis. He even taught himself how to make pixel art, playing Sonic the Hedgehog and other similar games so much that he started to see things in pixels. He eventually moved into game design. He had played games like Pictionary and was especially good at these kinds of games with his art background. Upon playing this, he realized that his friends were somewhat intimidated by the game play. Several years later, he was working on multiple board games—one that took a while to explain and another colorful checker-boarded game. He was quickly reminded of his pixel art days and went to his kid's room, grabbed the construction paper, and thought to himself, "There might be a game here!"

Scott went on to show Cryptozoic Entertainment several of his games at a board game convention but didn't think that his game, at the time named Who's Hue?, would be a great fit. However, the

Release Date: 2018
Publisher: Cryptozoic Entertainment
Designer: Scott Rogers

WHEN TO PLAY:

- When you're in a large group
- When you want something fun and easy
- When you're at a dinner party

PARTY GAMES

team asked to see the game anyway. At the time Cory Jones, the CEO of Cryptozoic, had been wanting to make a Pantone game for some time; however, he wasn't certain of the direction he wanted to take the game design. When Scott sat down to show him Who's Hue?, there was a perfect marriage between Cory's idea and Scott's game design. The lesson here is that anything can be turned into a game. Always bring all of your games to show off. You never know when everything is going to perfectly come together.

Pantone is a party game where players are tasked with using solid-colored cards to re-create iconic characters by arranging them on the table in front of them with a limited amount of time. There are four copies of each color swatch card, and they're available to all of the players. The character cards are randomized and shuffled, and then each player is given four of these. You discard one of them. The other three are the characters you need to create on the table, hoping the other players can guess them accurately!

To start the game the artist that round chooses one of the three characters in her hand and places the other two cards to the side; these are used in future rounds. Then she looks at it, remembers it, and keeps it secret from the other players. She can reference it at any time. Then a player sets a one-minute timer and uses the color swatch cards to create a representation of the character card chosen. She may stop before the time runs out but must stop at the one-minute mark. During the first round, she may use as many of the Pantone cards as she likes. Then all players must guess, starting with the player to the left of the artist, what the artist was attempting to depict. They are limited to just five seconds, and if a player fails to come up with a guess or guesses incorrectly, then the player to the first guessing player's left takes a guess. This continues clockwise until each nonartist has had a chance to guess. If one of the players guesses correctly, both the artist and the player are given points based on the clue number on the card.

If none of the players correctly guess the first time around during the no-hint round, the artist gives the first hint on her character card and every player receives another opportunity to guess. This continues until a player correctly guesses the character or the players fail to guess the character after the fourth and final hint is given.

The game takes place over three phases using all three of the cards the players selected. The game difficulty increases as it goes on:

1. In the **first phase**, the artist can use all of her color swatch cards.
2. In the **second phase**, the artist can only use one of each color swatch card to create her character.
3. In the **third phase**, the artist can only use three swatch cards total, regardless of her color selection.

Once a player has guessed correctly, points are awarded to the person guessing as well as to the artist who made the "painting." The points are based on the number of hints given, and they decrease with the number of hints. After they are scored, the player to her left becomes the new artist and is given the color swatch tray. The game ends when every player has created three characters.

EXPANSIONS

There are currently no expansions for this game.

Red Flags

Release Date: 2015

Publisher: Skybound Entertainment

Designer: Jack Dire

WHEN TO PLAY:

- When you want to learn more about your gaming friends

- When you're in a large group

- When it's time for a little competition

Difficulty: ★ ★ ★ ★ ★

Age Recommendation: 16+

Number of Players: 3–10

Play Time: 30 minutes

 **THE GOAL**

Find true love so you have the most points at the end of the game.

 **LET'S PLAY!**

Terrible dates. We've all been on one, or many. Red Flags is the game of terrible dates. In this game, players are tasked with finding their one true love, but what's a good love story without a catch? No, not a catch in a good way, a catch in a bad way. They say nobody's perfect, and you're going to find out plenty of good traits your potential partners possess, along with some really, truly unfortunate ones.

To start the game a player is selected to be the "single" player. He goes on dates and judges each round. The starting player is the player with the most real dates under his belt, and everyone at the table knows exactly who he is. This game either fills the players with hope and excitement or existential dread, depending on their past Tinder experiences.

Before starting play each player draws four perk cards and three red flags cards. As you can imagine, the perks are the good qualities your date might possess while the red flags are the ghastly ones. Using what you know about the "single" going on the date, pick two perks to create the ideal date for him.

Starting with the player to the left of the single, each player plays his two perks and reads the cards aloud to the table. Storytelling is highly encouraged during this segment of the game. After each player has read his picture-perfect date to the "single," begin again with the player to the single's left. Each player then adds a red flag to the player to his left's date.

Here's an example:

Perk: Has all of the same interests as you
Perk: Loves animals
Red Flag: Farts every time he smiles and it smells ghastly

The game even comes with some blank cards for players to make their own perks and red flags. As the players argue why the single should pick his character to date and reject the other candidates, the single must imagine that he dates this person long-term and does all of the normal things he would do with anyone else he dated. As you can imagine, this can lead to some really swell, or incredibly terrifying, experiences.

EXPANSIONS

- Dark Red Flags:
  A Filthy Expansion
  2015

- A Geeky Expansion
  2016

- Sexy Red Flags:
  A Seductive Expansion
  2016

- Expansion One
  2017

- Fairy Tale Red Flags
  2017

- Festive Red Flags
  2017

- The Date Deck
  2017

Happy Salmon

Release Date: 2016

Publisher: North Star Games

Designers: Ken Gruhl and Quentin Weir

WHEN TO PLAY:

- When you want something fun and easy

- When you need to relax

- When the whole family is around

Difficulty: ★ ★ ★ ★ ★

Age Recommendation: 5+

Number of Players: 3–6
(3–12 with the expansion)

Play Time: 2 minutes

 THE GOAL

Be the first player to complete all of your actions and discard all of your cards.

 LET'S PLAY!

Happy Salmon is one of the simplest games in this book, which also means it's easy to play with younger kids. Each person only needs to know four total actions, and it's likely that she already knows at least two of them.

Each player starts the game with twelve cards. There are four different cards in the deck, three of each card. When a player shows a card, another player who has that card must also show it, and together they must complete that action. There are two modes to the game: loud mode, where all of the players shout the action they need, and silent mode, where all players silently motion the actions of the cards in their hand!

There are four total actions a player may take:

1. **Pound it:** make a fist and bump fists with another player
2. **High five:** players, well, high five
3. **Switcharoo:** switch places with another player
4. **Happy salmon:** you and another player put your arms together and wag them back and forth as a happy salmon would in shallow waters, slapping each other's forearms, gently

If you're playing around a table, it's easiest to place the cards gently down on the table. However, if you are playing in an open circle and don't mind if your game gets a little wear and tear, it makes for a more entertaining, if chaotic, time.

EXPANSIONS

• Happy Salmon: Blue Fish

Time's Up!

WHEN TO PLAY:

- When the whole family is around

- When you're in a large group

- When you want to play on a team

Release Date: 1999
Publisher: R&R Games
Designer: Peter Sarrett

Difficulty: ✶ ✶ ✶ ✶ ✶   **Number of Players:** 4–18

Age Recommendation: 12+   **Play Time:** 90 minutes

 THE GOAL

Be on the team that guesses the most clues correctly.

 LET'S PLAY!

Everyone has played or heard of charades, the game where players act out clues to other players, trying to get them to say a certain word or phrase. Time's Up! is a variation on charades but adds in additional rules for every round and is played over a total of three rounds.

Before starting the game players divide into two teams, and the team members sit across from each other. The game is played using a set of randomly chosen name or word cards depending on the version of the game the players are playing. These are typically pop culture references from a specific time. Players can even make up their own if they so choose. Each team is given thirty seconds to guess as many names as possible with one clue giver giving clues to the guessers. Players can always use sound effects, but speech becomes more restricted as the game goes on:

1. In the **first round,** the clue giver can say anything short of the answer, but passing is not allowed.

2. In the **second round,** the clue giver can only say one word and the players are only allowed a single guess. Passing is allowed. Clue givers may want to reference something from the first round, so paying attention is a critical aspect of this game.
3. In the **third round,** the clue giver cannot say anything and may only mime and use sounds. The other players only get one guess, but passing is allowed.

This sounds impossible, but it's important to know that the players see the same clues recycled over and over again from round to round for both teams, making it as important to pay attention to what the other team is doing as it is for the players to pay attention to their own team. This makes the game not only more engaging for everyone; it also makes every second count.

FACT

Time's Up! is a variation on charades, which was originally published in 1550!

EXPANSIONS

- Expansion Set #1
  2001

- Expansion Set #2
  2002

- Game Geek Expansion
  2009

- Limited Expansion
  2016

FIELD

CYCLE

HOTEL

SPOT

PARK

GREECE

PIRATE

FACE

MOUNT

HOOK

DECK

BEACH

GIANT

BOLT

POUND

CONDUCTOR

SINK

LIFE

BAT

YARD

MOLE

Codenames

Difficulty: ✳ ✳ ✳ ✳   **Number of Players:** 2–8

Age Recommendation: 8+   **Play Time:** 15–20 minutes

WHEN TO PLAY:

- When you're in a large group

- When you want something fun and easy

- When you're at your local game store

Release Date: 2015
Publisher: Czech Games Edition
Designer: Vlaada Chvátil

 THE GOAL

Have your team successfully find all of your code words before the other team does!

LET'S PLAY!

Codenames took the world by storm when it exploded in 2015. What started out as a small word game became so popular so quickly that supply couldn't meet demand on the first-, second-, or even third-print runs. Codenames now has more than 4.5 million copies in print and has been translated to more than forty languages. What sets Codenames apart from other party games is the way it forces players to think outside of the box. In a typical party game, a player might be asked to act out or perform, maybe even sing, to convey his message. In Codenames, players are asked to do one thing: state one word and one number. That sounds simple, but it really challenges the players to ask themselves, "How well do we really know our friends?"

Split the players into two teams of similar size and skill. You need at least four players but can have up to eight. Someone shuffles up all of the cards and creates a grid of cards, five words high and five words wide. Two players are selected to be the clue givers, one for the red team and the other for the blue team. These

PARTY GAMES

two players can see a key, which they use to identify their team's words on the board. Whichever team started the game has nine words on the key while the second team has eight, and they're indicated by that team's color on the key along with one blacked-out tile with an X on it. This tile is also known as the assassin.

The key card corresponds to the grid on the table. The blue squares on the grid identify the words that the blue team must guess, and the red squares on the grid identify the words the red team must guess. Players also notice one black crossed-out square, which is the assassin. This is the one word on the grid players absolutely do not want their team to guess because if they do, they automatically lose the game. All of the tan squares are innocent bystanders, and you don't necessarily want your team to accidentally guess them. However, if they do, nothing terrible happens outside of ending your team's guessing turn immediately.

If a player is a spymaster, he tries to give his team a one-word clue that relates to some of the words on the board. He may only say one word followed by the number of clues on the board it corresponds to. This might take a minute, so it's important to be patient when it comes to your clue giver; he has a challenging job! When giving his clue it can only be one word and no additional hints may be given. The guessers can always guess one card more than the number given to them so that they might be able to guess clues that they missed from previous rounds.

When the spymaster gives a clue, his field operatives are tasked with sorting out what it means. They can debate it among themselves, but the spymaster needs to keep a straight face or in some cases simply temporarily walk away. When the field operatives touch a card, the spymaster immediately covers the word with the appropriate colored card that was assigned to that word. The team can keep guessing until they guess a card that is not their team's color. This could be a word from the other team, an innocent bystander, or, heaven forbid, the assassin. It's always a good idea for the clue givers to double-check the assassin card before saying their word out loud to the players guessing.

There are penalties for invalid clues and not keeping a straight face, so it's important to work hard to get your game face on.

Codenames is one of those games that gamers, serious or casual, want to play again and again. It's simple enough that you can teach it to virtually anyone, and it's as easy for children to pick up as adults. There are also themed versions of the game for Marvel, Disney, and Harry Potter, and more are coming out every year! For $20, this is a must-try title for anyone with even the smallest game collection.

FACT
Once a field operative has made contact with a card, his fate is sealed and the spymaster must put the appropriate color tile over that word.

EXPANSIONS

- Codenames: Pictures
- Codenames: Duet
- Codenames: Deep Undercover
- Codenames: Disney Family Edition
- Codenames: Marvel
- Codenames: Harry Potter

Hellapagos

Release Date: 2017

Publisher: Gigamic

Designers: Laurence Gamelin and Philippe Gamelin

Difficulty: ★ ★ ★ ★ ★

Age Recommendation: 12+

Number of Players: 3–12

Play Time: 30–45 minutes

 **THE GOAL**

Escape the island!

 **LET'S PLAY!**

Hellapagos is a game of survival at all costs. You and your fellow castaways struggle to assemble enough rafts to escape while having enough food and water to sustain yourselves. It's a "semi-cooperative" game; while you want to work together to achieve your goals, sometimes the odds aren't in your favor. When this happens you discover the darker side of the game: eliminating other castaways until there isn't a deficit. This might be good practice for a future in politics?

To start each round, the starting player flips over the top card of the weather deck. Then each player has the choice of one of four actions to take on her turn: gather wood to build a raft for escape, collect water, go fishing for food, or hunt in the shipwreck for something to help her stay in the game.

Collecting water and food are straightforward and simple actions, though both are scarce. Some rounds, no water is available to be collected! You need one unit of water and one unit of food for each surviving player at the end of each round, otherwise you find yourselves having to vote one or more players out until you have met this condition. These votes are the real meat of the game experience and provide a lot of tension around the table.

Gathering wood is the riskiest activity in the game. You need six wood tokens to build a raft seat for one person, and there is no guarantee that person is you. You can collect one wood token safely at the edge of the woods, but gathering more means venturing in deeper and potentially getting bitten by a snake! Left alone, you recover, but during this time you are very vulnerable to other castaways: you can't play cards, and you can't vote. Worse, you lose your next action but still require food and water. Do you trust the other players to be ruthless or merciful?

In the shipwreck, you find various interesting and useful cards to help you stay in the game. There is food and water to be stashed away to help you survive a vote and escape the island, items to help you gather resources more efficiently, and pistols. The pistols are useless without bullets, but if you have a pistol and a bullet you can potentially eliminate another player from the game, instantly.

Surviving Hellapagos involves a careful balance of building rafts, collecting supplies, and a bit of luck. And you need to do all of this under the pressure of time as well, because once the weather card reveals a hurricane you must escape the island that round or perish!

While eliminating players is part of the game, it is wise not to do so if it isn't necessary. An eliminated player is one less mouth to feed and one less seat needed on the raft, but it is also one less person to gather water, food, and wood to help the rest of the castaways.

You can play your food and water cards to help other people stay alive. You should also remember that you may be targeted for a vote later if supplies are short. Playing one of these supplies can help you survive a vote against you.

Some shipwreck cards are extremely powerful. The fruit basket can save the entire group from starvation and dehydration. The cannibal BBQ kit turns eliminated players into food. And the

> **ESSENTIAL**
>
> Wooden marbles provide two functions in the game. When you are gathering fish, the black marble is terrific; you catch three fish, feeding three people for the round! When gathering wood, it is the opposite; grabbing the black marble means you have been bitten by a snake and are poisoned!

voodoo doll can even bring an eliminated player back into the game! However, when a person spends a lot of time hunting through the shipwreck, she is probably doing so to ensure her own survival; don't be surprised if she plays a pistol and some bullets later in the game to improve her chances of survival.

Escaping the island is very difficult. You need one seat on the raft for each surviving player, plus enough food and water for each person to survive a full round at sea. When the hurricane comes, you might be forced to vote for seats on the raft if you don't have enough!

Geek Out!

Difficulty: ★★★★★ **Number of Players:** 2–99

Age Recommendation: 10+ **Play Time:** 30 minutes

WHEN TO PLAY:

- When you're in a large group
- When you want to learn more about your gaming friends
- When you're having a game night

Release Date: 2013

Publisher: Playroom Entertainment

Designers: Elisa Teague and Dan Rowen

THE GOAL

Answer questions as best you can to be the geekiest of all your friends!

LET'S PLAY!

Geek Out! is a party trivia game that does more than just ask questions of the players. It's a challenge game that asks the players to test their geeky knowledge against each other. Do you have a friend who is always claiming to be the most knowledgeable science fiction nerd out there? Maybe you have a close friend who knows everything there is to know about comics. This might be the perfect game for those friends to settle once and for all who is the geekiest of them all.

The game has a number of cards inside the box, all of which have several categories of geek-culture trivia. The categories are sci-fi, fantasy, games, comics, and miscellaneous. On his turn, each of the players rolls a die and draws a card from the top of the deck. He must answer the question on the card. For example, one might be asked to list two *Battlestar Galactica* locations or four enemies of Batman. The player should only take the challenge if he thinks he can answer the trivia, in which case he says, "Challenge accepted!" If he doesn't believe he can answer the question he

can pass play to the next player. Then the turns proceed around the table. If the player clockwise from the person answering the question says she can beat the answer (for instance, if the players can name two *Battlestar Galactica* locations but the person sitting next to her can name three), then she steals the question. If the next player claims he can name four, then he steals it. This proceeds around the table until all but one player passes!

Then the players have to decide if they accept the player's answers. If the player successfully answers the question, she gains the card in front of her and it counts as a point. The first player to get 5 points wins the game.

If the player fails her challenge, she is given a -2 point token. This means that the players must be very confident in their geek-culture answers if they want to win. You can imagine how challenging it would be to make a comeback from -2 points!

PENCIL AND PAPER:

ROLE–PLAYING GAMES

Imagine for a moment that you and your friends decide to embark on an epic adventure, and along the way you come across hardships and trials that none of you could have possibly anticipated. After a close friend suddenly vanishes and is nowhere to be found your party agrees to dedicate your lives to searching for him. After all, he was a core member of your community and you can't imagine life without him. You set out to search, and along the way you find chaos, violence, and evils you didn't know existed, all of which you and your friends must work together to overcome. Eventually, you stop off in a small tavern and hear rumblings of a local troublemaker. His description sounds oddly a lot like your friend who went missing. Last they heard your friend was headed west, which leaves only one option for your party as you set out. You walk for what seems like days and eventually come across a dingy and dank cave with signs of a recent entry. Your party has no choice but to enter. The cave is overrun with foul-mouthed grungy little goblins, and slime drips from every crevice of the wall. Your party asks for directions but is met with only violence. Thankfully, you came prepared for battle. With a little bit of teamwork you injure enough of the goblins that they back off and let you pass. As you near the end of the cave, you worry that you might never see your friend. Suddenly, you see him, sitting in the corner, laughing to himself while enjoying a goblin burger next to a fire he's made. One of you scurries over and pulls a vial out of your pocket, tilting your beloved friend's head back, making him drink the potion to cure what ails him: a cure for madness. After a couple of minutes the light re-enters his eyes.

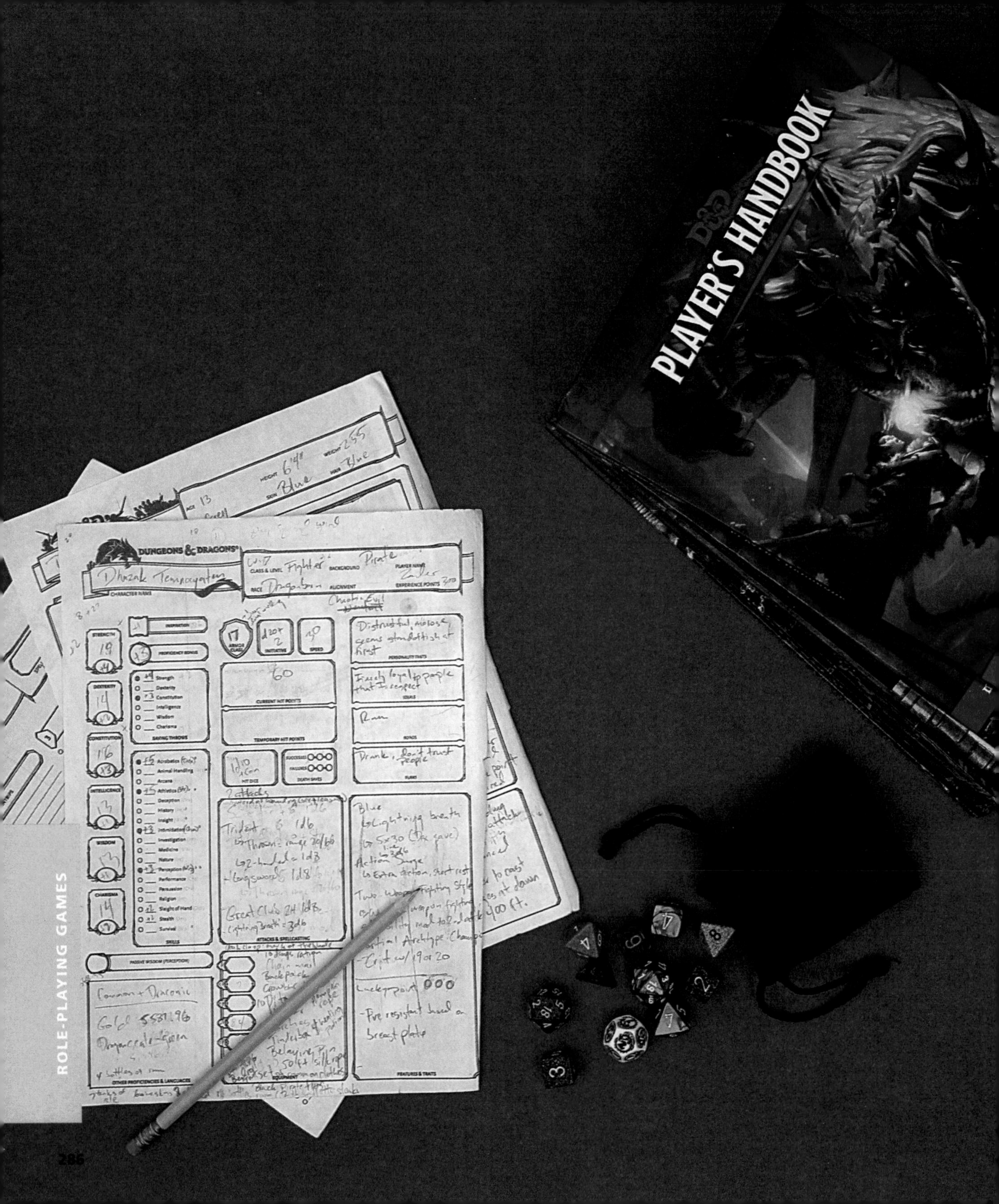
PLAYER'S HANDBOOK
DUNGEONS & DRAGONS

Dungeons & Dragons

Difficulty: ★ ★ ★ ★ ★

Age Recommendation: 7+

Number of Players: 3–6+

Play Time: Varies

 **THE GOAL**

Have adventures and watch your character level up.

 **LET'S PLAY!**

Not all heroes wear capes. In Dungeons & Dragons players pick a character class and build a backstory for their characters. At its core, Dungeons & Dragons is collaborative storytelling in which players guide their carefully crafted heroes through battles with unimaginable horrors, questing for riches and treasure and meeting fantastical otherworldly beings that challenge the players to explore and solve problems. Their collaborative efforts may or may not pay off because this game is a structured yet open-ended role-playing game that allows the players to explore a lush world filled with wonders and, best of all, dungeons and dragons.

Before starting a game of Dungeons & Dragons, it's typically a great idea to set out to find just the right Dungeon Master (DM) for you. A Dungeon Master is a player who runs the game and plays as all of the non-player characters, also known as NPCs. As the players quest through the magical world they're exploring they meet plenty of NPCs that the DM voices and acts out for the other players. They're also in charge of keeping track of all of the damage dealt to the baddies and they roll against the players.

WHEN TO PLAY:

- When you want to play on a team
- When you feel like adventure
- When you're at a gaming convention

Release Date: 1974

Publisher: Wizards of the Coast

Designers: Gary Gygax and Dave Arneson

ROLE-PLAYING GAMES

This is a tough job, so if you don't have a friend who is ready and willing to put a lot of work and research into this position, it's probably a good idea to hire someone to take this role on. There are plenty of professional Game Masters and Dungeon Masters out there. Some are even paid actors who are up for the task of creating an incredible and immersive tabletop gaming experience.

Before starting the game each player (except the DM) needs to design a character. There are a huge slew of character classes and races to choose from. First, it's important to ask yourself what kind of role you would like in the party. Are you a lovable but clumsy person who is always finding herself in lots of trouble? Are you a stoic and fearless leader ready to stand in the way of anyone who threatens your friends? What persona do you want to take on? Then ask yourself what your real-life strengths and weaknesses are. If you want, pick something completely opposite of who you are, because what fun is a role-playing game if you don't become someone else entirely?

There are six different statistics players need to know and think about within the game. Strength, dexterity, constitution, intelligence, wisdom, and charisma. Strength is pretty self-explanatory. Can your character beat things up? Yes or no? Dexterity is how mobile and graceful your character is. Does he react well in high-pressure situations? Is he capable of dodging things with ease or does he struggle to get around without an intense amount of pain and effort? Constitution is a character's physical endurance. Does she get sick often or is she damn near immune to disease? How is your character's intelligence? Does he know how to speak, or is he a genius capable of solving the most intricate problems? Wisdom is more about your character's ability to read other people, environments, and situations. A genius might be able to solve problems, but can she tell that she's just enraged an angsty sorceress who's ready to blight her into oblivion? Finally, we have charisma, which is a combination of your character's personality, appearance, and overall wit. Maybe your character is an absolute bore who makes everyone around him uncomfortable, or maybe he is literally Freddie Mercury.

Players use these character traits throughout the game to navigate the environment they've been thrown into, whether that is the famed city of Waterdeep or a musky old cavern. It's important for them to do what they can to play up their character. When faced with tasks they typically roll a check, which means that the Game Master determines a level for the challenge. The player must then roll at least that number or better to "pass" the check. Players use a twenty-sided die and modify the results based on their stats that they get to add to that roll. Each player is also given moves and abilities that they are able to use in limited quantities each day and at some point need to rest to refresh. Depending on the move, they might roll one four-sided die for damage or roll eight eight-sided die for damage in their efforts to thwart or even kill their opponents on the field. Each opponent they face will have a limited amount of health and only the GM will know what that number is. As the players deal damage, those opponents lose health, and when they have no health left, they are removed from the board.

No matter what problems arise, at the end of the day, it's up to the players to work together on whatever may be thrown at them. Most importantly, never split the party. Stick together, work together, and solve problems together, using each of your characters' strengths and weaknesses to your advantage.

ALERT!

Back in the 1980s, there was panic in some circles about Dungeons & Dragons. Critics said the game taught its players demonic magic and that players were emotionally injured when their characters were injured or died. This became the basis for a movie, starring Tom Hanks, *Mazes and Monsters*.

CAN I MAKE UP MY OWN ADVENTURES, OR DO I HAVE TO BUY THEM FROM WIZARDS OF THE COAST?

You can absolutely make up your own adventures. In fact, that's what most people do. These are sometimes called "homebrew campaigns." In addition, Wizards of the Coast publishes premade adventures set in one of their campaign worlds.

13th Age

Release Date: 2013

Publisher: Pelgrane Press

Designers: Rob Heinsoo and Jonathan Tweet

Difficulty: ★ ★ ★ ★ ☆   **Number of Players:** 3–6+

Age Recommendation: 13+   **Play Time:** Varies

THE GOAL

Have fun with a group of friends while using your unique powers and meaningful relationships with the region's iconic leaders to accomplish your collective goals, which are determined together throughout the game and can change.

LET'S PLAY!

13th Age is a tabletop board game born from Dungeons & Dragons. Some of the same great minds that made D&D great took on a new RPG called 13th Age. What makes this game unique is the way the game play flows and the ways in which relationships are everything. Instead of worrying about each of your statistics, instead worry about the ways in which you're able to convince your Game Master (GM) why you deserve this. If you fail, don't worry about it too much! In this game, players fail forward.

13th Age takes place in a rich fantasy world with portals to other worlds and glorious owlbears violently ripping people's extremities off their bodies. However, what sets 13th Age apart from other RPGs is its story-focused game play. Each character is given a unique backstory that impacts the play itself because their relationships are their most powerful resource. When something goes wrong, the story fails forward, making things more interesting as opposed to halting the story in its tracks like failures in most games. This means that no matter what, the GM knows the players are going to make mistakes, and these mistakes will serve as stepping stones along the way. The story will progress no matter what but there might be something funny that happens to the players as a result of the failure. If a player is aiming for someone with their bow and arrow but then rolls a natural one, the lowest possible roll, perhaps their arrow strikes a closer enemy, initiating a combat the players are unprepared for.

Backgrounds for each character are established at the start of the game. Instead of giving the players skills, the characters assign points or jobs to positions they have held in the past that help them in the future with in-game actions. It's up to the players to be creative with their backstory and up to the Game Master to decide if they've done a good enough job convincing him of their past experience. In addition to backgrounds, each player has one or more icons. These are power factions that can be used to alter the state of the game by sacrificing gained icons to change an aspect of the story.

Each player also has relationships with one or more different icon-based powerful being in the realm. This could be an all-powerful druid or a dwarf king. The players decide at the start of the game which of these thirteen beings they would like to have a history with and then tell the other players how that relationship came to be as well as the nature of it. For example, perhaps the player was a personal guard for the dwarf king because he was found in the forest alone at a young age and the dwarf king kidnapped him, making him his personal guard. The nature of the relationship isn't as cut-and-dried as some would like to think. However, the guard may be able to call in a personal favor from the person he spent most of his life protecting.

Finally, each player is given one unique thing that separates them from every other individual in the campaign's universe.

FACT

Jonathan Tweet, one of the designers of 13th Age, was also a lead designer on the third edition of Dungeons & Dragons. Tweet has a long career of game design behind him and is also the author of *Grandmother Fish*, a book that teaches evolution to preschoolers.

EXPANSIONS

There are currently no expansions for this game.

It defines them, and it's important that a lot of thought is put into this because some aspects of the story are going to revolve around it.

13th Age is different from Dungeons & Dragons because it's not mathy and its relationship-based focus allows for creative, collaborative storytelling in a way that keeps the story moving, engaging, and incredibly fun. It's one of those games that everyone should try at least once because once it's picked up, it's almost impossible to put down.

Fiasco

Difficulty: ★ ★ ★ ★ ★

Age Recommendation: 13+

Number of Players: 3–5

Play Time: 60+ minutes

 THE GOAL

Have fun adventures, with a twist!

 LET'S PLAY!

When most people think of pen-and-paper tabletop games, they think of something like the classic Dungeons & Dragons. Players roll dice, fight monsters, get treasure, and rescue the village over several three-hour campaign sessions. However, Fiasco is completely different. Fiasco is a storytelling system that can be played in two or three hours; doesn't require a Game Master (GM), the person who develops an adventure and guides the players through it; and focuses on storytelling more than combat. While some of the other pen and paper tabletop games require lots of peripheral material to get started, all you need to get started in Fiasco is three to five people, four six-sided dice per person, some index cards/Post-it notes, pencils, and the desire to make some really, really poor decisions.

    Fiasco was inspired by caper/heist movies such as *Fargo* and morality plays like the TV series *Breaking Bad*, in which ordinary people get caught up in their own ridiculously self-centered machinations and struggle to make it out. If they are lucky they do, but will probably be a little worse for wear. The action in Fiasco takes place over two acts, with each player taking turns

Release Date: 2009
Publisher: Bully Pulpit Games
Designer: Jason Morningstar

ROLE-PLAYING GAMES

establishing or resolving scenes. The directions of the scenes are determined by pulling dice from a large, shared pool of six-sided dice. These dice are also a clock, and the pool of dice is slowly diminishing as the game stretches toward the climax.

Everyone plays a role in the game, and that role is usually a desperately unethical one. This is ultimately a collaborative rather than competitive experience with more similarity to an improv exercise where players work together within an established set of circumstances. In Fiasco this set of circumstances is called the play-set. Each play-set provides an era (say, the 1950s) and lists numbered one to six to help players develop their unique situations.

After the players decide on a setting, it is time to work on the core of the game: the relationships. All those six-sided dice are rolled into a pile in the middle of the table. Then, using the play-set as a guide, players take turns looking through the lists and choosing dice to determine the relationship, a detail of the relationship, and a few needs/locations/objects. At the end of the set-up there is one relationship between each pair of players, a detail about the relationship (the devil is definitely in the details), plus one need, one location, and one object for the entire group depending on size.

This interconnected web of relationships, locations, needs, and objects (maybe it's a suitcase full of cash, maybe it's a poisonous snake. Who knows?) drives the story along as each player takes her scene. Remember, this is a game of powerful ambition, bad decisions, and even worse impulse control.

In act one players take turns developing their plan using the relationships to guide them. On a player's turn she chooses to either establish or resolve a scene, picks dice out of the dice pool to determine positive or negative outcomes, and generally makes it up as she goes along. At the end of act one, there is a Tilt. The Tilt is a random occurrence or two that throws a monkey wrench into everyone's plans. Then in act two, everyone gets to watch it all fall apart using the same process of establishing and resolving scenes. At the end of the game, the collected dice are used to determine the aftermath of all this drama.

Star Crossed: The Two-Player Game of Forbidden Love

Difficulty: ★ ★ ★ ★ ★

Age Recommendation: 13+

Number of Players: 2

Play Time: 2 hours

 THE GOAL

To fall in love—or not!

 **LET'S PLAY!**

Forbidden Love is a beautiful and alluring temptation that no one ever wants to admit they have, but it often makes your relationship grow even stronger. At times, when we overcome something with an additional barrier to entry, it can feel more satisfying. When people have had obstacles to overcome and had to fight to get where they are, they feel more motivated to make the situation work even if it's a relationship doomed for failure. Sharing secrets increases intimacy and can even strengthen relationships. While forbidden relationships often bring disapproval in the short term, in the long run they're likely to endure.

Star Crossed is like being pulled in two directions at once. Each player needs a character sheet and a pencil as well as a tumbling brick tower. These can be picked up at any major retailer. Together you and the other players work together to craft two characters who are powerfully attracted to each other but have a good reason to not act on their feelings. Perhaps if they do, the world

Release Date: 2019
Publisher: Bully Pulpit Games
Designer: Alex Roberts

WHEN TO PLAY:

- When you want to learn more about your gaming friends

- When you have a few spare hours

- When you need to relax

ROLE-PLAYING GAMES

There are currently
no expansions for this
game.

ends. Maybe one of the characters has an alien symbiotic living in her brain. Perhaps one of you is Harry Potter and the other is the Dark Lord. As you can imagine, things can get fan-fictiony fast. If you ever wanted Captain Kirk and Spock to fall for each other, now is your chance. If the tumbling tower falls, the characters act on their feelings, and the combined attraction score determines if the characters' love is doomed, triumphant, or something in between. Sometimes the tower never falls, in which case there is a final scene and the characters never act on their feelings, and sometimes that's exactly what they should do.

Before starting the game the players set out the scene cards between them, numbers one to eight, and flip over the first scene. Then they take turns doing one of the moves listed on their character sheets. One player takes the lead and adds dialogue to her actions while touching the tower. Some of the moves may only be done once per scene, and others once per game, so it's critical to use them at the appropriate times. Then each player fills a star beneath the move on her character sheet. The player who is following along can end the scene whenever she likes, and then the players repeat through all of the scenes until the tower falls or until the end of the eighth tower.

If the tower falls, the player who last touched it describes her character acting on her feelings for the other character. Knocking the tower over voluntarily is also a perfectly valid move. Add up the players' filled stars on their character sheets and combine them to compare the results on the epilogue chart, and the story is resolved. If the tower never falls then the players explain why their feelings were never acted on. Maybe they go their separate ways, or perhaps that's not all there is to the story.

Tales of the Arabian Nights

Difficulty: ★ ★ ★ ★ ★

Age Recommendation: 12+

Number of Players: 1–6

Play Time: 2+ hours

WHEN TO PLAY:

• When you want to play something challenging

• When it's time for a little competition

• When you feel like adventure

Release Date: 2009

Publisher: Z-Man Games

Designers: Anthony J. Gaella, Eric Goldberg, Kevin Maroney, and Zev Shlasinger

 THE GOAL

Fulfill the destiny foretold for you at the game's beginning.

 LET'S PLAY!

Between all of the players sits a massive map, and each player is given a character, whether that be Sinbad, Scheherazade, Ali Baba, Zumurrud, Ma'aruf, or Aladdin. Players take a total of three quest markers, which they place on the board as they adventure and explore. While this game is technically a board game, it also acts as a role-playing game provided everyone wants to get into character. Place each character token on the board in Baghdad. Before starting the game the players take a number of destiny and story point markers adding up to a total of twenty between the two.

Every player starts with his wealth marker in the poor box, and he has to scrounge his way up from poverty. The encounter cards are shuffled and placed facedown on the board, and the morning marker is placed faceup. Treasure and status cards are placed near the board. Then each player gets to take his skill markers by type. Each player in turn chooses one marker and repeats this a total of three times. All skills begin at talent level, but over time and with certain experiences, players can eventually upgrade these to master level skills.

ESSENTIAL

You are the hero or heroine in a story of adventure, wonder, riches, and imprisonment! Travel the lands near and far and seek your own destiny and fortune. Learn stories and gain wisdom that you might share with others. Your only goal is to fulfill the destiny chosen by you at the start of the game, so what are you waiting for? The next tale is yours to tell.

EXPANSIONS

There are currently no expansions for this game.

On his turn each player passes the book of tales to the player on his left; that person reads to him on his turn. Then the first player gives the reaction matrix to the player on his right. He checks treasures and statistics and announces any effects they have before moving. Then the player moves his standee based on the number of spaces he is permitted to move; this is based on his current wealth level. After moving, the player remaining at that location draws the top card of the encounter deck and encounters whatever is indicated on the card.

If the player draws a character encounter card the card directs the reader to paragraphs in the book of tales based on the number showing and the time of day. If he draws a terrain encounter he determines the kind of terrain in the matching paragraph number. If he encounters a city card he immediately goes to the paragraph printed at the bottom of the card for an encounter. Finally, if he has an encounter in a palace of power, he does not draw a card and simply finds the paragraph number shown on the board in the book of tales.

During his encounter the player must decide how to react. The encounter chart directs the matrix reader to one of fifteen reaction matrices labeled from A to O. The player chooses how he is going to react to the encounter and then the reader with the book of tales opens the book and reads the segment aloud to all of the players. Sometimes the player makes the right choices and is rewarded with riches beyond his wildest dreams or is sent to faraway lands where fantastical things happen! His skills might even help change the outcome of a story. Other times, he ends up imprisoned and has to bribe, or even fight, his way out past the guards. Either way, along the way he gains those precious story and destiny points he needs to win the game.

Weave

Difficulty: ★ ★ ★ ★ ★

Age Recommendation: 12+

Number of Players: 2–5

Play Time: 1+ hours

 THE GOAL

Overcome challenges and outscore the other players.

 LET'S PLAY!

Weave starts by handing the players a number of tarot-sized cards and then asking them to download the companion app for the game. The Game Master invites each of the players to the game they are playing, and then they have easy access to information about each of the characters after they build their character. What makes Weave unique is its seamless character creation process. After being dealt character cards, each player "scans" them into the app one at time. With every card scanned, new character traits are revealed for each player to pick from.

There are play-sets to choose from within the game: Goblins 'R Jerks, Xorte/IO, Gloomies, Solar Age, and Clique. Goblins 'R Jerks is your classic dungeon crawl setting, similar to Dungeons & Dragons, in a magical fantasy world. Xorte/IO is a cyberpunk adventure set where the players get into all kinds of mischief but they don't necessarily do as much fighting as one might think. Solar Age is a space adventure set in 1950s pulp science fiction. It's exactly as epic as you'd hope. Gloomies is a 1980s kid movie trope in a small town. Clique is a high school drama, and it's as catty as you think it's going to be.

WHEN TO PLAY:

- When you want a game you can carry with you
- When you feel like adventure
- When you love solving puzzles

Release Date: 2017
Publisher: Monocle Society
Designer: Collaborative effort

FACT

Tarot cards are not the first thing one would think of when thinking about role-playing games, but Weave takes tarot cards and mixes them with augmented reality in an app to create an immersive game play experience that has an incredibly low barrier to entry. The artist, Brianna Johnson, worked with Kyle Kinkade to create a stunning game that's fun, bold, and sophisticated.

Each character is given a backstory and options to choose from. Maybe she is a warlock who worships a magical relic she obtained in a cult she was once a part of. Maybe she's a disgraced detective who has been kicked off the police force and hasn't told anyone when she moved across the country. Next, she is given six talents that she may use during the game play. Perhaps the player is really good with ranged weapons, or maybe she knows a specific spell or is particularly hard to kill. Then the characters are each given flaws like being afraid of the dark or being super-excitable. On top of that each character gets a signature move. Maybe she's really good at blocking hits or she's incredibly stealthy. Finally, each player is given an inventory of items, typically armor or weapons, but you never know what kind of magic a player might be hiding.

Within the game there are four different kinds of challenges the player can face: brooks, flame, stone, and gale. Every challenge starts with a difficulty of one, but the storyteller can play a challenge card from his hand that matches the suit to replace the original challenge level. The players must then roll the weave dice and roll at least that many of that symbol in order to succeed at the challenge. Each player starts with three dice but may argue for more based on her skills and abilities as a character. Each die is six-sided and has one of each challenge symbols as well as one strike and one weave symbol. Weave symbols act as wilds. If the player fails she may receive a strike. If a player ever has three strikes, she cannot act for the rest of the scene but can come in at the start of the next scene. To pass these challenges the player needs to roll higher than the challenge of the task, so if it's a brooks two challenge, she needs to have at least two brooks faces showing on her dice, keeping in mind that a Weave not only gives her an additional brook but also lets her roll one additional die as a bonus for rolling a Weave.

Because of the collaborative efforts of Kyle, his team, and the writers for each play-set, Weave is a magical world of endless exploration that takes immersive settings and simple dice rolls and turns them into a story you can't turn away from. Its loose rule-set means that a lot can fly, and that means all kinds of shenanigans.

LORDS OF WAR:
WAR GAMES

When talking about war games, people often think of a huge map on the table with lots of miniature figures and armies like Warhammer (1983) or a paper map with lots of chits and tokens and is deep in strategy. There is so much more to the genre than that. War games are usually based on historical conflicts and simulate warfare. This can be through themes or mechanics and almost always includes direct conflict. There are also many war games with a fictional fantasy setting; these are among the most popular games in the genre. As the popularity of war games increases, designers are exploring themes that haven't been done before.

Historical war games are a great gateway to learn about the past. You get to learn about historical events in a way that's different from reading a book or watching a movie, while at the same time you have fun socializing and playing a game with friends. War games also include a lot of strategy. Like a lot of other tabletop games, war games tell a story, and that's what interests so many people. They provide a different, exciting, and challenging experience for players of all ages.

Star Wars: X-Wing Miniatures Game

Difficulty: ★ ★ ★ ★ ☆

Age Recommendation: 14+

Number of Players: 2

Play Time: 30–45 minutes

WHEN TO PLAY:

- When it's time for a little competition

- When you're ready to explain the rules

- When you want to play something challenging

Release Date: 2012
Publisher: Fantasy Flight Games
Designer: Jason Little

 THE GOAL

The player who destroys all the opposing player's ships wins the game.

 LET'S PLAY!

Star Wars: X-Wing Miniatures Game is a tactical ship-to-ship combat game set in the Star Wars universe, where players get to take control of the powerful Rebel X-Wings and Imperial TIE fighters facing them against each other in fast-paced space combat. The rules for X-Wing are based on Wings of War, which is a tactical-level historical war game simulating World War I aerial dogfights. The rules merge card and board game mechanics to re-create aerial combat.

X-Wing is a miniatures war game that re-creates Star Wars space combat throughout several scenarios that are included in the base game, which consists of just three ships to start out, two tie fighters, and one x-wing. The game is really popular, and tournaments are held at game stores and conventions all over the world.

X-Wing is different from many tabletop games as it is not played on a board. Instead, it can be played on any flat surface

with at least 3-by-3 inches (7½ centimeters by 7½ centimeters) of space. Players sometimes use a felt or cloth surface, which provides a little friction and helps to prevent players from accidentally bumping or moving the ships. As the game has grown in popularity so have the expansions and components that you can buy for the game.

Before starting the game, both players choose a faction that they want to play during the game. One player controls the Rebels while the other controls the Imperials. All components belonging to a player's own faction are considered friendly throughout the game, and all components belonging to his opponent's faction are considered an enemy.

X-Wing is played over a series of game rounds and ends when one player has destroyed all of his opponent's ships. During each game round, players perform four phases in order:

1. **The Planning Phase:** Each player secretly chooses one maneuver for each of his ships using a maneuver dial. The maneuver dial is a dial that is assigned to a ship and controls the movement of that ship during the game.
2. **A System Phase:** In this phase, players resolve any special abilities that their ships may have. The ships contained in the X-Wing core set do not have any special abilities, but some expansion ships do.
3. **An Activation Phase:** Players move each ship and perform an action. Performing actions in the game are some of the most important decisions players make. Actions provide several benefits during the game including the ability to reposition a ship in the game and so on.
4. **The Combat Phase:** Each player may perform one attack with each of his ships. During the combat phase, each ship declares a target: the attacker chooses which enemy ship he wants to attack, and the attacker rolls a number of attack dice equal to the ship's primary weapon value, which is on the ship card.

Both players can spend action tokens and resolve abilities that reroll or otherwise modify attack dice results, and then the defender rolls a number of defense dice equal to his ship's agility value, which is also a number on the ship card. The players then have a chance to modify their defense dice. This is really useful if they get some serious damage. They do this by spending action tokens and resolving abilities that allow them to reroll or otherwise modify defense dice results. As in many other war games, players compare the final attack and defense dice results to determine if the defender is hit and how much damage their ship suffers. If the defender is hit, that ship loses shield tokens, which act as defense, or receives damage cards.

Finally there is the end phase during which players remove unused action tokens from their ships and resolve any end phase abilities they may have on their cards. Then a new game round begins, starting with the planning phase. This continues until one player destroys all of his opponent's ships.

X-Wing is one of those war games that has simple actions but lots of strategy—you must think through the movement of ships and action selection during the planning phase—combined with luck from the dice rolling.

EXPANSIONS

- Galactic Empire/First Order Expansions
- Rebel Alliance/ Resistance Expansions
- Scum and Villainy Expansions
- X-Wing and Armada Game Mats

WAR GAMES

Root

WHEN TO PLAY:

- When you want to play something challenging

- When you're at a gaming convention

- When you're at your local game store

Release Date: 2018
Publisher: Leder Games
Designer: Cole Wehrle

Difficulty: ★ ★ ★ ★ ★

Age Recommendation: 10+

Number of Players: 2–4

Play Time: 60–90 minutes

 **THE GOAL**

The first player to reach 30 victory points immediately wins the game. If there is a tie and more than one player reaches thirty or more victory points simultaneously, the player taking the current turn wins.

LET'S PLAY!

Root is a war game with a difference. It has been in the running for the best game of 2018 on lots of lists and has created a huge, well-deserved buzz. Root has a woodland theme and has made a huge impact in the tabletop game community for creating a new style of war game that has become extremely popular with people who may not have been interested in playing war games before. It's an asymmetric war game, meaning that each player has different actions and different goals to take throughout the game. It has four different factions: marquise, eyrie, alliance, and vagabond.

The map, combined with the different factions and single-use cards, makes for a very interesting game. The game uses a single deck of multipurpose cards. Each player uses those cards in very different ways. This makes for a very tense game, swapping cards, potentially knowing what card your opponent has, only wishing that it was yours. Designer Cole Wehrle took inspiration from the GMT Games COIN series, a selection of war games based on modern-day conflicts using counterinsurgency and guerilla warfare as the main theme. He wanted to create an accessible war game that was out of the ordinary and appealing to most board game players.

The factions in Root share some features with some of the COIN series. A series that can often seem overwhelming to most has been transformed into an enticing game filled with action and adventure. It's easy to see which faction would take on which role.

Being an asymmetric game, each faction has a different selection of actions that it can take during the game. The first faction is Marquise de Cat, who wishes to exploit the Woodland. She has many resources she can use during the game to help her run her military and economic game engine. She scores points by constructing buildings in the Woodland. The Eyrie Dynasties are trying to reclaim the glory of their once-great aristocracy and retake the Woodland from the Marquise. They score each turn by building and protecting roots in the Woodland. It can almost feel like a cat-and-mouse chase throughout the game. The Woodland Alliance is a faction who spends their days trying to unite the creatures of the forest. Their goal during the game is to spread sympathy for their cause across the Woodland and revolt. The Vagabonds are the outcasts of the forest; they wish to gain fame and pick fights around the forest. This faction scores by completing quests for the creatures of the Woodland and by aiding and harming the other factions.

As mentioned earlier, each faction has a unique way to score victory points, but all four factions can score victory points during the game by removing buildings and tokens from the game board. Whenever a player removes an enemy's building or token, she scores a victory point. Players can also score points during the game by crafting items, which is an action that any faction can take. The player who does so scores the victory points listed on the card.

> **ESSENTIAL**
> If you aren't aware of it, the COIN series is designed by war game designer Volko Ruhnke. The system includes a central "government" faction with three competing but different "rebellion" factions.

Root is played in rounds with each faction taking actions that are noted on a player aid during the game. In front of each player sits a board with their unique character board depicting whichever race they are playing and actions they can take. This helps each player understand the game clearly. Asymmetric games can sometimes take a bit longer to learn than other board games since players must learn four different players' actions, but the payoff is worth it in the end.

Some more key actions that can be performed during the game include move; when the player moves, she can take any number of her warriors and move them to an adjacent space on the board. This is how players move around the board. Then there is the battle action. This is, of course, a war game full of area control and combat. When players battle, they choose a space on the board where they have warriors and choose another player in the space to be the defender. There are different combat rules for each faction, but these are essentially resolved by dice rolling and removing units (warriors) from the game.

EXPANSIONS

- Root: The Riverfolk Expansion

Twilight Struggle

Difficulty: ★ ★ ★ ★ ★

Number of Players: 2

Age Recommendation: 13+

Play Time: 120–180 minutes

 THE GOAL

There are various ways to win the game. The two most common ones are:

- Being the first player to reach 20 victory points.
- Being the player who controls Europe when it's time to score Europe in the game.

LET'S PLAY!

Twilight Struggle is a political two-player game based on the Cold War and doesn't involve any direct conflict. It has won many awards and is one of the most well-known and well-loved two-player card-driven games and is a staple in many collections. Being a quick-playing, low-complexity game compared to many other war games makes Twilight Struggle a great entry game into war games or card-driven political strategy games.

Players take on the role of either USA or USSR. Game play takes place on a world map that represents the events that happened in 1945. During the game players move units and exert influence in attempts to gain allies and control for their superpower.

Release Date: 2005

Publisher: GMT Games

Designers: Jason Matthews and Anada Gupta

WHEN TO PLAY:

- When you have a few spare hours
- When it's time for a little competition
- When you're at your local game store

WAR GAMES

Twilight Struggle is primarily driven by cards, each of which depict a real-life event during the Cold War. These cards are split into three decks for the early, mid, and late periods of the war with the historical events organized into a timeline throughout the game.

At the beginning of the game, the early war deck is used. At the beginning of turn four the mid war deck is shuffled into the remaining early war cards. At the start of turn eight, the late war deck is shuffled in. Players each have a hand of eight cards. At the start of each turn, they each pick a card to play as the "headline event." They then take turns in playing cards, with the USSR going first. The next turn each player is dealt more cards from the deck to bring his total up to eight.

The cards in Twilight Struggle can be used for various actions during the game. A card can be played either for the event (which are the historical events) or for its operations points. The operations that can be played during the game include:

- **Placing Influence:** The player can place influence in any country where he already has influence or in an adjacent country. The player can place as many influences as it states on the card he is playing.
- **Attempting a Coup**
- **Realignments**
- **Attempting to Advance in the Space Race**

If a player uses a card to attempt to advance in the space race, the event on the card does not happen. This makes it a useful way of disposing of an opponent-favorable event.

A player wins by reaching 20 victory points, "controlling" Europe when Europe comes to be scored, or if DEFCON degrades to one (i.e., thermonuclear war breaks out) during the opposing player's turn, irrespective of which player's actions "caused" this to occur.

Another way a player can claim victory is if war games are played, and the phasing player has at least 7 victory points or a player under influence of Cuban Missile Crisis coups any country, regardless of which player's turn it is, without first removing influence from certain countries. If neither player wins by the end of turn ten, each region is scored and this, coupled with the victory point track, determines the winner.

EXPANSIONS

- Twilight Struggle: Turn Zero
  2015

Eclipse

Difficulty: ★ ★ ★ ★ ☆

Age Recommendation: 14+

Number of Players: 2–6

Play Time: 60–180 minutes

 THE GOAL

After nine rounds, be the player with the most victory points to win.

 LET'S PLAY!

Eclipse is a game that places you in control of a vast interstellar civilization. It combines area control, dice rolling, and player elimination, and is a highly thematic sci-fi–themed strategy game. During the game, players explore star systems, research technologies, and build spaceships, which are used in war. Eclipse has been nominated and won many awards over the years and is the perfect game to talk about as an example of 4X strategy war games. A 4X game is a strategy-based game in which players control an empire and proceed to explore the area, expand their empire, exploit resources available to them and exterminate their opponents. It has the perfect combination of narrative and game play and is a favorite among many tabletop game fans.

During the game, players manage a population of people. When a player's civilization expands to a new sector, it may be colonized by moving the population cubes from the player board to the squares on the sector hex.

WHEN TO PLAY:

- When you want to play something challenging

- When you feel like adventure

- When you're ready to explain rules

Release Date: 2011
Publisher: Lautapelit.fi
Designer: Touko Tahkokallio

WAR GAMES

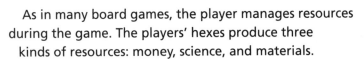

As in many board games, the player manages resources during the game. The players' hexes produce three kinds of resources: money, science, and materials. Money is used for placing influence during the game, controlling hexes, and taking actions that require players to pay money at the end of the round. Science is used for researching new technologies during the game, which give players' civilizations different advantages. These can be broken down into three categories: military, nano, and grid. Materials are needed to build new ships and structures throughout the game.

Players in Eclipse have miniature ships, which represent their army during the game and are used for fighting against other players. It is worth nothing that each kind of ship has its own blueprint on the player board. Players can customize their ships during the game to help with combat and can add more weapons.

The game board in Eclipse is built from hexagonal tiles. Each hex represents a sector of star systems and may contain a number of colored population squares, which represent star clusters with worlds that produce resources.

The game is played in four phases. There is the action phase, which allows players to take different actions. These include:

- **Explore:** A player adds more hexes to the board.
- **Upgrade:** A player upgrades her ships with new weapons.
- **Move:** A player moves her ships.
- **Research:** A player researches for different technologies.
- **Build:** A player builds on the board.

The next phase in the game is the combat phase. This is where the war game comes in! During this phase, battles are resolved and different sectors of the board are conquered, gaining the player points.

After the combat phase is the upkeep phase. Players pay for upkeep costs for their civilizations that they have built up during the game.

Finally, there is a cleanup phase in which players move their influence discs that they used during the game to play actions, and new tiles are drawn.

Players' influence during the game is represented by the wooden influence discs. These are used to mark the hexes on the board that are controlled by each civilization. Also, it's important to remember that taking an action requires players to move an influence disc on the corresponding action space. After nine rounds, be the player with the most victory points to win. Victory points are gained from controlling galactic sectors, fighting battles, forming diplomatic relations, researching technologies, making discoveries, and controlling monoliths.

EXPANSIONS

- Rise of the Ancients **2012**

- Ship Pack One **2013**

- Shadow of the Rift **2015**

- Four mini expansions were also released.

- The iOS version of the game was released in **2013** and Android and Steam versions were released in **2016**.

INDEX

INDEX

ABOUT THE AUTHOR

Bebo is a tabletop gaming expert who has been playing table-top games for more than twenty-five years. She has been work-ing in the board game and tabletop RPG industry professionally since 2012, starting in the marketing department of a large board game distribution company. In 2018 she launched her own marketing and production company called Be Bold Games. She also writes, films, produces, directs, and acts in all of her own videos celebrating the wonder and joy of tabletop gaming.